Digital Curation for
Libraries and Archives

DIGITAL CURATION FOR LIBRARIES AND ARCHIVES

Stacy T. Kowalczyk

LIBRARIES
UNLIMITED™

An Imprint of ABC-CLIO, LLC

Santa Barbara, California • Denver, Colorado

Library of Congress Cataloging-in-Publication Data

Names: Kowalczyk, Stacy T., author.
Title: Digital curation for libraries and archives / Stacy T. Kowalczyk.
Description: Santa Barbara, California : Libraries Unlimited, [2018] | Includes bibliographical
    references and index.
Identifiers: LCCN 2018003078 (print) | LCCN 2018015897 (ebook) | ISBN 9781610696326 (ebook) |
    ISBN 9781610696319 (paperback : alk. paper)
Subjects: LCSH: Data curation in libraries. | Data curation.
Classification: LCC ZA4080.4 (ebook) | LCC ZA4080.4 .K69 2018 (print) | DDC 025—dc23
LC record available at https://lccn.loc.gov/2018003078

ISBN: 978–1–61069–631–9 (paperback)
       978–1–61069–632–6 (eBook)

22 21 20 19 18   1 2 3 4 5

This book is also available as an eBook.

Libraries Unlimited
An Imprint of ABC-CLIO, LLC

ABC-CLIO, LLC
130 Cremona Drive, P.O. Box 1911
Santa Barbara, California 93116-1911
www.abc-clio.com

This book is printed on acid-free paper ∞

Manufactured in the United States of America

In loving memory of Kerry and Megan, my amazing daughters, who made such an impact on the world and the people that they loved. Their loss has led me to care so deeply about preserving memory.

CONTENTS

ILLUSTRATIONS

FIGURES

TABLES

PREFACE

Digital curation is an area of increasing importance in libraries, archives, and other knowledge-based organizations as these organizations need to maintain more and more data in digital form, access that information quickly and accurately, and keep the data viable for long periods of time. It is a cross-disciplinary field of study in library science, information science, and computer science. New jobs are being created with titles such as digital curator, digital archivist, repository manager, digital preservation manager, and many others.

One might ask why is digital curation an emerging practice? Why now? Is this a fad or a long-term trend? Digital curation has been a concern of labor and information professionals since the early 1990s when the digital age began. The need for digital curation has increased as the amount of digital data has increased. As big data has emerged, digital curation has become part of the public discourse. But the principles of preserving digital content were established more than 20 years ago.

This book, *Digital Curation for Libraries and Archives*, was written as introduction to digital curation. The book is based on the experiences of a digital librarian, curator, and researcher who has had many years as an instructor in the classroom. It can be used as a textbook for students in information, library, and archival sciences. It can also be used by working librarians, archivists, and information professionals to learn and understand the basics of digital curation. This book takes the broad view of looking to provide an overview of all of the elements of curating digital contents. The details of technologies and specifics of solutions change rapidly. But the big picture elements—file formats, metadata, and repositories—have been relatively stable for nearly 20 years.

As with any introductory book, this is a starting point for learning about curation. Digital curation is an active field in both practice and research. It changes as technology changes. It expands its scope as new types of data are created. Many journals, both scholarly and professional, publish articles on curating digital content. In addition, many library, information science, and computer science conferences have programs or tracks on digital preservation. These resources can supplement this book and enhance the students understanding of digital curation.

Section I

Preservation Overview

Chapter 1

INTRODUCTION TO DIGITAL CURATION

Our capacity to record information has increased exponentially over time while the longevity of the media used to store the information has decreased equivalently.
—Paul Conway

INTRODUCTION

Over the past 25 years, a revolution in the way that data, information, history, and communications are created has occurred. This revolution has been documented in newspapers, broadcast media, and academic journals. This information revolution has been called the data deluge as digital materials are coming to us at an ever-increasing pace.

Digital data is created in a number of ways. One very familiar way to librarians and archivists is analog to digital conversion. Since the mid-1990s, libraries and archives have spent considerable time and money digitizing their treasures: photographs, letters, and other original source materials, rare books, and special collections. Goals for digitizing included providing new and easier access to archival materials and outreach to scholars and scholarly communities by extending the scope and reducing the cost of primary research. Some digitizing projects, in addition to increased access, were designed to preserve the physical artifact by reducing exposure.

While analog to digital conversion has been a major initiative in libraries and archives, it is not the primary source of the digital deluge. Born-digital materials, data that was created in its original format as digital, are the true source of the digital content revolution. Born-digital data is generated by businesses, governments, research organizations, and academic institutions—and by individuals. Current communication technologies produce exabytes of born-digital materials in the forms of emails, text messages, photographic images, moving images, and social media such as Twitter and Facebook. Scientific research has produced many more exabytes of born-digital materials.

Curating for digital material has become a field of study and a profession. Digital curation, the processes and technologies needed to maintain digital materials over time, is an interdisciplinary field that draws strongly on the fields of library and information science (LIS) and informatics/computer science (CS). Each discipline brings different perspectives to the field, which can be reflected in the differing definitions of the field itself. Baker, Keeton, and Martin (2005) use a CS perspective in their definition of digital preservation—storing immutable data over long periods of time. The CS perspective is clearly focused on the technology.

In LIS, digital preservation is defined as "the managed activities necessary for ensuring both the long-term maintenance of a byte stream and continued accessibility of its contents" (Research Libraries Group & OCLC, 2002, p. 11). Another LIS definition of digital preservation is "the planning, resource allocation, and application of preservation methods and technologies necessary to ensure that digital information of continuing value remains accessible and usable" (Hedstrom, 1997, p. 190). The LIS definitions of digital preservation highlight the requirement of management, stewardship, and long-term availability and usability of the data. In LIS, the definition of preservation has been recently expanding to include digital archiving and digital curation. These definitions are still evolving and are regularly used interchangeably, much to the detriment of clear and concise communication (Beagrie, 2006).

Digital curation is important outside of libraries and academic organizations. As more information is created and stored in digital form, the legal system needs to account for maintaining digital data. A legal definition of digital preservation is "long-term, error-free storage of digital information, with means for retrieval and interpretation, for the entire time span the information is required" (Digital Preservation, 2016). This definition includes not only the long-term storage but also the means of access and rendering. The data is meaningless if it cannot be read by both machines and people. Unlike libraries, archives, and other cultural heritage organizations, the legal view of the longevity of curation is less than eternal. In legal terms, the data should be preserved only as long as necessary. This aligns with records management retention philosophy. Some data is required for life; other data has a limited usefulness based on specific requirements—one year, three years, four years, seven years, and so forth.

But in general, digital curation concerns longer timeframes looking to preserve data for future generations. Digital curation "is concerned with 'communication across time'" and endeavors to provide "interoperability with the future" (Rusbridge et al., 2005, p. 31) for uninterrupted access to the intellectual content.

Throughout the literature, the terms *digital curation, digital preservation,* and *digital archiving* have been used interchangeably. In order to address the growing need for specificity and clarity related to the issues important to digital preservation, Lord, Macdonald, Lyon, and Giaretta (2004) developed a set of differentiated definitions. They describe *curation* as a process of managing and enhancing data throughout its life—from curation to purposeful deletion—with the goal of long-term access and usability. They define *archiving* as a subset of the curation, which involves assessment and selection, appropriate archival storage, and ensuring authenticity of the data. *preservation* is a subset of archiving and involves the individual processes that ensure accessibility over time.

The granularity of these definitions indicates a maturity of some of the thinking about digital preservation. However, these definitions are not widely used with this level of precision. This book will attempt to use these definitions.

How is this digital deluge, this digital revolution, changing the world? It has increased the pace of knowledge creation, changed the nature of our communication patterns, and undermined our ability to record and preserve our own history. To understand how the digital revolution has made our history more vulnerable, we need to understand more clearly the nature of digital things.

THEORETICAL OVERVIEW

The Nature of Digital Things

It might be helpful to first define the difference between digital and physical things. Digital things are defined as intellectual expressions that exist *in silico*, in a computer. A digital thing is generally referred to as a digital object, which can be defined as "an information object, of any type of information or any format that is expressed in digital form" (Thibodeau, 2002, p. 6).

A book is an information object. As a physical object, it has a cover, either soft or hard, and a set of pages in between. The pages could have text, images, or be left intentionally blank. A digital book has digital representations of those same elements—covers and pages with text, images, or left intentionally blank. While a physical book has many component elements, it is generally a single object. However, a digital book in a digital library, such as the HathiTrust Digital Library,[1] is made up of hundreds of individual components—files that must be coordinated and managed. A small book of 100 pages can be comprised of at least 301 individual digital things: 100 archival images (large files with as much information as possible for future uses), 100 web delivery images (smaller, faster to load, and easier for web browsers to display), 100 files containing the text of the book generated by optical character recognition processing (OCR), and a file with structural metadata (data that indicates which file is page 1, which file is page 2, etc.) that allows the software to display and return the pages. It is likely that more digital things could be part of this digital book—descriptive metadata such as a MARC or Dublin Core record, perhaps a PDF of the entire book, PDFs of each chapter, edited and encoded files for research use, and so on (see Figure 1.1).

When working with digital materials, one must decide the level of the object. Many curators decide that the digital object is the intellectual object. In the case of a book, the digital object should include all of the files that contain the intellectual content of the physical book.

Thus, the first principle of the nature of digital things: digital objects are inherently complex. This complexity has several underlying causes. The first is that

Figure 1.1.
Physical and Digital Versions of a Book

(Source: Hathi Trust)

digital objects contain multiple digital elements. As described previously, a digital book has many image files—one for each page. But even a simple object such as a photograph can have multiple files. A photograph could have a thumbnail image, a small image to display on a web page, a larger image, also for web delivery that has more details, and a very large archival version that is not appropriate for web viewing—four files for one single, simple physical object. Providing both access to and preservation of digital materials adds complexity. As described previously, digital things are tied to formats. Formats for access are often different than formats for preservation. Generally, access formats are smaller, have less data, and are easier to transmit and display, while preservation formats are larger, as more data, and are difficult to transmit and display (see Chapter 3 for a fuller discussion of these issues).

The second reason that digital objects are complex is that people expect more functionality from digital objects than physical objects. People expect that a digital book will provide searching functions that are substantially more than browsing the table of contents or an index in a physical book. This additional functionality creates complexity—additional files, additional links documenting the relationships between files, and additional software.

To fulfill their functionality, digital objects require electricity and equipment to render on a screen in order to be perceived. It is difficult to see the digital object outside of its technology. It is possible to hold a disk drive. It is possible to hold the display screen. It is possible to hold the printed version of the digital thing, but it is not possible to touch the digital thing itself.

Thus, the second principle of the nature of digital things: digital things are opaque. They are tied to a specific technology environment. This technology environment requires computational, display, and storage hardware. Some digital things may require very specific additional peripheral equipment. Each component of this hardware environment needs to communicate with the other; thus, operating systems, device drivers, communication buses, and file systems must be included in this technology environment. Digital things are tied to specific format, an organization scheme with a specific syntax that allows a computer program to interpret, process, and render; thus, in addition to hardware, digital things require software—software that can access the digital thing, display or render the digital thing, or manipulate, modify, or use the digital thing.

Frustration is a common experience for people who use digital things via the Internet. Resources available yesterday are inaccessible today. The search term previously used is no longer successful. Links are broken resulting in the 404 File Not Found error and a blank browser screen; rights have changed, so access is denied. Digital resources that worked fine previously no longer load or render properly.

Thus the third principle of the nature of digital things: digital things are fragile. The fragility of digital things has multiple levels: access, fixity, and obsolescence. Access to digital things can break easily because links break as data is moved. Digital things rarely describe themselves. Often, context of a digital thing is external to its instantiation; that is, the description, the metadata for that thing exists as a different digital thing in a separate system. Context for a digital thing can be visible when it exists within a web page, a library or archival system, or publicly available database; context can be hidden when it exists within another digital document such as a Word file or PDF or in a secured, off-line database.

Digital things are easy to copy, move, and manipulate. These are features that make digital content so appealing but also cause issues when curating these materials. Because digital things can be copied and manipulated so easily, it is difficult to know whether the digital object "in hand" is an exact replica of the original.

Digital things can be changed either inadvertently or maliciously. Digital things are copied and moved via software over networks. During this process, data can be corrupted or lost. Digital things can be corrupted by an inadvertent error in the software or by an intended feature designed to do damage. Digital things can be corrupted by the hardware technologies both computational and storage. This is the problem of fixity. Unlike books and other analog things, digital things are not fixed in a physical medium. Curators must be able to ensure that the digital things they have are exact copies of the original.

Obsolescence is a significant issue in digital curation. As described under curation principle two, digital data is tied to a specific technology. Technology ages quickly. Some technologies change and evolve while others left behind. Digital things in formats and technologies that are maintained and growing are more easily curated. Digital things in technologies that are not maintained and growing are more difficult to curate. The obsolescence of the technology creates challenges for the curators: how to detect obsolescence, how to plan for new technologies, and how to choose technologies as to minimize future obsolescence.

Open Archival Information System Conceptual Model

The Open Archival Information System (OAIS) is a conceptual model, a conceptual model, a representation of the relationships of the major components of an archival organization (see Figure 1.2). The OAIS is an abstract model, not an architecture, a system, or a cookbook for digital preservation success, but a communications vehicle for complex constructs. The OAIS was developed by the Consultative Committee for Space Data Systems (CCSDS). In 1995, the CCSDS held its first international workshop proposing to develop the OAIS. Drafts were circulated in 1997 and 1999; it was published as a draft standard in 2000 and approved as an ISO standard (14721) in 2002. The CCSDS created a collaborative and inclusive environment when developing the standard and included librarians and curators as well as scientific domain experts to develop this conceptual model. A revised version was published in 2012 and focuses on recommended practice. This conceptual model was designed to help organizations develop systems, both human and technical, to archive and preserve digital materials. An Archival Information System is "an organization of people and systems that has accepted responsibility to preserve information and make it available for a designated community" (CCSDS, 2012, p. 1.1).

An Archival Information System exists in an environment that includes producers of information and consumers of that information. The system itself sits as a mediator between these two sets of information users. The entire Archival

Figure 1.2.
OAIS Conceptual Model Overview

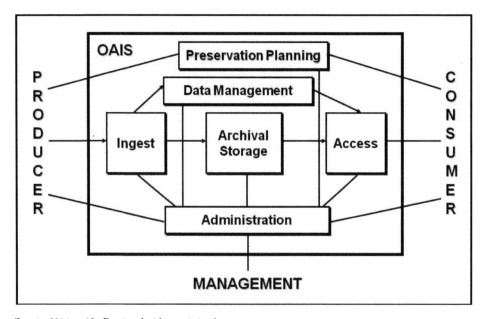

(Lavoie, 2014, p. 12. Reprinted with permission.)

Information System needs regular and ongoing management to be successful. An Archival Information System has a number of components to help it fulfill its mandatory responsibilities.

- *Ingest* is the process to accept information from data producers and successfully store the data.
- *Archival Storage* is described as technology, the long-term storage and maintenance of digital objects.
- *Access* describes the processes in which consumers of the data, that is, users, can discover request and receives information.
- *Data Management* is the process to maintain and manage data about the digital objects, including descriptive and administrative metadata.
- *Preservation Planning* includes developing strategies for the Archival Information System and managing changes in technology, user communities and expectations, and funding.
- *Administration* involves the day-to-day operations of the archive.

An Archival Information System has a number of mandatory responsibilities. It must accept content from producers. It must obtain control over that content, including, if necessary, intellectual property rights. The Archival Information System must be able to modify the files and make copies of the files as necessary, hence the requirement for data management. The Archival Information System must ensure that the consumers of the information are able to independently understand the information; that is, that the user community can access and render the data. An Archival Information System needs to develop and follow procedures to preserve information and make the preserved information available by the dissemination of authenticated copies.

The OAIS has had a significant impact on digital curation. It has provided framework for discussion and a vocabulary to define complex concepts so that curators, librarians, technologists, and research community can communicate and collaborate to develop solutions.

Mental Model of Curation

A mental model—a map of concepts, connections, and relationships—can be an effective way of organizing and visualizing complex concepts and/or systems. In the mental model of digital curation found in Figure 1.3, Rusbridge (2007) shows five primary branches of curation: timescales, preservation and archiving, access and reuse, data resource, and sustainability and exit strategy.

These branches are interconnected at various points. Timescale refers to the duration for which one wishes to curate data; this is the primary driver of all other options and decisions. If it is necessary to keep data viable for three months, the technical requirements, including hardware, software, metadata, are significantly different than the technical requirements for materials to be preserved for 50 or 100 years. Understanding the timescale is the critical first step in Preservation

Figure 1.3.
Mental Model of Curation

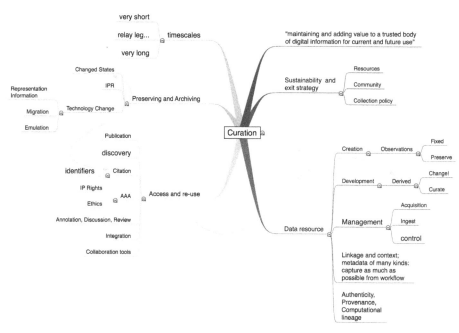

(Rusbridge, 2007, p. 2. Used with permission of Chris Rusbridge and the Digital Curation Centre.)

Planning (see Chapter 9). The Preservation and Archiving branch covers strategies and techniques for managing technology changes. Preservation and archiving will be discussed in Chapters 2, 3, and 4. According to this model, the goal of digital curation is to provide current and ongoing access to the digital materials. The Access and Reuse branch and the Data Resources branch are, then, the desired outcomes of the other processes. In Chapters 10, 11, and 12, topics of data resources and access and reuse for three major categories of data will be covered. Sustainability and exit strategy will be discussed in Chapters 5–9.

TECHNICAL IMPLICATIONS

The technical implications of digital curation are substantial. As digital objects are instantiated within technical environments, one could expect the technology challenges to be daunting. And they are. However, the technical issues are not insurmountable. These technical issues can be resolved with creativity, thoughtful planning, and concerted effort.

One of the most interesting technical challenges that digital curators face involves the nature of digital things—digital objects are made of multiple types of digital files. It may not be immediately clear why this would be a difficult technical challenge. As mentioned earlier, digital content is tied to technology environment. Different types of files require different technology infrastructures. Curating that digital book requires an understanding of all the types of files used: TIFF, JPEG, JPEG2000, PDF, XML, txt, and perhaps others. Each of those types of files requires a different technology to process, read, write, edit, and display. In Chapter 3, files and file formats will be covered in detail.

The construct of time has significant technical implications. Managing technology over time means managing change. Obsolescence is built into technology. As soon as one version of hardware or software is released, work begins on new versions. The general expectation of technology longevity is three to five years. The implication is technology must be replaced on a rotating three- to five-year schedule. This should not be surprising. People who have computers, whether desktop, laptop, tablet, or cell phone, understand that new versions are released on a regular basis and that their technology is out of date quickly. Chapters on preservation planning (Chapter 9), data management (Chapter 7), and disaster planning (Chapter 8) will address technology management over time.

While the OAIS model is explicitly not technical, it does have a number of technical assumptions. It implies, by its very structure, a system for managing digital objects. Such a system is often referred to as a digital repository. One of the outcomes of the OAIS model has been a focus on developing digital repositories. Fedora, DSpace, CONTENTdm, and ePrints are but a few of the repository systems developed and deployed since OAIS began. This work on digital repositories has helped digital libraries and digital archives implement infrastructures specifically developed for their environments. Chapter 6 will have a full discussion of the functionality and technologies of a variety of repository systems.

PRACTICAL APPLICATION

Digital curation is a growth area in libraries, archives, museums, and many other types of information-centric organizations, such as research institutes and businesses. David Lewis predicts that "in the next 20 years only 25% to 40% of libraries resources will go into purchasing collections and 40% to 60% will go into curating digital content" (Lewis, 2007, p. 12). Curating digital content is becoming a profession. Digital curation is a function in many jobs: digital librarian, digital asset manager, data manager, and data librarian, as well as many others. A number of job titles focus completely on digital curation: digital archivist, digital curator, digital assets librarian, data archivist, and others. For this discussion, the term *digital curator* will be used as the inclusive term for all possibilities.

Digital curators, whether in for-profit businesses or not-for-profit cultural heritage organizations, deal with similar projects and problems. Many organizations are digitizing their analog holdings—photos, films, audio, and records of all types. These mass digitization projects have many similar characteristics. They require standards for uniform digitization, standards for descriptive and technical metadata, decisions on rights and permissions, decisions on software for storage and end-user access, and decisions on hardware and operating environments. Digital curators will participate in these projects—working with a team providing advice, doing research, determining the requirements, and choosing standards. The choices made will be determined by the needs of the organization, the technical environment, and the human and financial recourses allotted.

Digital curators also work with born-digital materials including email, websites and web contents, social media contents such as Twitter and Facebook, documents of all sorts such as contracts, memos, minutes, correspondence, newsletters, and presentations. Some born data comes to the digital curator as historical data on failing media. Many organizations produce research data—manufacturers' product testing, pharmaceutical clinical trials, academic research, and surveys. This data comes in a variety of formats, on a variety of media. The work of digital curators will include all of these types of data.

Digital curation and archiving are relatively new job categories. While the terms are used widely, the LIS literature has been reluctant to clearly define them (Radick, 2013). However, various job search websites and practitioners have not been so reluctant. Digital curators "are responsible for acquiring material for a collection, preserving these materials for future generations, helping users locate items from the collection and providing contextual information so they can better understand them, and designing exhibits for the benefit and enjoyment of the public . . ." (Reside, 2011, para. 2). In addition to these tasks, digital curators digitize analog materials, preserve born-digital materials, create contextual information for digital materials, and provide access to and tools for as much of the collection as possible within the bounds of ethics and the law (Reside, 2011). Digital archivists organize large collections of digital materials applying historical context and modern technology standards to preserve data for the future (Study.com, 2016). Several of the job websites indicate that market demand for digital curators will grow. ". . . [B]ecause of the universal need for digital preservation (companies need a place to keep their old records and files and putting them on a hard drive makes more sense then filling up space with large filing cabinets or boxes), this job will open a lot of different doors: For example both universities and law firms have a high need for this position, but each have very different types of archives" (Chegg, 2016, para. 4).

Skills Needed for Digital Curation

Regardless of job title, curator, archivist, or asset manager, the skills needed are very similar. A number of studies have reviewed job posting and developed lists (Dooley, 2014; Kim, Warga, & Moen, 2013; Smith, 2013). The digital curator needs the following:

- An excellent understanding of archival principles, functions, and tasks
  - Appraisal and evaluation
  - Description
  - Collection management

- An excellent understanding of digital preservation and curation
  - Strategies
  - Repositories
  - Formats
  - Metadata
- A good understanding of a variety of metadata standards
  - Descriptive
  - Technical
- The ability to work in a technology intensive environment
- The needed skills in risk assessment
  - Assessment
  - Mitigation
  - Planning
- A good understanding of copyright and intellectual property rights as related to preservation and access
  - Project management skills
  - Project planning
  - Resource allocation
- An understanding of the needs of both born-digital and analog-to-digital materials
- The ability to collaborate with staff in other units of the organization

LeFurgy (2011) emphasizes creative, interpersonal, and communication skills. Bridging the gap between the highly technical and the nontechnical, outreach to both internal and external audiences, finding new and unique ways to apply technology to current problems, and great writing skills are more important than a deep understanding of technology or any specific technology skill, such as programming.

No single person can be an expert in all areas of digital curation. In many organizations, digital curation is a group effort. Even with full-time, dedicated digital curators, teams are essential to successful curation of digital materials. Working well with others, collaboration, cooperation, and a willingness to learn new approaches are some the most important skills needed.

SUMMARY

Digital objects are complex, opaque, and fragile. They consist of multiple files and multiple types of files. They need specific technologies to be useable. A digital object many need unique and proprietary software to process or render on a screen. Digital objects are fragile. They are breakable—locations change, making the objects inaccessible, their bits can be corrupted, and their supporting technologies become obsolete.

The OAIS is the overarching conceptual model for digital curation. An Archival Information System exists in an environment that includes producers of information and consumers of that information. An Archival Information System has a number of components to help it fulfill its mandatory responsibilities, including data ingest, archival storage, end-user access, data management, and preservation planning. The OAIS provides a common understanding and vocabulary of the primary components of digital curation.

Technology challenges abound, but the more challenging task in digital curation is developing policy, training staff, and developing institutional will and funding streams.

Questions for Discussion

1. How would you define digital curation?
2. What concepts would you include in a mental model of digital curation?
3. Have you ever lost any digital data or files? What happened? Could any of the concepts in this chapter have helped?
4. How would you describe the nature of digital objects?

NOTE

1. http://hathitrust.org

REFERENCES

Baker, M., Keeton, K., & Martin, S. (2005). *Why traditional storage systems don't help us save stuff forever* (Technical Report 2005-120). Palo Alto, CA. Found at http://citeseerx.ist .psu.edu/viewdoc/download?doi=10.1.1.65.2375&rep=rep1&type=pdf

Beagrie, N. (2006). Digital curation for science, digital libraries, and individuals. *International Journal of Digital Curation, 1*(1), 3–16.

Chegg. (2016). *Digital archivist.* Found at https://www.chegg.com/career-center/explore/ digital-archivist

Consultative Committee for Space Data Systems (CCSDS). (2012). *Reference model for an Open Archival Information System (OAIS).* Issue 2. Recommendation for Space Data System Standards (Magenta Book), CCSDS 650.0-M-2. Washington, DC: ISO 14721:2012. Found at http://public.ccsds.org/publications/archive/650x0m2.pdf

Digital Preservation. (2016). Digital preservation law and legal definition. In *USLegal Definitions.* Found at http://definitions.uslegal.com/d/digital-preservation

Dooley, J. (2014). What's in a digital archivist's skill set? In *hangingtogether.org from OCLC Research.* June 9, 2014. Found at http://hangingtogether.org/?p=3912

Hedstrom, M. (1997). Digital preservation: A time bomb for digital libraries. *Computers and the Humanities, 31*(3), 189–202. doi:10.1023/A:1000676723815

Kim, J., Warga, E., & Moen, W. (2013). Competencies required for digital curation: An analysis of job advertisements. *International Journal of Digital Curation, 8*(1), 66–83.

Lavoie, B. F. (2014). *The Open Archival Information System (OAIS) reference model: Introductory guide* (2nd ed.). The Digital Preservation Coalition. Found at http://www .oclc.org/research/news/2014/12-04.html

LeFurgy, W. (2011).What skills does a digital archivist or Librarian need? In *The Signal: Digital Preservation*. July 13. Found at http://blogs.loc.gov/digitalpreservation/2011/07/what-skills-does-a-digital-archivist-or-librarian-need/

Lewis, D. W. (2007). A model for academic libraries 2005 to 2025. Paper presented at "Visions of Change," California State University at Sacramento, January 26. Found at https://scholarworks.iupui.edu/handle/1805/665

Lord, P., Macdonald, A., Lyon, L., & Giaretta, D. (2004). From data deluge to data curation. In S. J. Cox (Ed.), *e-Science All Hands Meeting 2004* (pp. 371–375). Nottingham, England. Found at http://citeseerx.ist.psu.edu/viewdoc/download?doi=10.1.1.111.7425&rep=rep1&type=pdf

Radick, C. (2013). Ambiguity and the digital archivist. *Provenance, Journal of the Society of Georgia Archivists, 31*(2), 5. Found at http://digitalcommons.kennesaw.edu/cgi/viewcontent.cgi?article=1008&context=provenance

Research Libraries Group & OCLC. (2002). *Trusted digital repositories: Attributes and responsibilities: An RLG-OCLC report*. Mountain View, CA: Research Libraries Group and OCLC. Found at http://www.oclc.org/research/activities/past/rlg/trustedrep/repositories.pdf

Reside, D. (2011). What is a digital curator? In *The New York Public Library for the Performing Arts, Dorothy and Lewis B. Cullman Center*. April 4. Found at http://www.nypl.org/blog/2011/04/04/what-digital-curator

Rusbridge, C. (2007). Create, curate, re-use: The expanding life course of digital research data. In *EDUCAUSE Australasia 2007*. Melbourne, Victoria, Australia: EDUCAUSE. Found at http://hdl.handle.net/1842/1731

Rusbridge, C., Burnhill, P., Ross, S., Buneman, P., Giaretta, D., Lyon, L., & Atkinson, M. (2005, June). The Digital Curation Centre: A vision for digital curation. In *2005 IEEE International Symposium on Mass Storage Systems and Technology* (pp. 31–41). IEEE. Found at doi:10.1109/LGDI.2005.1612461

Smith, K. R. (2013). Defining the role of digital archivist. In *Engineering the Future of the Past*. February 26. Found at https://libraries.mit.edu/digital-archives/defining-role/

Study.com. (2016). *Digital archivist: Job description, duties and requirements*. Found at http://study.com/articles/Digital_Archivist_Job_Description_Duties_and_Requirements.html

Thibodeau, K. (2002). Overview of technological approaches to digital preservation and challenges in coming years. In *The state of digital preservation: An international perspective*, 4–31. Found at http://www.clir.org/pubs/reports/reports/pub107/pub107.pdf

Chapter 2

CURATION STRATEGIES AND MODELS

Once a new technology rolls over you, if you're not part of the steamroller, you're part of the road.

—Stewart Brand

In the early 1990s when the digital revolution was beginning, librarians and archivists were concerned with their ability to fulfill their mission as knowledge keepers over time. They saw the digital steamroller starting up and did not want to be part of the road. As anyone who is facing a steamroller approaching, librarians in the early 1990s felt some level of panic. The technology was changing rapidly; and more surprisingly, the technology was accepted and adopted more rapidly than could have been predicted. Initial reactions to this digital revolution were mixed. Some saw it as the great equalizer of information, providing access to those who would never had before. Others saw it as the beginning of the end of libraries. Yet others saw the technology as a black hole from which knowledge could never escape. Despite the differences in perspectives, librarians, archivists, and technologists worked together to develop strategies and models for dealing with the new reality of knowledge in digital form.

When dealing with a complex topic such as digital curation, it is often helpful to view it from different perspectives. Viewing a topic from different perspectives can help gain a deeper understanding. It can be difficult to find different perspectives if one is overwhelmed by details. Abstracting the details of a given problem, that is, to analyze and categorize the details, helps develop models that can provide these different perspectives. In this chapter, a variety of models of curation are shown, each of which gives a different view and helps develop new insights into the primary issues of digital curation.

In this chapter, three distinct types of models are described. First, we will look at strategic models of curation. Then lifecycle models of curation are proposed. The chapter ends with a variety of cost models.

THEORETICAL OVERVIEW

Curation Strategies

Curating digital materials requires a strategy. That is, curation requires a plan of action to accomplish the goals of an organization. Three primary strategies for curating digital materials have been developed: technology preservation, technology emulation, and data migration. Each of these strategies has strengths and weaknesses. Most organizations will have a primary strategy for the majority of their materials but may need to implement others as the need arises.

Technology Preservation

As discussed in Chapter 1, digital materials are bound to a specific technology; that is, digital files need specific software for rendering, manipulation, and/or use. This software requires specific operating systems and hardware in which to function. One strategy for preserving access to objects that require obsolete software and hardware is to preserve the original technology environment. This involves maintaining old computers, old storage devices, old operating systems, and old software. In many ways, this can appear to be the reasonable strategy. Keeping the original technologies seems to be straightforward. But in actuality, this is a difficult strategy to implement. Technologies become obsolete so quickly that the number of hardware and software configurations that must be maintained can grow rapidly. Finding resources, both human and technical, to maintain the machines and software becomes increasingly difficult. Imagine a scenario in which an organization needed to maintain applications and data running in DOS, Windows 3, Windows XP, Windows NT, a variety of UNIX operating systems, and Mac OS up to release 10; finding or developing staff with expertise in all of these technologies would be difficult.

Providing access to this material to researchers and the general public would also be a significant challenge. Few of these technologies could be made available via the Internet; researchers would need to physically visit the organization to be able to access the information. Not only would researchers need physical access to the computers, but they would also need access to reams of documentation. For example, DOS, the Disk Operating System, was the ubiquitous operating system from 1974 through 1995.[1] New generations of computer users have had no experience with MS-DOS and would be completely confused by a blinking cursor at the C: prompt (see Figure 2.1). Instructing users to be able to use DOS commands to find programs and data would be difficult. Scaling the instructions would be daunting. Imagine multiplying this by dozens of technologies. Technology preservation is an impractical large-scale solution.

Figure 2.1.
Windows DOS C: Prompt

```
C:\Users\Public>
```

Technology preservation has been referred to as the museum-style approach (Caplan, 2008). Not surprisingly, this approach has been used by museums specifically for art installations where the look, feel, and functionality of the original, proprietary, and unique hardware are considered by the artist to be significant components of the art itself.

Technology Emulation

Technology emulation is the second of the three digital curation strategies. This strategy involves creating a technical environment that is able to execute existing software. This strategy was considered very controversial when it was introduced in the late 1990s. There were concerns about developing, implementing, and maintaining an emulation engine (Rothenberg, 1998a, 1998b). However, as time has passed, a number of emulation engines have been developed and are deployed very successfully.

The computer gaming community is one of the driving forces for the emulation strategy. This community has taken upon itself the task of preserving access to computer-based games. The problems of preserving access to computer-based games are many and complex, the sheer number of game platforms being first among them. Microsoft, Sony, Nintendo, Atari, and more have their own proprietary gaming systems that include hardware, peripherals, operating systems, and, of course, games. The second significant problem with preserving access to computer-based games is the primary requirement to exactly replicate the look, feel, and interactive functionality of the original. Because of these issues, emulation is considered to be the best strategy for preserving games. Historically, there has been a close tie between gaming and computer science. One result of that close tie has been the development of a number of emulation engines specifically for gaming platforms. Gaming websites listed dozens of emulators. As an example, the FantasyAnime[2] gaming website lists 71 emulators.

Data Migration

The OAIS model refers to four types of data migration: refreshment, replication, repackaging, and transformation. The first three—refreshment, replication, and repackaging—are types of file copies for good data management, including disaster recovery planning and data repurposing. These "three Rs" will be discussed more fully in the disaster planning chapter. When we talk about data migration as a pres-ervation strategy, we mean data transformation—a change from one data format to another.

The data migration strategy acknowledges that technology will change and that data formats will become obsolete. To ensure that data will be accessible over time, the data migration strategy expects to convert data from the obsolete format into new formats. This is the prevalent strategy in place in most organizations with a digital curation program. This strategy requires organizations to be able to recognize format obsolescence and have sufficient management control of their objects and adequate technical metadata to identify the objects that require migration.

Data migration strategy has two approaches: one is preemptive, that is, data is migrated when it is accepted into the repository; the second is a just-in-time strategy that expects plans to migrate data at time of format obsolescence. Using a preemptive data migration strategy means that data is migrated upon accession. This process is also referred to as normalization. In general, an archivist would choose several optimal preservation formats. An archivist could expect to receive documents in a number of different formats, including a variety of Microsoft Word formats (.doc, .docx), plain text (.txt), rich text (.rtf), Apple compressed/encrypted format (.dmg), and many others. To implement the preemptive data migration strategy, the archive would convert all of these files to a more preservable format such as PDF/A. To follow best archival practice, this archive would save and commit to ongoing to bit-level maintenance of the original documents. But the normalized version would be the file that would be preserved for access.

Using the just-in-time data migration strategy means that the archiving organiza-tion needs to be aware of the file formats in its repository and must monitor for obsolescence of these formats. When the organization recognized the need to migrate, the resources needed to plan and implement a migration project must be marshaled. These resources could include systems analysts, programmers, project managers, format experts, and systems administrators, as well as the collection own-ers and other organizational stakeholders.

In order to migrate data, software to read the existing file, modify the data to the new format, and write the new file out must be created. In order to write such a pro-gram, the file format must be knowable; that is, there must be sufficient documen-tation for programmers to be able to deconstruct the current file, map the existing data into the new format, and validate the data transfer. This means that format becomes a significant indicator of preservability. In Chapter 3, this will be explored from both a theoretical and technical perspective.

Data migration is a well-understood phenomenon. It is a regular practice of any organization that deals with information systems. Whenever a system is modified and requires new data elements, data must be migrated. New data formats, whether for long-term data preservation or for transactional systems, require migration. The data migration process has six steps: assess, plan, extract, cleanse, load, and verify (Data Recovery Labs, n.d.). As with many system-related activities, assess-ment and planning are the first two steps. Assessment and planning include review-ing the existing data and the new data format target and determining the best method for implementing the changes. The assessment and planning processes should produce a set of requirements. Once the requirements are established, data can be extracted from the current data format. Data is then cleaned, meaning that it is changed to meet the new format, errors in the old data are fixed, and inconsistencies are reconciled. The modified data is then loaded into the new system in the new format. And, of course, the new data must be tested and verified.

While data migration is the most common primary strategy, it is not without issues. Unlike the technology preservation and emulation strategies, data migration does not allow for the preservation of the original "look and feel" of the interface. For some applications, such as games, this is an unacceptable loss. However, for documents, photographs, and other types of materials, the content is more important than the experience. Again unlike technology preservation and emulation strategies, data migration can introduce error into the preservation process by actually changing the format of the data. Errors can be introduced during the mapping process by misidentifying fields, misunderstanding the meanings of fields, or the inability to find an appropriate new format for one that is obsolete. Errors could be introduced through bugs in the programs that read, transform, and write the files.

Lifecycle Models

Digital preservation is often defined as the management of data throughout its lifecycle. Lifecycles are models that explain complex and interactive processes. In digital curation, lifecycles describe the process by which digital data is created, analyzed, managed, and used.

Lifecycles have been proven to provide an important and useful framework for understanding digital curation. As with other types of modeling methodologies, lifecycles allow organizations to abstract, that is, to categorize and generalize the details of these complex processes, allowing the big picture to emerge. Organizations are dealing with an increasing amount of data created in a variety of formats with different equipment and for different purposes. In addition, the number of individuals and processes to manage the complex data environment has increased, again adding significant complexity. Lifecycles are generally path dependent, meaning that decisions made early in the process can significantly impact the options available later in the process. For example, if an organization used the data migration strategy of preemptive normalization (they convert data to a common, preservable format at a very early stage) and decided to not preserve the original files, that organization will no longer be able to access the original files for future use.

Many organizations and research projects have developed lifecycles for describing their data processes. Some of these lifecycles describe the research process and include steps such as ideation, data creation and/or data gathering, and data analysis. Others of these describe the lifecycle of data and include such steps as creation, describing, and managing. Yet others describe the actual curation process and include such steps as curate, manage, and preserve. We will look at several examples of each of these lifecycles.

Research Lifecycles

In general, although there may be significant differences in the individual stages, research lifecycle models generally include the design and capture, cleaning/integration, analysis, publication, and preservation processes, which occur in an iterative fashion. This is shown in Figure 2.2.

The social science community has been very active in the data preservation movement and has developed several lifecycles to describe the basic research model. The Data Documentation Initiative (DDI), a metadata standard for data description used in the social sciences, is based on a lifecycle model (Green, 2008). The model describes an eight-stage linear research model that includes study concept, data collection, data processing, data archiving, data distribution, data discovery, data analysis, and data repurposing. The DDI model is based on the concepts of production, the actual creation of the data, and data reuse. The conception of the study and data collection phases are considered preproduction stages; the data processing is considered production; data archiving and data distribution are considered postproduction activities; and data discovery, analysis, and repurposing are considered secondary use. Another social science research lifecycle model is a five-stage cycle that includes discovery and planning, initial data collection, final data preparation and analysis, publication and sharing, and long-term management (Green & Gutmann, 2007).

These two research lifecycle models were developed as part of the research agenda of ICPSR[3] (Inter-university Consortium for Political and Social Research). ICPSR is a data repository for social science research. As a long-term data preservation repository, they consider preservation and long-term data management as part of their mission. Other research domains are unlikely to consider preservation as part of their processes.

Data Lifecycles

Data lifecycles, sometimes called information lifecycles, describe the processes and states of data (or information). Different data lifecycles have different levels of granularity and detail (see Figure 2.2). The Digital Content Lifecycle from the National Library of New Zealand was developed to capture a digitization process. The lifecycle includes functions such as creation of data and metadata as well as steps that the patrons will use for discovery and use. The lifecycle includes selection as a prestep to the digitizing process and preservation as an offshoot of management. The lifecycle developed by the Interagency Working Group on Digital Data (IWGDD, 2009) for the Committee on Science of the National Science and Technology Council is at a totally different level. While it does contain the data creation and data use, it also includes steps of security and documentation. The lifecycle is situated in an organization with policy, technology, and human infrastructures that impact the cycle.

Digital Curation Lifecycles

Many digital curation lifecycles have been developed. We will look at three as exemplars. As with research and data lifecycles, each of the digital curation lifecycles is trying to communicate different aspects of curation. Some focus on generic processes while others represent the needs and requirements of a specific organization.

The Library of Congress (2011) has developed a generic preservation lifecycle that compares the traditional preservation model of nondigital materials to an emerging model for digital preservation (see Figure 2.3). The traditional model focuses on "fixing information to physical objects; the conservation of the physical objects becomes the mode of preserving the information" (Rumsey, 2010, p. 29). In the digital preservation lifecycle, preservation actions are initiated at every stage of the lifecycle. Preservation actions are of particular import when responsibility for the data changes hands. These handoffs, from the creator to the curator, involve technology and policy that can affect the long-term viability of the data to be preserved (Rumsey, 2010).

An early preservation model (see Figure 2.4) was developed for the Joint Information Systems Council (UK) and includes data capture (ingest) and a cycle for multiple levels of storage with preservation actions (Beagrie, 2004).

Figure 2.2.
Data Lifecycles

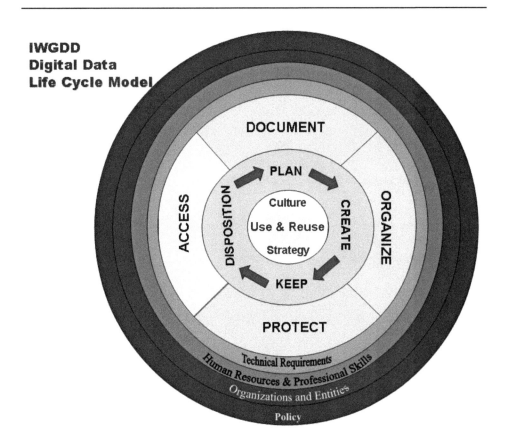

Figure 2.3.
Traditional and Digital Preservation Lifecycles

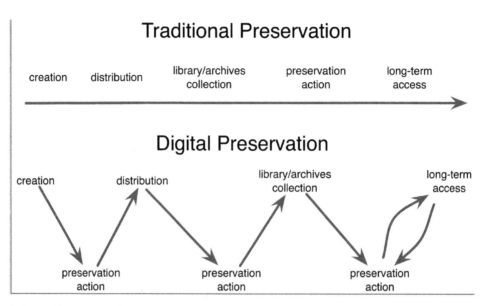

(Library of Congress, 2011)

The Digital Curation Centre (DCC, 2016) designed a high level and broadly situated curation lifecycle to be used by curators (see Figure 2.5). The DCC model has multiple levels that depict both data stages and preservation actions.

Figure 2.4.
Simplified Model for the JISC Information Environment

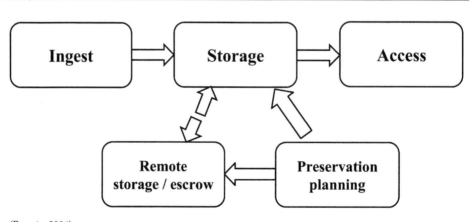

(Beagrie, 2004)

Figure 2.5.
The Digital Curation Centre Lifecycle Model

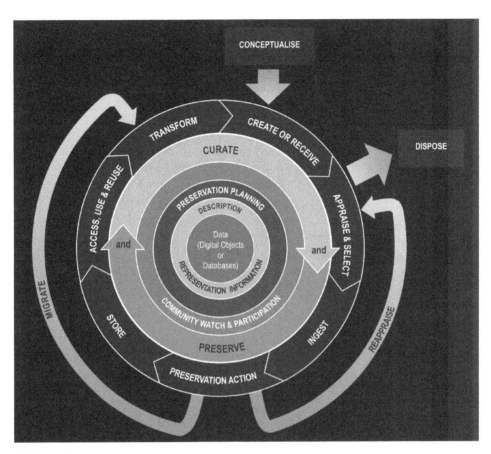

(DCC, 2016)

It is important to note that the model is an ideal. In reality, users of the model may enter at any stage of the lifecycle depending on their current area of need. For instance, a digital repository manager may engage with the model for this first time when considering curation from the point of ingest. The repository manger may then work backwards to refine the support they offer during the conceptualisation [sic] and creation processes to improve data management and longer-term curation. (DCC, 2016)

Cost Models

As the importance of digital materials increases, the number of people who care about digital curation increases. And as the amount of digital content increases, concern about cost increases. Thus, cost models become increasingly important.

Stakeholders, those who care deeply about the costs of ongoing access to digital content, include research funders, government agencies, content creators, research institutions, and businesses. Research funders want to ensure that their limited funds are well spent and that the research output is available for other research uses. Content creators include such diverse roles as research scientists, game developers, and artists, such as photographers and musicians, often bear the brunt of the cost of maintaining their materials over time.

Modeling the costs of the lifecycle of digital materials is fundamentally different than modeling costs of analog or physical objects in that the infrastructure for digital materials has a significantly shorter lifespan than the infrastructure of a library or an archive. For a book, acquisition is the most significant cost; the purchase cost, metadata creation, and physical processing, including such activities as barcoding, labeling, and shelving, are upfront onetime costs. Once the book is on the shelf, the incremental cost is negligible. In general, libraries do not amortize the cost of electricity, heat, cooling, and building maintenance over the lifespan of each book on the shelves. When a traditional collection of papers, letters, and other analog documents comes to an archive, again it is the upfront processing that is the most expensive; organizing, boxing, describing, and shelving are the primary costs. It is infrequent and unusual to reprocess collections. The infrastructure for these collections—the boxes, the shelves, and the buildings—is intended to last for generations.

Digital objects also have front-loaded acquisition costs analogous to physical materials. In addition, digital objects have an ongoing infrastructure cost. On a three- to five-year cycle, the servers, storage devices, network connections, and software applications need to be upgraded or replaced as they become obsolete. Ongoing budgeting for digital curation must then include not only the incremental costs of new materials but also the reengineering and architecting of the entire infrastructure on a regular schedule.

Components of a Digital Curation Cost Model

A number of components must be considered when developing a cost model for digital curation (see Table 2.1). A set of variables about the organization needs to be analyzed and quantified. The capacity of the organization, that is, the entirety of the resources in equipment, people, and skills, must be accounted for in a cost model. Building capacity and capability are expensive in both time and money. The organization's tolerance for risk is another component to be factored into a cost model. The more risk averse, the more backups and failover plans need to be developed and financed. An organization that has an established robust technical infrastructure may need only model incremental costs, while an organization with a minimal technical infrastructure may need to include significant infrastructures into its model. Overall organizational funding models also play a role in developing cost models for curation. Cost recovery organizations will need to have many more components covered in the cost model than organizations with persistent operational funding.

In addition to the organizational variables, there are cost drivers to be considered. Cost drivers are the elements having the highest direct impact on cost (see Table 2.1). For curation, these drivers center on the nature of the data to be curated. Volume, both in terms of number of bytes and number of files, is one of the most significant cost drivers. And this seems logical; the higher the number of files, the more administration and management are required; the higher the sheer number of bits, the more storage capacity is required. Volatility of the data can also impact the long-term cost of curation. If we are curating data from its inception and if this data undergoes multiple changes during its lifecycle, administration, management, and data storage costs will increase. If the volatility is low, that is, the data does not change after its initial creation, the costs will be lower. It may be difficult to quantify the volatility of the data. It may be dependent on the source. Velocity, the speed at which data is created and must be processed, impacts capacity requirements. Lots of data coming quickly require greater capacity in the entire infrastructure, including the network, computational and processing systems, and storage systems. Access requirements impact network, storage, and computational infrastructures. Large data files that require fast delivery require higher bandwidth and faster storage mechanisms. If those large data files need to be processed as part of the delivery process, the computational infrastructure may need to be more robust.

Think of costs as predictable recurring costs and unique event-based costs (see Table 2.2). A number of costs are recurring. Recurring costs can be thought of as either on an annual or multiple year schedule. Annually recurring costs can include such operational budget items as staff, such as systems administrators, software developers, iteration staff, and support staff, as well as ongoing technology operations costs, such as data center charges, power, cooling, and hardware and software maintenance.

Technology replacement cycles are generally on the order of three to five years, the time period in which technology becomes obsolete and/or begins to fail. The technology for digital curation is not dissimilar technology for operational systems, such as library catalogs or human resources systems. Servers are required to run software; storage devices are required to hold digital data; network components are required for connectivity; and software is required for application functionality. It is the projected geometric growth in volume that is the significant differentiation.

Event costs are those that can be tied to a specific action. As with analog materials, the costs of acquisition activities can be calculated. There is the cost of creating or purchasing the digital object, creating descriptive metadata, and validating and

Table 2.1.

Cost Model Variables

Cost Drivers	Organizational Variables
Volume of materials	Capacity of the organization
Volatility of materials	Risk tolerance
Velocity	Overall technical infrastructure
Access requirements	Funding models

Table 2.2.

Cost Categories

Recurring Costs	Event Costs
Annual	*Acquisition*
• Staff	• Quality assessment
∘ Systems administration	• Technical metadata
∘ Software developer	• Ingest
∘ Digital curators	• Descriptive metadata
• Technology Operation	*Preservation Activities*
∘ Data center costs	• Integrity validation
∘ Maintenance costs	• Data migration
Technology Replacement Cycle	∘ Storage refreshing
• Storage	∘ Format obsolescence
• Servers	*Deaccession*
• Network components	• Identification
• Applications	• Safe and full delete
	• Verification

verifying that the object is complete. But unlike analog materials, an ongoing set of preservation activities must be planned and executed. The costs associated with these activities include software developers, system administrators, computational resources, network resources, and storage. Preservation activities can be integrated operational activities or onetime, special projects. One of the ongoing and regular operational preservation activities is integrity validation, the process of ensuring that the files have not been corrupted and that data has not been lost (see Chapter 5 for an extended discussion). This process has high computational costs. Data disposal could also be considered a regular operational process. Data that has a "delete by date" could be removed. While one could think that this could be a cost savings activity, it can be difficult to reclaim the storage space without an additional investment in staff.

Cost models can be highly complex representations of their organizations. As such, these cost models can also be highly idiosyncratic in that transferring principles between the organizations can be difficult. What works for one organization may be completely unthinkable for another. Centralized organizations may be able to absorb more overhead costs, such as personnel costs, hardware and software maintenance costs, and floor space, than decentralized organizations. Decentralized organizations may have no way to create an income stream to manage these overhead costs and thus must develop methods to account for and allocate overhead costs.

Examples of Digital Curation Cost Models

A number of cost models have been developed primarily in Europe. Many of these projects were developed for specific types of materials: research data, clinical data, digitized books, and cultural heritage materials. Each of these models has different goals and accounting assumptions (APARSEN, 2013). The digital preservation community has developed and continues to maintain a comprehensive list of digital preservation costing initiatives (Costing Digital Preservation, 2016):

- LIFE 1, 2, and 3[4]—projects developed a methodology to model an organization's digital lifecycle and calculate the costs of preserving digital information for 5, 10, or 20 years.
- Cost Model for Digital Preservation (CMDP)[5]—project at the Royal Danish Library and the Danish National Archives to develop a tool that calculates present and future costs of cultural heritage institutions' digital collections.
- Keeping Research Data Safe 1 and 2 (KRDS)[6]—a JISC-funded project to develop tools and methodologies to assessing costs and benefits of curation and preservation of research data.
- Presto Prime[7]—project out of University of Southampton in the United Kingdom developed the iModel, which projects costs by system components, such as storage, ingest, and access.
- Cost Estimation Toolkit (CET)[8]—from NASA Goddard Center used for estimating lifecycle costs for newly planned or modified long-term archival facilities.
- Cost Model for Small Scale Automated Digital Preservation Archives[9]—researchers Strodl and Rauber developed a cost model especially for small-scale automated digital preservation software system.
- APARSEN[10]—project based in Europe that tests digital preservation costing models.
- EPRSC and JISC Cost analysis of cloud computing for research.[11]
- DP4lib[12]—project out of Germany is developing a business and cost model for a digital preservation service.
- Blue Ribbon Task Force on Sustainable Digital Preservation and Access[13]—a project sponsored by the National Science Foundation and the Mellon Foundation to develop general principles and actions to support long-term economic sustainability of digital materials.
- ENSURE Project[14]—Enabling kNowledge Sustainability Usability and Recovery for Economic value looks at the preservation costs of industry.
- 4C project[15]—a European collaboration led by JISC to clarify the costs of curation.
- TCP[16]—a project of the University of California to develop an analytical framework for modeling the full economic costs of preservation, the "total cost of preservation."
- Cost model for digital preservation[17]—a project of the National Archives of the Netherlands to test and evaluate the costs of the different preservation approaches.

TECHNICAL IMPLICATIONS

The *technology preservation strategy* is considered a niche strategy for extremely rare and unique digital artifacts. This strategy is not technically sustainable as the equipment will eventually fail irreparably. Rare parts will be consumed and become irreplaceable. This strategy must be considered to be short term.

When the *technology emulation strategy* was proposed in 1998 (Rothenberg, 1998), librarians, archivists, and technologists had grave concerns about its feasibility and sustainability. With the advent of virtualization, wide-scale use of emulation as a preservation strategy has become possible. Virtualization is the process by which multiple "virtual machines" run on a single hardware platform. The virtualization software masks the physical server, allowing each application to have its own virtual view of resources on the physical machine creating a *virtual machine*. Each virtual machine has an allocation of the physical resources, such as memory, processors, and storage. In addition, each virtual machine has its own operating system with customized requisite parameters. Each virtual machine can run any number of applications. Virtualization is in itself software. It is used by hundreds of data centers around the world to maximize the utility of the expensive hardware platforms. As long as this technology is widely used in business, finding technical expertise to run a virtualized emulation technology will be possible.

While technology emulation is a more realistic strategy than technology preservation, it is not without its challenges. As with technology preservation, issues with user accessibility will be significant. For some applications, users will be dropped at the C: prompt. For others, cryptic commands will be required. Some applications will require a left mouse click, while others will not recognize that input.

One of the most daunting challenges of technology emulation is the setup process. Let us take the example of a set of documents in different technology formats—Word Perfect, Apple Claris Works, and WordStar. The correct versions of the software would need to be identified, located, and purchased. The software would need to be installed and configured. It might be necessary to create a separate virtual machine for each software package. Multiply this effort by scores of collections, formats, and software packages. Providing remote access to these resources remains a technical challenge.

The *data migration strategy* is the most straightforward of the strategies. As described previously, migrating data from one format to another is a normal part of most information technology environments and a normal task in many software development projects. Many programmers have experience with data migration. The major technical issues are the ability to adequately test the quality of the conversion and the size of the collection.

The biggest technical challenge in data migration is to be able to adequately test the quality of the conversion—to ensure that the conversion was correct and that the intellectual content is exactly represented in the new file. Automated process can verify that the file is well formed and meets standards. This is an absolute requirement of a migration. Verifying that the conversion adequately and appropriately converted the intellectual content is more difficult. Understanding the nature of the material, the content, and the feasibility of developing an automated process for validating the content requires a cooperative team effort of technologists, librarians, and/or archivists. Manual testing will need to be an integral component of the project. It is vital to ensure an accurate and complete conversion. A minor error introduced in one conversion may not be noticeable. However, because a file may have multiple conversions over its lifetime, that small error could cause a bigger problem in a future conversion. Errors have a cumulative effect.

The size of the collection impacts the infrastructure requirements for any data migration project. The larger the collection is, the more infrastructure is required. The original files need to be read from the storage device and copied into a temporary space for staging. Network bandwidth will impact the speed of this process and may impact other systems and processes if insufficient. Once the data is staged, the data must be processed. The computational environment will impact the migration: the size, number, and speed of the processors, as well as the amount and type of internal memory. When the conversion process is complete, the quality control process will need to be completed. The new file will need to be stored—more bandwidth and more storage required. And after the conversion, new technical metadata will need to be created (see Chapter 4 for a fuller discussion of metadata).

PRACTICAL APPLICATION

Lifecycles and models are inherently theoretical; they generalize details to create a high-level, abstracted view of an issue. But curation lifecycles and models are developed to be practical, to help librarians, archivists, and technologists find practical solutions to their curation and preservation problems. The HathiTrust Digital Library (HTDL) is an example of the application of curation strategies to a real-life situation. The HTDL is a very large digital collection, consisting primarily of book and book-like materials. As of this writing,[18] the HTDL has 16 million total volumes with 5.5 billion pages that take 721 terabytes of storage.

Technology Preservation—The HTDL has a significant and complex hardware infrastructure that includes multiple larger servers and a massive data store that is replicated in another organization in another state. While the HTDL will certainly want to use their hardware as long as possible, it is not realistic to keep the hardware for the long term. The hardware is not important for this collection; it is just the vehicle for delivering content.

Technology Emulation—The HTDL has a significant and complex software environment that includes a bibliographic search engine, a full text search engine, a page image delivery system with image and text download functions, and individual volume text indexing and searching. This software is implemented across servers for efficiency and redundancy. One option would be to preserve the software as it is right now—to "freeze" the software and functionality of the system. Another option would be to preserve each iteration of the software via emulation, allowing a longitudinal view of the look and feel and functionality of the system. A third option would be to emulate the underlying delivery services—the components that read the files and transform them for delivery and display on a screen. This option would allow for ongoing upgrades to the system's functionality and avoiding a data migration.

Data Migration—The HTDL has a large amount of data. Converting this data when formats become obsolete will be a huge undertaking. All of the issues raised and discussed in the previous section would apply—hardware needs, staffing issues, testing, and quality control. It would certainly be possible to convert the data in an ongoing process.

SUMMARY

Strategies

Each of the preservation strategies—technology preservation, technology emulation, and data migration—has strengths and weaknesses. Both technology preservation and emulation can provide the end user with the actual (or a very close approximation of the) experience of the original system. This is a strength, as experiential integrity is a key goal for archivists. However, the strength can become a weakness as time passes, and the user population is removed from the regular use of the technology. The original experience, while a rich source of information, could become a significant barrier to the underlying information. Documenting and training both archives and users about all of the systems required to support the curated data would be prohibitively expensive. In addition, staff to maintain multiple systems technologies could be very expensive. Emulation for a set of specific materials with a specific need may be feasible.

Data migration is seen as a more viable, long-term option for most organizations and most types of materials. While migration does not require multiple versions of old software and/or hardware to be maintained, it too has its issues. Data migration can introduce error and/or data loss. Inaccurate data mapping, inconsistent data coding, and software errors can all contribute to the problem. Data migration requires a level of technology expertise for analysts and programmers. Hiring and paying this specialized staff could be expensive. Finding the computing resources to execute the migration code could also be expensive. Imagine having to find resources to convert multiple petabytes of TIFF files while maintaining a production environment.

Lifecycles are useful models for conceptualizing complex issues. Types of lifecycle models include research lifecycles, data lifecycles, and curation lifecycles. Lifecycle models are developed with the specific goal in mind. Some were developed to be a universal model, applicable to many organizations, while others were developed for a specific institution to solve a specific problem. Some were developed to emphasize one aspect of the complete lifecycle, while others were intended to be complete. Lifecycles have different levels of granularity, that is, Lifecycles have different levels of granularity that makes it difficult to compare models. Lifecycle models can be useful to help curation professionals to find appropriate strategies, workflows, and processes for their organizations and collections.

Cost models are complex. Cost drivers, organizational variables, recurring costs, and event costs need to be identified and quantified. The organization itself needs to determine what costs are overhead, that is, built into overall budget structures, and which costs need to be accounted for separately. While a large number of cost models have been developed, they have not been widely adopted. Institutions are still in the early stages of developing predictive and consistent cost models for curation and preservation.

Questions for Discussion

1. Why is the data migration strategy the most prevalent strategy for digital curation in libraries and archives?

2. Can you describe scenarios where a technology preservation strategy would be appropriate? Or a technology emulation strategy?

3. How could lifecycle models help organizations when thinking about a preservation strategy?

4. Which curation strategy do you think would work best for the HathiTrust Digital Library?

5. Think about your favorite information organization (a library, archive, or other information-centric institution) or your favorite information collection. What strategies and lifecycles would you consider if you were developing a curation program for your organization or collection?

NOTES

1. https://en.wikipedia.org/wiki/DOS
2. http://fantasyanime.com/emulators as of January 23, 2014.
3. https://www.icpsr.umich.edu/icpsrweb/landing.jsp
4. http://www.life.ac.uk/
5. http://www.costmodelfordigitalpreservation.dk/
6. http://www.beagrie.com/krds.php
7. http://prestoprime.it-innovation.soton.ac.uk/imodel/faq/
8. http://www.pv2007.dlr.de/Papers/Fontaine_CostModelObservations.pdf
9. http://www.ifs.tuwien.ac.at/~strodl/paper/strodl_ipres2011_costmodel.pdf
10. http://www.alliancepermanentaccess.org/wp-content/uploads/sites/7/downloads/2014/06/APARSEN-REP-D32_2-01-1_0_incURN.pdf
11. http://www.webarchive.org.uk/wayback/archive/20140615025247/http://www.jisc.ac.uk/media/documents/programmes/research_infrastructure/costcloudresearch.pdf
12. http://dp4lib.langzeitarchivierung.de/downloads/DP4lib-One-Pager-08-eng.pdf
13. http://brtf.sdsc.edu/index.html
14. http://cordis.europa.eu/project/rcn/98002_en.html
15. http://4cproject.eu/
16. https://wiki.ucop.edu/display/Curation/Cost+Modeling
17. http://dlmforum.typepad.com/Paper_RemcoVerdegem_and_JS_CostModelfordigitalpreservation.pdf
18. February 4, 2018.

REFERENCES

Alliance for Permanent Access to the Records of Science Network (APARSEN). (2013). *Report on cost parameters for digital repositories* (Report number: APARSEN-REP-D32_1-01-1_0 2013-02-28). Found at http://www.alliancepermanentaccess.org/wp-content/uploads/sites/7/downloads/2014/06/APARSEN-REP-D32_1-01-1_0_incURN.pdf

Beagrie, N. (2004). The continuing access and digital preservation strategy for the Joint Information Systems Committee (JISC). *D-Lib Magazine, 10*(7/8). Found at http://www.dlib.org/dlib/july04/beagrie/07beagrie.html

Caplan, P. (2008). Preservation Practices. *Library Technology Reports,* 44(2), 10–13.

Costing Digital Preservation. (2016). *Digital preservation and data curation costing and cost modelling.* Found at http://wiki.opf-labs.org/display/CDP/Home

Data Recovery Labs. (n.d.). *Data migration/conversion services.* Found at http://www.werecoverdata.com/data-migration-conversion-services/

Digital Curation Centre (DCC). (2016). *DCC Curation Lifecycle Model.* Found at http://www.dcc.ac.uk/resources/curation-lifecycle-model

Green, A. (2008). *Data Documentation Initiative DDI. DataShare.* Edinburgh, Scotland. Found at www.disc-uk.org/docs/DDI_Green.pdf

Green, A. G., & Gutmann, M. P. (2007). Building partnerships among social science researchers, institution-based repositories and domain specific data archives. *OCLC Systems & Services, 23*(1), 35–53. doi:10.1108/10650750710720757

Interagency Working Group on Digital Data (IWGDD). (2009). Appendix B. Digital Data Life Cycle. In Harnessing the *power* of digital data for science and society. Report of the Interagency Working Group on Digital Data to the Committee on Science of the National Science and Technology Council. Found at https://www.nitrd.gov/About/Harnessing_Power_Web.pdf

Library of Congress. (2011). *Preserving our digital heritage: The national digital information infrastructure and preservation program 2010 report.* Washington, DC: A Collaborative Initiative of the Library of Congress. Found at http://www.digitalpreservation.gov/multimedia/documents/NDIIPP2010Report_Post.pdf

National Library of New Zealand. (n.d.). Getting started with digitisation. *DigitalNZ.* Found at http://www.digitalnz.org/make-it-digital/getting-started-with-digitisation

Rothenberg, J. (1999). *Avoiding technological quicksand: Finding a viable technical foundation for digital preservation.* Washington, DC: Council on Library and Information Resources. ISBN 1-887334-63-7. Found at http://www.clir.org/pubs/reports/rothenberg/contents.html

Rumsey, A. S. (2010). *Sustainable economics for a digital planet: Ensuring long-term access to digital information. Final report of the Blue Ribbon Task Force on Sustainable Digital Preservation and Access.* Washington, DC: National Science Foundation (NSF Award No. OCI 0737721). Found at http://brtf.sdsc.edu/biblio/BRTF_Final_Report.pdf

Section II

Preservation Technology
Fundamentals

Chapter 3

FORMATS

... [C]lassical Greek script in the stone is still legible after 22 centuries; words in Shakespeare's first printed edition of sonnet are legible after nearly four centuries; many microfilms carried by pigeons during the siege of Paris in 1870 are still readable today. Digital media, however, can become unreadable within a decade.

—Ziming Liu (2004, p. 279)

At its most basic level, digital curation is concerned with preserving computer files. Anyone who has used a computer has used files—written files, read files, and changed files. Because using files within their context of a computer with an operating system and software is relatively intuitive, people do not often completely understand what a file actually is. Having a clear and precise definition is useful when discussing curation. *A file is a collection of data stored as a single entity that is named and available to be used by a computer.*

Digital data is represented in a file format, which is defined as *the internal structure and encoding that facilitate computational processing as well as rendering for human use* (Brown, 2006). Abrams (2004) contends that the concept of representation format is the foundation of many, if not all, digital preservation activities. File formats need to be understood in order to document, describe, deliver, maintain, and change a file. File formats number in the hundreds.[1] The proliferation of complex formats greatly increases the complexity of preservation (Barateiro, Antunes, Cabral, Borbinha, & Rodrigues, 2008; Ross, 2007). The technical format of a file affects its probability of being preserved (Anderson, 2015; Kowalczyk, 2008).

Format change and/or obsolescence is a major threat to preservation (Anderson, 2015). When formats change, files may no longer be usable. Software may only support the most current version. Over time, some versions of the format may be deprecated, that is, no longer supported. Formats may become obsolete; that is, the systems that create, process, render, and use that format are no longer functional, viable, and/or available. An obsolete format is essentially dead. Format change and obsolescence is the primary focus of the data migration preservation strategy (see Chapter 2).

This chapter will discuss the nature of files and formats as well as ways in which digital curators can avoid format obsolescence and data loss.

THEORETICAL OVERVIEW

The Hierarchy of Data

Data is inherently hierarchical (see Figure 3.1). A bit is the smallest amount of information; a bit is a single electrical impulse that is either off or on, zero or one. Bits are organized into bytes; most modern computers have eight bits in a byte,

Figure 3.1.
Data Hierarchy

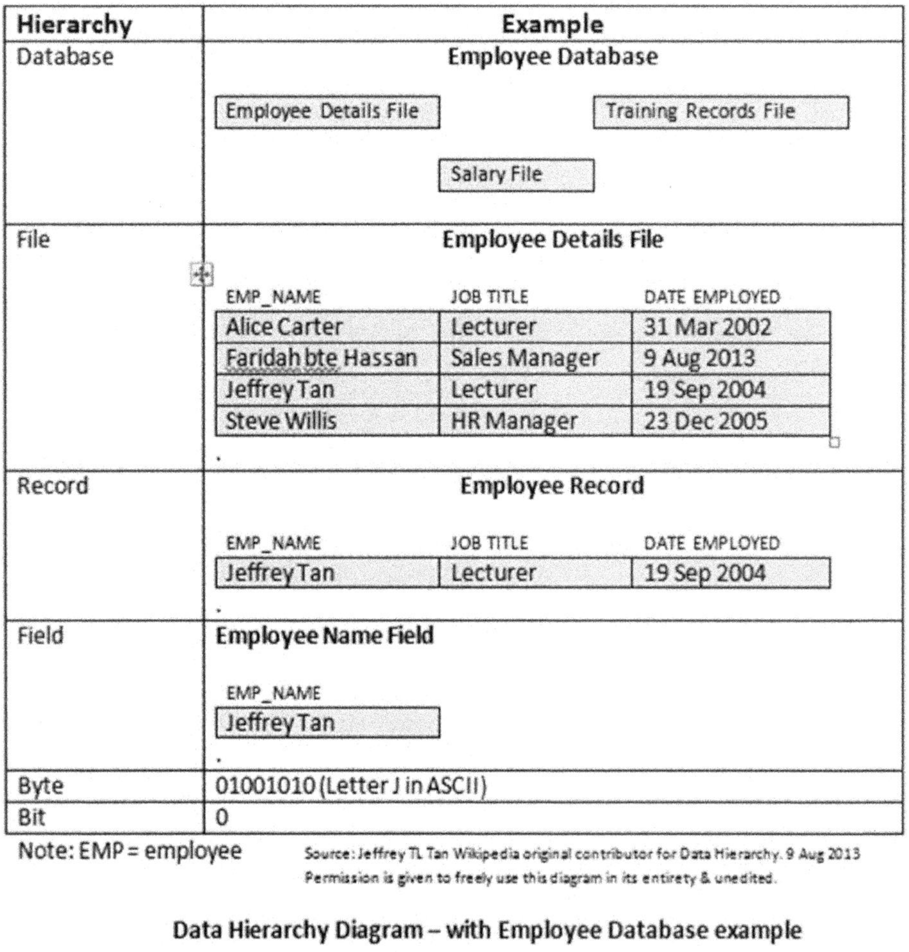

Hierarchy	Example
Database	**Employee Database** Employee Details File Training Records File Salary File
File	**Employee Details File** EMP_NAME JOB TITLE DATE EMPLOYED Alice Carter Lecturer 31 Mar 2002 Faridah bte Hassan Sales Manager 9 Aug 2013 Jeffrey Tan Lecturer 19 Sep 2004 Steve Willis HR Manager 23 Dec 2005
Record	**Employee Record** EMP_NAME JOB TITLE DATE EMPLOYED Jeffrey Tan Lecturer 19 Sep 2004
Field	**Employee Name Field** EMP_NAME Jeffrey Tan
Byte	01001010 (Letter J in ASCII)
Bit	0

Note: EMP = employee   Source: Jeffrey TL Tan Wikipedia original contributor for Data Hierarchy. 9 Aug 2013
Permission is given to freely use this diagram in its entirety & unedited.

Data Hierarchy Diagram – with Employee Database example

(Tan 2013)

sufficient to store a single ASCII[2] character. Moving from physical representation to logical information, characters (bytes) are organized into fields. Fields generally have a logical construct that represents the information. In the example, the field contains an employee's name. Multiple fields are organized into records, again representing an information construct. In the example, all of the information about an employee is gathered into an employee record. Multiple records are gathered into files. All of the employee records become the employee file. Multiple files can be represented as a database. In our example, we have the employee data, salary information, and training records.

Files can be a single character or complex information objects. Files are managed in file systems. File system organizing principles and access mechanisms are specific to the operating system. But in general, file systems are hierarchical in nature. Individual files can be gathered into directories; directories can be named, and they can be nested.

Formats

Data is stored in files. But in order to use that data, the layout of that data, how that data is represented in the file, must be understood. In other words, the format of the data must be known. *Format is defined as the internal structure, the arrangement of bits and bytes, that allows software to read, process, and render the data in meaningful ways.* As the primary goal in digital curation is to make data accessible and usable to the future, understanding file formats is a key component of digital curation. Abrams (2004) contends that "the concept of representation format permeates all technical aspects of digital repository architecture and is, therefore, the foundation of many, if not all, digital preservation activities." In other words, the technical format of a file determines its probability of being preserved; curation must include preserving access to the intellectual content of the file, which requires software to interpret the data, a process that requires an understanding of the representational format.

File Format Standards

File formats can be either proprietary or open standards. Proprietary file formats are defined as being owned by one or more organizations or individuals with legal restrictions of use, with limited transparency and/or software for rendering and processing. Open standard formats are defined as being in the public domain or owned by an organization that makes the format available with no legal restrictions and has publically available documentation and software for processing and/or rendering. Proprietary formats are often developed by and used in application software created by for-profit organizations. Some of the world's most popular and ubiquitous file formats are proprietary; all of the formats used in Microsoft Office are proprietary. Many other formats, however, are open: JPEG, TIFF, PNG, and many others are available to use without restrictions. Open standards are often controlled by national and international organizations, such as NISO and ISO. These organizations control and maintain the formal descriptions of these file formats. Changes are vetted by committees and approved on by communities.

Syntax and Semantics in File Formats

Syntax refers to the sequence or order of words or terms. Syntax is the set rules that govern the way the words come together to make sense. Syntax is grammar. Language consists of syntactical elements such as clauses, phrases, verbs, and subjects. In a technical context, syntax refers to the structure and grammar of files and markup languages. Just as with human language, files and markup languages have correct word orders and required punctuation. Syntax can be rigid or flexible. A rigid syntax requires that all the syntactical rules are met before the file will be usable. Depending on the nature of the error, it may not be readable. In the TIFF file format, the data elements, known as tags, are relatively flexible. But the size of each must be 12 bytes. This rule must be enforced. It is rigid. The TIFF format has an extensive set of public tags, fields that are known, well documented, and open for use. In addition, TIFF allows for private tags, data elements that can be created and used for a specific purpose by an application.

Delimited formats are also very rigid. The most common delimited file structure is the comma separated values syntax, often referred to as CSV. CSV files often can be represented as a table with columns and rows. In a CSV file, the data elements are separated by commas that act as the field delimiters. In this example—field1, field2, field3, field5—the record has five data elements and five commas. Field4 has no data but must have a comma as a placeholder. The names of the data elements may be explicitly expressed in the first row of the file.

XML, the extensible markup language, can be used to define a file format. Using the schema, the syntax of the file can be documented. Data elements are expressed as tags in angle brackets, which encapsulate the data: <tag>*data*</tag>. XML schema can express rules—certain tags must be present; certain tags depend on the presence of other tags, and so on. XML is generally a more flexible structure.

In addition to syntax, file formats also require semantics, the meaning of the data. The meaning of the data can be expressed in schema per XML and databases, column headers in CSV files, and data dictionaries. A sample of the TIFF public tags can be seen in Table 3.1.

File Format Sustainability

Since representational format is so significant to curation, understanding the factors that influence the probability of longevity is crucial. A number of researchers have developed criteria for choosing sustainable file formats. The most widely used and most inclusive list was developed by the Library of Congress. These factors focus on the *openness* of the format. The more open the format, the more sustainable the format. Proprietary formats are generally not open and thus are less sustainable. The seven sustainability factors from the Library of Congress are:

1. disclosure;
2. adoption;

Table 3.1.

TIFF Syntax

TIFF Public Tag	Description
256	ImageWidth
257	ImageLength
258	BitsPerSample
259	Compression
262	PhotometricInterpretation
273	StripOffsets
277	SamplesPerPixel
278	RowsPerStrip
279	StripByteCounts
282	XResolution
283	YResolution
296	ResolutionUnit
320	ColorMap
284	PlanarConfiguration
529	YCbCrCoefficients
530	YCbCrSubSampling
531	YCbCrPositioning

3. transparency;

4. self-documentation;

5. external dependencies;

6. impact of patents; and

7. technical protection mechanisms. (Library of Congress, 2013)

Disclosure describes the level of documentation, specifications, and tools that are available for verifying and validating the format. Disclosure is not a binary state; multiple levels of disclosure are possible. Proprietary formats will likely have lower levels of disclosure better open formats. Some proprietary formats may be well documented with few barriers to access while other proprietary formats may have virtually no documentation available. Open file formats may also have multiple levels of disclosure. Open formats that are supported by national standards organizations with documentation that is maintained and preserved would have a higher disclosure level than an open format that is no longer actively supported.

Adoption describes the level to which a format is used and supported. Formats used in multiple software packages with multiple options for creation, manipulation, and rendering are more likely to be maintained and supported than those formats with few tools. File formats with low adoption rates are more likely to become obsolete. Adoption can be measured by ubiquity of the format—integrated with web browsers; used by multiple, competing software products; and accepted as industry standards. The greater the adoption, the higher the investments made by content creators and the greater the probability of tools to maintain, sustain, and, if necessary, migrate the data into new formats.

Transparency describes the level to which a file format can be discerned and analyzed with the simplest of tools. Can the file be understood by viewing it through a simple text editor? The concept of transparency supposes that the simpler and more direct the file format, the easier it will be to maintain access to the file and migrate to a new format if necessary. Transparency includes technical readability, that is, using well-supported and standard encodings, such as UTF-8 for text. Transparency may require some loss of efficiency in processing. As an example, it is more transparent to save software as source code rather than as an executable file. And compression negatively impacts transparency.

Self-documentation describes the level that a file can describe itself by containing its own metadata. According to the Library of Congress (2013), the "ability of a digital format to hold (in a transparent form) metadata beyond that needed for basic rendering of the content in today's technical environment is an advantage for purposes of preservation" (para. 11). A number of file formats allow for self-documenting metadata. Some, such as TEI, have a formal set of XML tags for bibliographic data. Others, such as JPEG2000 and TIFF, allow for the inclusion of external metadata standards.

External dependencies describe the level to which a format requires a specific software or hardware environment for use—the more complex the set of external dependencies, the more difficult to sustain over time. External dependencies can be as simple as a specific software package to render a file. Microsoft PowerPoint is required to display and manipulate a .ppt file, as an example. Or external dependencies can be as complex as a complete software and hardware infrastructure to render and interact with a specific electronic game. In some cases, it is possible to mitigate the external dependency by providing surrogates in other less dependent formats. In our example, we could provide a PDF version of the PowerPoint file. While some functionality may be lost (editing for example), the intellectual content would still be accessible. But for more interactive content, such as an electronic game, the dependencies are too significant to be mitigated.

Impact of patents describes the level to which a format has intellectual property protections that could impact its *preservability* and inhibit its adoption. Patents could impact the development of open sources tools to encode and decode the file format, impacting the cost of using that format. The Library of Congress (2013) considers the "widespread adoption of a format may be a good indicator that there will be no adverse effect on the ability of archival institutions to sustain access to the content" of material in formats with active patents (para. 14).

Technical protection mechanisms describe the level to which a format or digital media has embedded functionality that prevents replication or impedes access to the intellectual content. Files stored on media with these types of protections cannot be considered archived per the Library of Congress.

Choosing an archival format is an important component of digital curation. Archival formats should be the most sustainable and store data of the highest quality. In general, high quality means capturing the most information possible, which generally relates to the highest bit rate possible. Of course, an archival format should be the most open and preservable format.

TECHNICAL IMPLICATIONS

High-quality archival objects in open, preservable formats create very large files, which require significant infrastructure for storage and networking. Storing and managing these very large files can be difficult. Compression, defined in the dictionary as the act of pressing or squeezing an object to reduce its volume or size (Compress, 2014), is a common data processing technique to save storage space and cost. Compression techniques fall into two categories: lossless and lossy. As its name implies, lossless compression does not remove or lose any data. It is reversible; that is, files can be restored to their original state. With lossy compression, data that is considered redundant or unimportant is removed. The process cannot be reversed; the compressed file cannot be restored to its former state (see Figure 3.2). Compression and file format are not synonymous but are often coupled. Some file formats integrate specific compression algorithms as files are created. JPEG, MP3, and other formats compress data automatically. Other compression algorithms can be applied to files after they are created. Zip compression can be applied to single files, directories, and nested directories.

Lossless Compression

From a data processing perspective, the process for losslessly compressing a file is really quite simple. The original data is processed by some compression software, which produces compressed data. This process can be run in reverse to restore the data to its original state.

While the overall data processing model is simple, the compression algorithms can be quite complex. While some compression algorithms can be generic (such as Zip) and used on any type of file, many are specific to a format type. In general,

Figure 3.2.
Compression Models

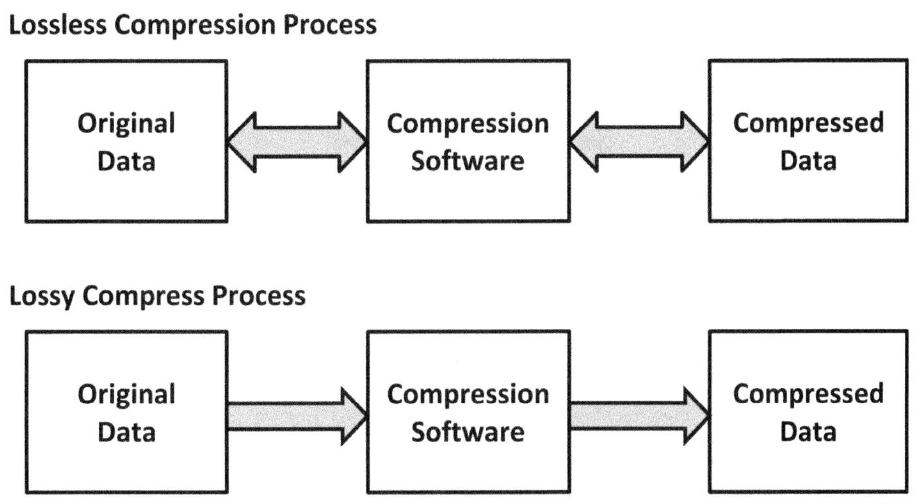

Lossless Compression Process

Lossy Compress Process

these algorithms reduce redundancy or create more efficient data encoding. Compression algorithms are specific to each data type.

- For images
  - Reversible color simplification
  - More efficient data encoding
    ◦ Replace redundant patterns with codes
    ◦ Most common pattern gets the shortest code

- For video
  - Temporal redundancy: because the sequential frames in a video change little, the differences between the frames are coded
  - Spatial redundancy: works similarly to the temporal redundancy, but focuses on the changes in colors across images with the video/film

Lossy Compression

Lossy compression reduces size by eliminating data. Lossy compression cannot be reversed; data is irrevocably lost. While lossy compression removes data, it generally does not change the sensory perception of the object. The algorithms generally reduce irrelevant information that should not impact perception. Using a photographic image as an example, a lossy compression algorithm would analyze the colors of all of the bits. If within a field of a single color value of red, random pixels have a different color, the lossy algorithm would ignore those alternate color values. Those pixels would be encoded as the majority color. The information of the color difference would be lost. Often, color values are rounded. Therefore, if in a photographic image colors fade one at a time across a number of pixels, a lossy algorithm would *smooth* the transition by rounding the numerical values or simplifying the color space. This again results in data loss. An image that has been compressed with a lossy algorithm will appear, at its optimal viewing size, to be whole. When viewed at magnification, the data loss will become visible—blurry lines and details missing.

Hardware Compression

Uncompressed data is preferred for archival storage. Archivists and curators may be surprised to learn that they do not always control how data is actually stored. Many enterprise-level storage devices have lossless compression embedded in their firmware. That is, lossless compression is automatically performed when data is stored; the data is uncompressed when read from the device. Hardware manufacturers see this as a great benefit to their customers by providing more efficient storage and retrieval mechanisms. Some network hardware and software also automatically compress data with a lossless algorithm. Again, this is transparent to the users—both the owners and the users of the data. Transporting compressed data across networks is considerably faster. The time savings in transport outweighs the time cost of compression and decompression. If the process is truly lossless, these transformations for storage and transport will do no harm. Curators and archivists can ensure that *wholeness* of data with various data assurance techniques that will be discussed in Chapter 5.

PRACTICAL APPLICATION

File Formats and Levels of Use

A significant goal of preservation is to make data available. Archival formats, the high-quality, high-resolution, preservable formats, are not always suited for end-user use. Often, archival files are very large causing them to be difficult to transport over networks. A number of archival formats are incompatible with web browsers; these formats have no applications for rendering, viewing, and using. A digital curator ensures that, in addition to the archival format, files are also saved in formats that are easy to deliver and easy to render. Often this means digital archives need to maintain multiple copies: archival copy and usable copies.

For digital photographs, best practice would require a master copy in an archival format, such as TIFF. As of this writing, TIFF is considered to be the archival file format of choice for digital images. However, high-quality TIFF files are very large, often in the hundreds of gigabytes. Large files are difficult to transport over networks and can take a very long time to render. Additionally, many browsers cannot natively display TIFF. In order to make these images available, the archive creates a smaller, more browser- and network-friendly file using such formats as JPEG, PNG, or GIF. The smaller files are often referred to as derivative files as they are derived from the master file. They can also be called a delivery file as they are delivered to web browsers. Digital archive or digital library may choose to have multiple derivative or delivery versions: very small version, also known as a thumbnail, that is suitable for an index or a result set page; a larger version for display on an item-level page; and a large derivative for full-screen viewing, that is, to see the image at 100 percent.

Depending on the nature of the materials, an item may require additional processing to be fully useful to researchers. When digitizing, it is best practice to create the archival version of the original object as it stands. If the analog object is damaged, the archival image is of its current state. However, the damage can obscure the meaning and value of the object. It is possible to "digitally repair" the object. Using software such as Adobe Photoshop, photographs can be fixed: colors can be adjusted, stains can be removed, and rips can be mended. Since the process of digitally restoring images can be time-consuming and expensive, it is reasonable that a library or an archive would want to have an archival version of the repaired image. The restored image in its archival TIFF format would then be used to create derivative/delivery versions of the image. The file that has been manipulated using software cannot be considered the master file but is often referred to as a production master. The production master is a derivative of the archival master file and can be used to create more network and browser-friendly derivative files (see Figure 3.3). Production master files are often used in audio conversion. The archival master file is a faithful rendering of the original material. The production master copy after the

Figure 3.3.
Levels of Use

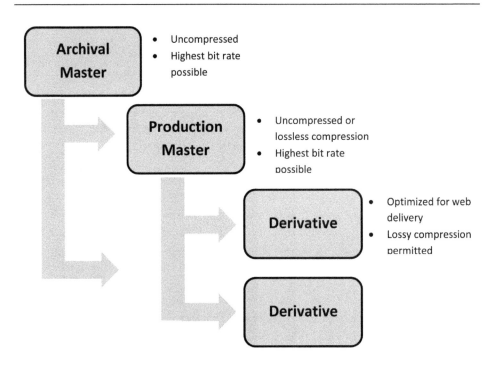

audio engineer cleans up hisses, pops, and other distortions is produced by the original recording process.

Best Practice in File Formats by Level of Use

Choosing file formats seems to be a complex, technical, and somewhat daunting process. Documentation for many file formats is densely technical and quite difficult to read. These documents can be intimidating. Understanding file format may seem too difficult for many digital curators. Digital curators are not required to understand the technical details of different file formats. It is unnecessary for a curator to understand the TIFF directory structure or the offsets of the tags. It is, however, important for a digital curator to know that TIFF is an open, transparent, and widely used archival format for images. Digital curators do not need to make decisions about archival formats by themselves. Fortunately, digital curation professionals can rely on a large network of both practitioners and researchers for advice. Organizations such as the Digital Library Federation,[3] the Library of Congress,[4] and the Digital Curation Centre[5] can provide digital curators with access to network of practitioners for support and guidance. In addition to listservs, conferences, and journals, these organizations provide reliable and authoritative curation resources that are freely available. The Federal Agencies Digitizing Guidelines

Initiative, the Library of Congress, and the Digital Curation Centre offer practical help and file formats and other technical issues.

However much digital curators would like to make informed choices about file formats, it is often out of their hands. Choices are made by the data creators that preclude curatorial options. Many software applications, including word processing applications, accounting software, statistical analysis tools, and scientific instrumentation, create proprietary formats. The ubiquity of these formats means that millions of files will be difficult to preserve.

Best Practice for Archival File Formats

As with many other technical fields, digital curation best practice changes as technologies evolve. What was best practice in 1993, when the digital revolution began, is significantly different than current best practice. As best practice changes, digital curators need to keep current by monitoring authoritative resources. Please verify current practice with reliable sources, such as the Library of Congress, the Digital Library Federation, and the Digital Curation Centre.

Photographic Images

Digital libraries and archives have large holdings of photographic images as film negatives (and occasionally positives), prints, and increasingly as born-digital files. Many libraries and archives were actively digitizing their analog materials. Best practice for digitized analog photographs is uncompressed TIFF. The best case scenario for digital photography is to digitize to the native raw file and convert to TIFF. Just as in the past as they received boxes of photographs from contributors, libraries and archives should expect to receive digital photographs. Many of these photographs will be in lossy compressed file formats, such as JPEG. Because these files have already lost data, it is impossible to recover that data. For files in compressed formats, many libraries and archives are maintaining them in their original format:

- Born digital—capture as raw or TIFF. Often archives and libraries must accept the file formats the creators uses.
- Analog to digital—when scanning, digitize directly to TIFF. For digital photography, capture as either TIFF or raw files, and convert raw files to TIFF. Some organizations are looking at uncompressed JPEG2000 as an archival format for some materials.
- Derivative files for delivery—JPEG is the most common deliverable format. The use of JPEG2000 is increasing.

Documents

Documents, including letters, journals, books, white papers, and so on, are a significant component of archives and library holdings. Libraries and archives are digitizing many of their unique holdings. Best practice calls for digitizing directly to uncompressed TIFF. Born-digital documents present greater challenges to do archives and libraries as they arrived in a wide variety of formats, many of which are proprietary. Some organizations make a choice to migrate files at the time the data is acquired. The National Library of the Netherlands, as an example, chooses to migrate all documents to PDF/A. This simplifies their curation requirements with only one file type to manage. For documents in proprietary formats, best practice would require the archive to maintain the original file in its original format in addition to the converted formats:

- Born digital—maintain the original file. For proprietary formats, convert to PDF/A.
- Analog to digital—digitize directly to TIFF.
- Derivative files for delivery—JPEG and/or PDF or PDF/A.

Audio

Digitizing audio holdings on tape, lacquer discs, and other vulnerable formats is of increasing importance to digital libraries and archives as these materials are deteriorating at an alarming rate. Because the original materials can often only support a single read, archival quality of the digital process as well as the format is of the utmost importance; thus, digitizing audio creates very large files. Most audio being generated currently is born digital. The National Archives normalizes born-digital audio for long-term preservation.[6]

- Born digital—normalize to archival formats if possible.
- Analog to digital—broadcast WAV.
- Derivative files for delivery—MP3 is a common delivery format.

Moving Images

Like audio, digitizing analog film and video is increasingly important for archives and libraries as the original media destabilizes. Best practice is to create uncompressed MPEG2 or MPEG4. However, these uncompressed files are huge. An hour of uncompressed video ranges between 70 gigabytes to nearly 1 terabyte, depending on the bit rate, frames per second, and other variables. For many libraries and archives, this is unsustainable; the cost of the uncompressed data is too high (FADGI, 2014). While uncompressed is preferred, lossless compression is acceptable. Born-digital video is a mainstay of social media. Once uploaded to a web service, such as YouTube, the file has been hyper compressed with lossy algorithms. For digital curators, the only versions may be one of these files. As with born-digital photographs, once the data is lost, it is not recoverable.

- Born digital—capture in archival formats, normalize if possible, or accept as is.
- Analog to digital—MPEG2 and MPEG4.
- Derivative files for delivery—compressed streaming formats.

SUMMARY

Data is hierarchical starting from the smallest amount of data—one bit, the on or off electrical switch—to a collection of organized information in a database. File formats are maps to the data that allow software and people to use and understand the data. Since the goal of curation is to make data accessible and usable to the future, understanding file formats is a key component of digital curation.

Archival files should be high-quality, uncompressed, open formats. Formats should be as sustainable as possible—open, transparent, documented, and widely adopted. Archival files may be compressed using lossless algorithms. Files for web or other forms of delivery can be made more efficient and usable by lossy compression schemes. JPEG and MP3 are some common formats that use lossy compression.

A digital file may need to be saved in multiple formats to meet the requirements of the users. Different levels of use may require different file formats. Archival formats are usually not network- or web browser-friendly, so smaller files, often compressed with lossy compression algorithms, are created as derivatives for end-user delivery. Some materials need to be *digitally repaired*. When the customized digital manipulations are completed, these files can be saved as production masters in an archival format to preserve the effort and expense expended on the repair. Derivatives can be created from production masters when available.

Best practice is a moving target. It changes as technology changes. Digital curators have a large community of practice upon which to rely for advice and counsel. A number of authoritative organizations provide excellent resources for digital curators.

Questions for Discussion

1. Why is file format such an important aspect of digital curation?
2. Why is sustainability of formats an important consideration?
3. What is a proprietary file format? List five open file formats and five proprietary file formats.
4. Have you had an experience with an obsolete file format? Were you able to retrieve the data from that file?

NOTES

1. As of February 2018, IANA (Internet Assigned Numbers Authority) has 1271 registered Mime T types, a rough equivalent of file formats. See https://www.iana.org/assignments/media-types/application.csv

2. American Standard Code for Information Interchange—the most common character encoding scheme. See http://ascii.cl/

3. https://www.diglib.org/

4. http://www.digitalpreservation.gov/
5. http://www.dcc.ac.uk/
6. https://www.archives.gov/preservation/products/products/aud-p3.html

REFERENCES

Abrams, S. L. (2004). The role of format in digital preservation. *Vine, 34*(2), 49–55.

Anderson, D. (2015). Preserving the digital record of computing history. *Communications of the ACM, 58*(7), 29–31.

Barateiro, J., Antunes, G., Cabral, M., Borbinha, J., & Rodrigues, R. (2008). Using a grid for digital preservation. In G. Buchanan, M. Masoodian, & S. J. Cunningham (Eds.), *Digital Libraries: Universal and Ubiquitous Access to Information*, 5362 (pp. 225–235). Berlin: Springer. Found at http://www.springerlink.com/content/k71v8x6081738x18

Brown, A. (2006). Automatic format identification using PRONOM and DROID. *Digital Preservation Technical Paper 1, Issue 2.* London: National Archives of the United Kingdom. Found at http://www.nationalarchives.gov.uk/aboutapps/fileformat/pdf/automatic_format_identification.pdf

Compress. (2014). In *Merriam-Webster's online dictionary.* Found at from http://www.merriam-webster.com/dictionary/compress

Federal Agencies Digitizing Guidelines Initiative (FADGI). (2014). *Creating and archiving born digital video: Part I. Introduction.* Found at http://www.digitizationguidelines.gov/audio-visual/

Kowalczyk, S. T. (2008). Digital preservation by design. In M. S. Raisinghani (Ed.), *Handbook of Research on Global Information Technology: Management in the Digital Economy* (pp. 405–431). Hershey, PA: Information Science Reference/IGI Global.

Library of Congress. (2013). *Sustainability of digital formats planning for Library of Congress collections.* Found at http://www.digitalpreservation.gov/formats/sustain/sustain.shtml

Liu, Z. (2004). The evolution of documents and its impacts. *Journal of Documentation, 60* (3), 279–288.

Ross, S. (2007). Digital preservation, archival science and methodological foundations for digital libraries. *Proceedings of the 11th European Conference on Digital Libraries (ECDL), Budapest (17 September).* Budapest, Hungary: Springer. Found at http://www.ecdl2007.org/Keynote_ECDL2007_SROSS.pdf

Tan, J. (2013). Data Hierarchy diagram showing employee database example. In *Wikipedia Data Hierarchy.* Found at Data_Hierarchy_diagram_showing_Employee_database _example_by_JeffTan.gif

Chapter 4

METADATA FOR CURATION

Think of [metadata] as a gift to the future.

—Library of Congress (LOC, 2011b)

Librarians and archivists have long been advocates of excellent metadata. Usually, this metadata has been descriptive in nature; that is, the metadata describes the object. The machine-readable records (MARC) metadata standard was established in the early 1960s as a way to encode bibliographic information. The Encoded Archival Description (EAD) was established in the early 1990s as a standard for describing finding aids and archival collections. This metadata is imperative for discovery of digital materials. Digital files without descriptive metadata can be considered lost—undiscoverable in an ocean of bits.

Traditional metadata, however, is insufficient to adequately curate digital objects. In addition to traditional metadata, digital libraries and archives need more information to manage their collections. One of the principles from the Framework of Guidance for Building Good Digital Collections indicates other requirements for metadata: "Good metadata supports the long-term management, curation, and preservation of objects in collections" (NISO Framework Working Group, 2007, p. 83). Curators need to know specific details about the technology that created the digital materials, how those digital materials can be used, what processes have been run against those digital materials, and how all the components of the digital object are related to each other. For these purposes, digital curators need metadata. And without that metadata, the digital objects may be unusable. Creating useful, accurate, and thorough metadata is, indeed, a gift to the future.

THEORETICAL OVERVIEW

The Nature of Metadata

Metadata is often described as "data about data." This definition is very close to the dictionary definition of "data that provides information about other data" (Metadata, 2016). This definition, while accurate, is vague and incomplete. A more technical definition is that metadata is the structured descriptions of the essential properties of discrete computer data objects that are stored as separate computer data objects (Gill, 2008). This definition more clearly represents the "meta-"[1] aspect. Metadata is more highly organized as it is structured, and it is specialized data.

Types of Metadata

Metadata needs to provide curators and users with sufficient information to be able to locate, use, and manage data. Metadata can be categorized as descriptive, structural, or administrative (NISO, 2004). Another metadata categorization separates administrative metadata into two categories: technical and administrative (NISO, 2010).

Descriptive metadata, also known as intellectual or access metadata, provides information about the intellectual content of the object. This metadata is used for search and discovery by end users as well as librarians, archivists, and curators. Common descriptive metadata formats include MARC, EAD, Dublin Core, MODS, and VRA. As libraries and archives have begun to manage and preserve more nontraditional materials, such as data sets, databases, research data, and so forth, new forms of descriptive metadata are required: Darwin Core,[2] Flexible Image Transport System (FITS),[3] and Ecological Metadata Language (EML).[4] Descriptive metadata is an important component of preservation as it allows access to the objects.

Structural metadata, as its name implies, documents the relationships between the components of the digital object. Digital objects can be complex with multiple types of files. Structural metadata can be thought of as a wrapper for the data. Structural metadata can provide information to allow navigation of the object. For a book-like object, structural metadata documents the internal features of a resource, such as pages, chapters, indexes, full text, and so on. Structural metadata also describes the relationships between the various files based on user requirements: image A is the archival master; image B is a derivative of the archival master and is used for full-screen display; image C is derived from the archival master and is a thumbnail. The primary structural metadata format for digital libraries and archives is the Metadata Encoding Transmission Standard (METS)[5] that was developed and is maintained by the Library of Congress. Of course, structural metadata is important for access and delivery. Systems that deliver digital objects often use structural metadata for display and for user actions, such as turning pages interviewing next object. Structural metadata is a vital component for curation. Documenting the components of an object is critical to ensuring its integrity. Without knowing all of the component pieces of the digital object, it is impossible for a curator to know that they are all present and accounted for.

Administrative metadata documents the information necessary to manage digital objects over time. Increasingly, administrative metadata is referred to as preservation metadata. The Digital Curation Centre defines preservation metadata as the

> [T]echnical details on the format, structure and use of the digital content, the history of all actions performed on the resource including changes and decisions, the authenticity information such as technical features or custody history, and the responsibilities and rights information applicable to preservation actions. (PADI, n.d., para. 2)

So in this definition, structural metadata becomes part of preservation metadata. This makes sense as understanding the structure of the object is integral to preserving it over time. Structural metadata is also an important component of authenticity, ensuring integrity. While authenticity is often thought of as fixity, maintaining the exact bits level representation of an object, ensuring that all of the files that are part of the digital object are present and accounted for, is also part of authenticity. A book missing a page is considered damaged. A digital object without one of its component files is also considered damaged. Provenance is the history of an object. And as in the provenance of an art object, digital provenance is a component of authenticity. Provenance documents the lineage of its ownership, the processes imposed. Preservation metadata includes technical information: details about the format, the technology environment in which this object can be used, such as software, hardware, and other information for rendering, processing, and understanding the data. Rights information, documenting the intellectual property rights that must be followed, is also included in administrative metadata.

In reality, the categorizing metadata formats by the three types is not necessarily straightforward. Some metadata formats include attributes from all of the categories. And some file formats contain metadata including provenance (the equipment and software used to create the object), technical (bit rates, visual or audio spectrum data), and structure (sequence of subcomponents). While there may not be a one-to-one correlation between the type of metadata and metadata format, each metadata format will have data elements that fit into one or more categories.

Context

Metadata provides curators and users with sufficient information for their needs. Metadata provides context; it describes the context of the object. Context is relative; it depends on the situation. Consider situational contexts of digital objects:

- A researcher needs to find a specific object created by a specific person.
- A researcher wants to know what software is required to process a certain digital object.
- The researcher wants to find the highest quality digital image available.
- A curator needs to find all of the objects created with a certain scanner.

- A curator needs to verify that a specific file has not changed over time.
- A curator needs to find all of the objects created within a specific time range.
- A curator needs to find all of the digital objects that contain file format.

If the primary goal of curation is to keep data accessible, then creating and maintaining descriptive information about the data is key. The descriptions are used for indexing, searching, and choosing data. However, researchers and curators need more information about digital objects than the description of the intellectual content.

Curators and researchers need to understand the technical environment required for the digital object. For many objects, that technology environment is ubiquitous; that is, it is everywhere. Viewing a JPEG image is straightforward in today's information environment. Click on a link and a browser will display the image. However, many objects require more substantial and specialized infrastructure. For example, a geospatial data set may require a specific software package that will require a specific operating system and so forth. Metadata can provide that information in a structured manner so researchers can search and discover the requirements and decide how best to get that data.

Digital objects may contain multiple versions of an intellectual entity; one photographic image may have a high-quality archival master file stored in as an uncompressed TIFF file as well as one or more JPEG files better suited for web delivery. A researcher may discover that JPEG version and view it on the web. For many uses, that web delivery version is perfectly sufficient for the research needs. However, there are circumstances under which a researcher would require a higher quality version. Metadata that describes the structure of the object can help with a researcher or a curator find that the appropriate high-quality image to satisfy that researcher's needs.

Curators need to manage their digital collections. Occasionally, due to quality or other issues, curators will need to know all of the files that were created with a certain piece of equipment over a specific time range or by a specific technician. When contemplating a data migration, curators will need to identify and locate all of the digital objects that contain a specific file format. And on an ongoing basis, curators want to make sure that all of the files within a digital object are present, viable, and unchanged.

Metadata can describe how that file was created, why that file was created, how the file can be used, and how the file should not be used. Specific attributes can be described such as data elements, dates and locations, creators' information, and so on. Metadata becomes its own object, a file stored in a file format with syntax and semantics. Metadata files need to be managed as part of the intellectual content digital object.

Preservation Metadata in Open Archival Information System

Metadata is a key component of the Open Archival Information System (OAIS) reference model. OAIS uses the conceptual framework of an information object. As seen in Figure 4.1, the information object contains the intellectual content as

Figure 4.1.
OAIS Information Object

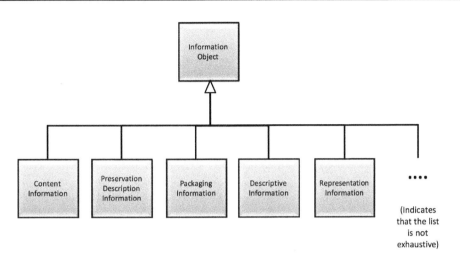

(Reprinted with permission of the Consultative Committee for Space Data System.)

well as a variety of metadata. The content information is the intellectual content; structural metadata, preservation metadata, common technical metadata, and descriptive metadata become part of the entire information object package.

The OAIS situates metadata within three conceptualized contexts: data submission, data distribution, and data archiving. Within the OAIS, these contexts are associated with metadata requirements. The metadata is not expected to be in a single format but maybe multiple files in multiple formats; however, the metadata will be *packaged* for each context. Submitting data to an archival system requires a Submission Information Package (SIP). The SIP is created by the information producer and sent to an archival system. The SIP contains the digital content and usually descriptive metadata, some type of structural metadata, and perhaps some technical and/or preservation metadata. The exact contents of the SIP are generally negotiated between the archival system and the data producer. The OAIS does not have a specification for the contents. While some metadata may be explicitly encoded in standard formats, it is possible that producers may provide metadata in nonstandard or implicit forms. Implicit metadata, that is, metadata that is not encoded in a structured form, can be found in file names and directory structures or assumed based on project, policy, and/or experience.

Delivering information is the context for the Dissemination Information Package (DIP). The DIP is the information that is sent to end users to decode, render, and process the digital objects. Digital objects may be disseminated to either an individual person or a system. Dissemination information packages may take different forms depending on the identity of the requesting system. A DIP for a remote requester, another archival information system perhaps, would need substantially

Figure 4.2.
OAIS Archival Information Package

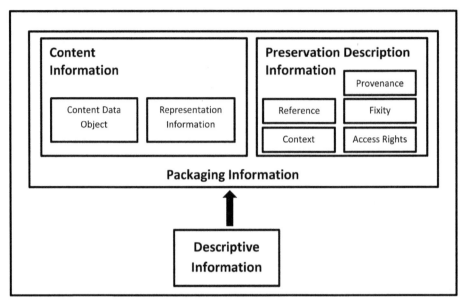

(Lavoie, 2014. Reprinted with permission.)

more information for rendering and use than the user interface for the owning institution's system. If archive A has an object, its system would need less information to display that object than archive B would need if they had asked for a copy of the object. Archive B would require rendering information specific to that object.

Archival Information Package is known as an AIP (see Figure 4.2). The AIP is the core of the OAIS. The AIP contains all of the information necessary for curating the digital object over time. The AIP encapsulates three conceptualizations of metadata. The first is descriptive metadata. Just as in the three types described previously, descriptive metadata is what is considered to be the traditional form of metadata. This would contain title, creator, subjects/topics, publication information, and so on. The second conceptualization of metadata is content information. This includes the data object itself and the representation information necessary to render and use the object. Representation information could be of codebook for a data set or a link to the file format schema at a standards website/repository. Representation information could include names and links of two specific software versions and/or specific hardware environments required. Structural metadata would be included in the representation information. The third conceptualization of metadata is of preservation information that includes provenance, rights information, and other technical metadata. As with other aspects of the OAIS reference model, the AIP does not prescribe a specific format, values, or practice. The AIP does provide a comprehensive view of metadata for preservation.

TECHNICAL IMPLICATIONS

The AIP is a conceptual view of preservation metadata. The information represented in the AIP conceptual view needs to be instantiated in a metadata format. While the AIP is a single conceptual entity and might appear to be a single digital representation (see Figure 4.2), the AIP is actually a set of individual, separate metadata files. Over time, the librarians, archivists, and technologists in the digital curation community have developed a number of metadata standards for preservation metadata. Each of these standards has a unique syntax and semantic structure and was designed to meet a specific need. Some of the standards can be used across multiple content types, while others are specific to a format or function. This section will review the primary metadata standards for specific technical metadata, structural metadata, and a widely used preservation metadata format.

File Type Specific Technical Metadata

Digital objects are made up of numerous computer files. Each type of file—whether image, audio, or video—has specific technical aspects that impact curation. And file formats within each type of file have specific technical features that again impact curation. Many file types and file formats have specific technical metadata standards. Images, very common in digital libraries and archives, often have technical metadata embedded in the EXIF metadata standard, which includes information such as type of capture equipment (camera or scanner information), bit rate, color space, and so on. This information is really useful for the digital curator. However, as the data is embedded within the file, it is difficult for a curator or an archival system to access. If a curator wanted to find all of the images created by a specific camera or scanner, each image within the system would need to be opened and processed. This could be hundreds of terabytes of data to find a small subset. Replicating that data in a separate metadata file would be much more efficient. The metadata could be indexed so that a curator or archival system could easily find the subset of images that were created by a specific piece of equipment.

Metadata for Images in XML (MIX) is a metadata schema supported by the Library of Congress and the NISO Technical Metadata for Digital Still Images Standards Committee to support curation and management of digital images. MIX makes technical information explicit. The MIX data dictionary describes five primary data sections:

1. Basic Digital Object Information includes information about identifiers, format, compression, and fixity.

2. Basic Image Information includes information about size, color, and encoding.

3. Image Capture Metadata includes information about time and location, image source, equipment, equipment specifications, and orientation.

4. Information Assessment Metadata includes information about sampling, bit rates, color maps, and targets.

5. Change History includes information about image processing, such as the software used and the processing actions period (NISO, 2006).

Text is another very common format for digital libraries and archives. Text has a number of characteristics that present challenges for curators. Besides the numerous software packages that process text documents and the unique and proprietary formats that are created, text can be created in a number of character sets, that is, the code set of the actual characters. Current common character sets are Unicode, UTF-8, and ASCII; however, additional obsolete character sets exist, such as EBCDIC, an IBM mainframe encoding scheme. Curators and archival information systems need to know character sets in order to properly render and process documents. Knowing the language of the document helps curators and systems create appropriate indexes and interfaces for search and retrieval. If a document has been encoded with a markup language, the system needs to have information about the SGML, XML, or other schemas used in order to process and render that document. A metadata format schema for capturing technical information about text was developed in the libraries at New York University. In 2007, the Library of Congress assumed responsibility for the standard, textMD. The textMD metadata format includes information about the document's encoding, character set, language, font, markup language, page order and sequence, and requirements for viewing and printing (LOC, 2016).

The Library of Congress maintains standards for technical metadata for both audio and video data; audioMD and videoMD are XML schemas that document the technical characteristics of audio and video. Audio and video are both time-based media; that is, they include duration as a characteristic. Archival information systems need to know about the amount of data overtime—how much information was captured per time segment. This is often called the sampling rate. If the digital files were created as part of an analog to digital conversion, information about that transfer is important, including playback rates, manual adjustments, conversion equipment, and so on. The specific data encoding is also important; this is often called the codec. File format, fixity, and other data elements are also included in these technical metadata standards (LOC, 2011a).

Many metadata standards are a combination of descriptive, structural, and technical. The Society of American Archivists[6] has a Metadata Directory with a comprehensive list of metadata standards with descriptions and links. The Library of Congress has excellent resources on technical metadata for digital materials.[7]

Structural Metadata

Information objects are complex. Often, multiple files are required to represent a logical set of information. These complex information structures are often referred to as digital objects. A digital object could contain hundreds or even thousands of files. Structural metadata maintains the relationships between the components of a digital object.

For example, a library decides that it wants to digitize its Gutenberg Bible in order to provide greater access to this iconic work and promote its other unique and valuable collections. A complete Gutenberg Bible has 1,286[8] pages. Creating a scanned image for each page results in 1,286 image files. If the library follows best practice for scanning, the original scans would be the master files and would create these as TIFFs. But because the files are very large and are not supported in most browsers, the library would need to provide more suitable and network-friendly deliverable files by generating derivative files as JPEG or JPEG2000. So with just a master file and a deliverable file for each page, the library has nearly 2,500 files for this book. The library could decide that it wanted the transcription of the text. If the text transcription is created and stored at the page level, as it often is, another 1,286 files are added. Again following best practice, the library would want to have technical metadata appropriate for images, adding another 1,286 files. The derivative files are excellent for web delivery but are difficult to print. To provide efficient and useful printing capability, the library decides to create PDF files for each chapter, resulting in an additional 1,189[9] files. Adding the descriptive metadata, in this case a bibliographic record, the library has a total of 6,334 files for one large book.

Digital documents have a natural sequence and hierarchy. The intellectual whole, the document, has components—pages, chapters, front matter, indexes, and so on. It is possible to represent the hierarchy of a digital object (see Figure 4.3).

Figure 4.3.
Digital Book Components

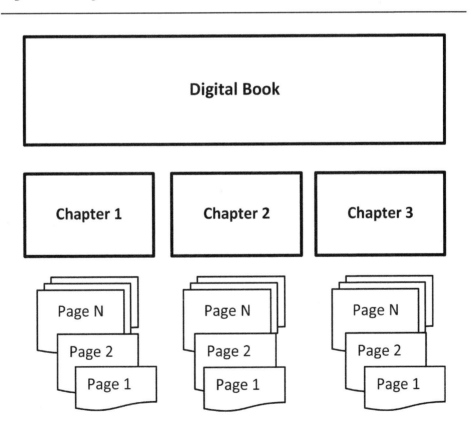

METS is an XML schema used by digital archives and libraries to document the relationships between files and create a wrapper to package digital objects. The METS schema has seven sections: the METS Header, Descriptive Metadata, Administrative Metadata, File, Structure Map, Structural Link, and Behavior (METS Editorial Board, 2010).

The METS Header is the first element of the METS document. This section contains information about the METS document itself, who created the file and when. The next section is for Descriptive Metadata. METS does not have its own descriptive metadata scheme. The format allows curators either to embed an existing metadata record within the METS file or to include a pointer to an external descriptive metadata record. Curators can use any descriptive metadata scheme that suits their needs, either library and archival formats, such as Dublin Core, MARC, EAD, and TEI, or domain-specific metadata schemes, such as FGCD for geospatial data. The descriptive metadata applies to the entire METS record and not to individual components of the digital object.

To support administrative metadata, the METS schema supports four elements for rights metadata, technical metadata, source metadata, and digital provenance. The rights element describes the nature of the access rights and the constraints of intellectual property for the entire digital object. An object can be declared to be in the public domain or under copyright. METS allows for a full text description of usage rights. As with the descriptive metadata, the technical metadata is expected to be in another file format, such as MIX or textMD. The technical metadata in METS can be embedded or a pointer to an external file or record. Unlike the rights element and metadata section, the technical metadata should be associated with individual files. The MIX record for TIFF file A should be associated with TIFF file A and that file only. The source element describes the origins of the digital object. As an example, the source element would describe the original media for analog-to-digital conversion—reel to reel tape, video, document information, and so on. The digital provenance element allows curators to insert information about processes to create or maintain the digital objects. Again, METS does not have a specific provenance scheme but allows inclusion of locally developed provenance data or to establish standards.

The Structure Map is the only required section and is the core of the METS standard. When used in conjunction with the file section, METS can faithfully represent most any digital object. The file section is an inventory of all of the individual files that comprise the digital object. Files can be grouped to better represent the object. File groups have an attribute to identify the levels of use—archival, screen, thumbnail, and so on. Each file in the file section is given an identifier that can be used to define the relationships, such as sequence and hierarchy, in the Structure Map. Sequence is documented through an element Divisions, the way that hierarchy is defined via an attribute of the file element in the structure map. Hierarchy can be defined via division. Each division can be labeled. As an example, divisions could be labeled with chapter names. These labels can be used for navigation in user interfaces. The Structure link section allows for hyperlinks between the divisions of the Structure Map and is used primarily for archived websites.

The behavior section is used to document the manner in which the data should be displayed and processed. The behaviors are documented in an interface definition element by a description. The mechanism element identifies executable code, software that has implemented the specific behavior. As an example, a behavior section could point to a page-turning system or a search interface. This optional section is not frequently used.

Preservation Metadata: Implementation Strategies

Preservation Metadata: Implementation Strategies (PREMIS) is an international standard for preservation metadata that provides the data dictionary that defines elements necessary to support the curation of digital objects. PREMIS is technology neutral; that is, it has been designed so that it can be implemented in any number of technology environments. As a data dictionary, PREMIS can be used as a stand-alone metadata file format or implemented in a database for use and archival system. While PREMIS is technology agnostic, it has been implemented as an XML schema.[10] When implemented as an XML document, PREMIS can be embedded in a METS file; this creates a very complete preservation package. The PREMIS data dictionary and schema are maintained by the Library of Congress (PREMIS, 2015).

The PREMIS data dictionary has four primary components: objects, agents, events, and rights (see Figure 4.4). The object is the digital entity to be preserved. In version 3 of the PREMIS data dictionary, the technology environment, descriptions of the hardware and software, becomes part of the digital object itself. The agent component describes the people, organizations, and/or technologies that can be associated with any of the other PREMIS components. Agents act on objects. Events are actions involving one or more objects or agents. Events could include such activities as migrating formats, creating derivatives, changing physical file locations, and so forth.

The object is a unit of information, such as a photograph, a sound recording, a book, or a chapter of a book. The unit is defined by the nature of the materials and the needs of the curator and the user community. As with METS, PREMIS is very flexible. The object contains all of the files necessary for intellectual entity. The Object can also contain information about the representation of that object; in fact, the Object may contain multiple representations of the intellectual entity. For example, an archive may have a Word file and a PDF of the certain document. Each of these different formats is a representation of the same intellectual entity. The archive may choose to create one PREMIS object for both representations, or the archive may choose to create two separate PREMIS records. An environment can have events and agents.

PREMIS provides a mechanism for documenting the technical environment for the object. The environment is its own semantic unit and has its own container. It is an object in its own right with specific elements. The environment can be related to multiple objects and other environment containers. For example, an environment unit could scribe a web browser, and the second environment unit could describe required plug-in. An environment can have supporting objects; an environment that

Figure 4.4.
PREMIS Data Model

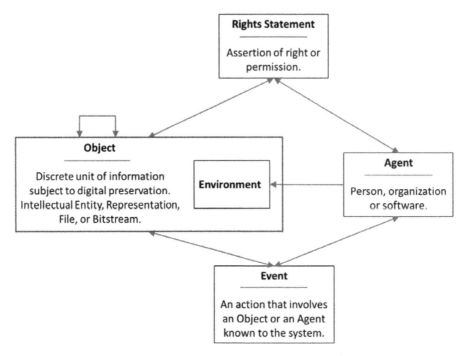

(PREMIS, 2015, p. 6. Reproduced with permission from the Library of Congress.)

describes an operating system could be related to an object that defines an operating manual or specification. Throughout the lifecycle of an object, environment can change; changes are recorded in events. Agents are actors who implement change; people, systems, and/or processes can be agents. Environments can also have rights associated with it; software can have a license, copyright, or policies that need to be documented and preserved.

PRACTICAL APPLICATION

The primary goal of metadata is to make the implicit explicit, that is, to explicitly record information that is implicitly known and understood. In order to preserve digital content over time, it is vital that the assumptions about and the understanding of the current infrastructure are recorded clearly and accurately.

Multiplicity of Standards

Certainly, there is no shortage of metadata standards. A reasonable person might ask why so many are needed. Is it really necessary to have separate technical metadata standards by type informant? Is it really necessary to have a metadata standard to define the structure of an object? Could it not be possible to have one metadata standard that could encapsulate all of the information necessary for long-term preservation? Attempts have been made to create an "uber" standard for metadata. These have failed due to the complexity of the technologies, competing priorities, and great variety of requirements and needs. Having a super standard may be useful to some; however, the complexity of that standard could outweigh its usefulness. A standard that could deal with still images, moving images, audio, and text would be huge. The software to process that metadata would be large and complex. It would be difficult to maintain. Every change to a technology would require upgrades to all of the metadata for all of the file types. It would violate the modularity principle of computer science that promotes separating functionality into independent components that contain what is necessary for only one aspect of that functionality and that can be combined and recombined as necessary. With multiple technical metadata standards for each type of material and a wrapper standard such as METS, digital libraries and archives can combine components as they need to adequately and accurately describe their materials.

Digital libraries and archives often use multiple metadata standards. The HathiTrust Digital Library, a partnership of the hundred libraries with nearly 15 million digital volumes, uses both METS and PREMIS for its structural and preservation metadata and MARC for its descriptive metadata (HathiTrust, n.d.). The Public Television Digital Archive uses METS and PREMIS for its structural and preservation metadata and its own standard, PBSCore, for descriptive metadata (Rubin, 2009). The California Digital Library uses METS, elements of PREMIS, MIX, and other standards as necessary (California Digital Library, 2017).

Data Duplication

Technical metadata is generally created by extracting data from file headers; time and date stamps, geospatial locations, file size, character encoding, equipment specifications, color space, sampling rates, and other technical information are often all available within the file itself. Why then is technical metadata important? If the data is available within the file itself, why is it important to explicitly encode in an external metadata? In many ways, it seems that technical metadata duplicates existing data in a file. And data duplication, having the same data stored in multiple places, violates best data practice. Having data stored in multiple places can cause a number of issues. Besides wasting storage space, storing the same data in multiple places can cause currency and consistency issues. Changes in data that have been in one place need to be duplicated or the data gets out of sync. This is primarily a problem in dynamic databases with the data changing frequently. For most data in a digital archive or library, data does not change often. While data duplication is an issue, for digital archives, the benefits greatly outweigh potential problems.

Technical metadata provides a convenient way for libraries and archives to have fast and easy access to the technical information about files. Without technical metadata, curation systems would need to open and read the file headers to locate the technical information. In any number of situations, looking file by file for technical information becomes dauntingly difficult. A common scenario is that a curator needed to find all of the files that were created using a specific piece of equipment during a specific time range; if a specific scanner malfunctioned and could not fully digitize the items, creating images with a black spot in the middle, the curator would want to fix those images. It would be possible for the curator to find all of the TIFF files that were created in the time range using the file system, but to determine which of those TIFF files were created with the specific piece of scanner, each of the TIFF files would need to be opened and parsed to find the specific scanner identifier. Depending on the number of TIFF files created and the bit rate used when digitizing, the process could involve multiple terabytes and many hours of computational processing. If each TIFF file had a MIX metadata record, the technical metadata could be indexed and the appropriate set of image files could be located in a matter of seconds. Explicit technical metadata makes managing digital content faster and more accurate.

Representing Objects with Structural Metadata

When digitizing an analog object, libraries and archives often capture metadata implicitly using a set of directories capture the structure of the digital contents. Using the example of a book, the top-level directory is created for the entire book. A subdirectory could be created for each chapter. All of the files associated with a chapter are stored in that subdirectory. Often, the directories are named with the control number, the number associated either with a physical object or with a system number. For digital books, the files have the bibliographic record number. For archival documents, the archival control number is often the identifier.

For the example of the Gutenberg Bible, the hierarchy has an additional level. The whole book is a compilation of other books—66 to be specific. Each of these books has chapters. Each chapter has pages. Each image needs to have a sequence number: first image, second image. These sequence numbers may bear no relationship to the printed page number. The cover of a book is the first file in the sequence, and page one may be the 15th file.

METS is a very flexible standard and can model most any type of digital object. Curators have many options for how they package their materials. Curators may make decisions based on delivery systems, that is, the software that researchers use to search and display materials. Curators may make decisions based on the repository systems that they use (see Chapter 6 for more information on repository systems). Representing serials presents more options for modeling structure in METS. A curator could model the serial at any level of granularity: the article, the issue, the volume, or the run. While it would certainly be possible to include an entire hundred-year run of a serial in a single METS file, it would be awkward; the file would be very large and difficult to process both by people and software. It would be equally possible to create a METS file for every article with a METS for every issues file that associated all of the METS for articles, a METS file for every volume that associated all of the METS for issues, and a METS for the run that would associate all of the METS for volumes.

Creating technical and structural metadata for digital objects is generally an automated process. Programs or scripts are created that process the implicit structure of directory and file names or that extract technical information from file headers. This data is then formatted into the specific metadata format. For more information about creating technical and structural metadata, please see Chapter 5.

SUMMARY

Contextualized curation needs drive the requirements for metadata. The three types of metadata—descriptive, structural, and administrative—support specific functions. The OAIS conceptual model describes three major functional contexts for metadata: ingest, preservation, and use. Each of these functions requires an information package. The Submission Information Package (SIP) includes all of the data and metadata required for ingest. The Archival Information Package (AIP) includes all of the data and metadata required for storing, managing, and preserving the data. The Dissemination Information Package (DIP) includes all of the data and metadata required for end users.

Specific metadata standards are used to meet specific curation needs. Structural metadata is used to package all of the elements of a digital object together. The primary structural metadata standard is METS, an XML schema that documents the relationships between files. Technical metadata is often specific to the type of data; the Library of Congress maintains a set of technical metadata standards for still images, text, audio, and moving images. PREMIS is the primary metadata schema for preservation information. PREMIS is a flexible XML schema that can stand as its own record or be included in another metadata document, such as METS. PREMIS can document the technical environment and the provenance of an object.

Multiple metadata standards may seem confusing but are necessary to adequately describe digital objects for long-term preservation. Digital libraries and archives use the standards that best meet their needs. Many use a combination of METS, MIX, and some elements of the PREMIS standards.

Questions for Discussion

1. What is preservation metadata?
2. Why is preservation metadata important?
3. Why are preservation metadata standards instantiated in XML?
4. Why would creating a single technical metadata standard be difficult?

NOTES

1. *Merriam-Webster* defines the prefix "meta" to be "more highly organized or specialized form" of the subject (Meta, 2016).

2. http://rs.tdwg.org/dwc/index.htm

3. http://fits.gsfc.nasa.gov/fits_home.html

4. https://knb.ecoinformatics.org/#tools/eml

5. http://www.loc.gov/standards/mets/

6. http://www2.archivists.org/groups/metadata-and-digital-object-roundtable/metadata-directory#.V5Dmz67EKYA

7. https://www.loc.gov/standards/

8. Biblia Latina (the "Gutenberg Bible"). Mainz: Johann Gutenberg, 1454–55. HOLLIS 005779380.

9. *Blue Letter Bible.* http://www.blueletterbible.org/

10. http://www.loc.gov/standards/premis/premis.xsd

REFERENCES

California Digital Library. (2017). *CDL guidelines for digital objects.* Found at https://www.cdlib.org/gateways/docs/GDO.pdf

Consultative Committee for Space Data Systems (CCSDS). (2012). *Reference model for an Open Archival Information System (OAIS).* Issue 2. Recommendation for Space Data System Standards (Magenta Book), CCSDS 650.0-M-2. Washington, DC: ISO 14721:2012. Found at http://public.ccsds.org/publications/archive/650x0m2.pdf

Gill, T. (2008). Metadata and the Web. In *Introduction to Metadata* (2nd ed., pp. 20–38). Edited by M. Baca. Los Angeles: Getty Publications.

HathiTrust. (n.d.). *Digital object specifications (METS and PREMIS).* Found at https://www.hathitrust.org/digital_object_specifications

Lavoie, B. F. (2014). *The Open Archival Information System (OAIS) reference model: Introductory guide.* (2nd ed.) (DPC Technology Watch Report). Found at http://www.oclc.org/research/news/2014/12-04.html

Library of Congress (LOC). (2011a). *About audioMD and videoMD.* Found at https://www.loc.gov/standards/amdvmd/

Library of Congress (LOC). (2011b). *Adding descriptions to digital photographs: Your gift to the future.* Found at http://www.digitalpreservation.gov/multimedia/documents/photometadata_script.pdf

Library of Congress (LOC). (2016). *TextMD: Technical metadata for text.* Found at https://www.loc.gov/standards/textMD/

Meta. (2016). In *Merriam-Webster.* Found at http://www.merriam-webster.com/dictionary/Meta

Metadata. (2016). In *Merriam-Webster.* Found at http://www.merriam-webster.com/dictionary/Meta

METS Editorial Board. (2010). *Metadata encoding and transmission standard: Primer and reference manual (Version 1.6).* Washington, DC: Digital Library Federation.

NISO. (2004). Understanding metadata. In *National Information Standards.* Bethesda, MD: NISO Press. Found at http://www.niso.org/publications/understanding-metadata

NISO. (2006). *Data dictionary—Technical metadata for digital still images.* Bethesda, MD: NISO Press. Found at https://groups.niso.org/apps/group_public/document.php?document_id=14697

NISO. (2010). Digital preservation metadata standards. *Information Standards Quarterly, 22*(2). Found at https://www.loc.gov/standards/premis/FE_Dappert_Enders_Metadata Stds_isqv22no2.pdf

NISO Framework Working Group. (2007). *A framework of guidance for building good digital collections. [2013-08-15]*. Found at http://www.niso.org/sites/default/files/2017-08/framework3.pdf

PREMIS Editorial Committee (PREMIS). (2015). *PREMIS data dictionary for preservation metadata*. Found at http://www.loc.gov/standards/premis/

Preserving Access to Digital Information (PADI). (n.d.). *Preservation metadata*. National Library of Australia. Found at http://pandora.nla.gov.au/pan/10691/20110824-1153/www.nla.gov.au/padi/topics/32.html

Rubin, N. (2009). Preserving digital public television: Not just an archive, but a new attitude to preserve public broadcasting. *Library Trends*, *57*(3), 393–412. Found at http://www.thirteen.org/ptvdigitalarchive/files/2009/10/library-trends-spring-2009.pdf

Chapter 5

DATA ASSURANCE

Quality is never an accident; it is always the result of high intention, sincere effort, intelligent direction and skillful execution; it represents the wise choice of many alternatives.
—William A. Foster[1]

Data is produced through a variety of processes. Data can be created by typing into word processing software. Data can be created during research, including experiments, interviews, and surveys. Data can be created through various digitizing processes. Data can be created via social media, such as Twitter, Facebook, and Snapchat. The quality of that data depends on the nature of the process, the purpose for which the data was created, and the circumstances under which the data was created (Karr, Sanil, Sacks, & Elmagarmid, 2001). A photograph that was digitized for a family reunion would most likely have a different quality signature than a photograph digitized in a professional digital library or archives lab. The process, the purpose, and the needs for quality can range widely.

Quality matters in preservation. For both physical preservation, such as paper conservancy, and digital preservation, high-quality originals have a higher probability of lasting over time. For digital materials, this means not only high bit rates but also using standard formats for both the data itself and its metadata. Standards have been the foundation of computer technology. Without commonly agreed upon formats, computers would be unable to process data. Libraries and archives have been champions of file format standards, starting with Z39.02, the MARC record, which was first approved in the 1960s. However good standards are, they are not perfect. It is possible for different systems to interpret a standard differently and produce different records for the same object. In a recent study, a team researching the variability of implementations of PDF found wide variations in the files (Termens, Ribera, & Locher, 2015).

It may be surprising to learn that standards can be interpreted and implemented in ways that impede interoperability. For digital curators, this can be a significant problem. Curators want to make sure that the data they are preserving is high-quality, free from error, consistent, and exactly the same today as it was when it was received. Fixing errors in data is always expensive. But for digital archival systems, it is absolutely essential to get the correct digital file, descriptive metadata, and technical metadata when the data is accepted into the system. According to the National Archives of England, Wales, and the United Kingdom, the cost of creating data for sustainability should be the goal because "attempts to bring electronic records into a managed and sustainable regime after the fact tend to be expensive, complex and, generally, less successful" (A. Brown, 2003, p. 4).

Assuring the quality of the data helps build a trusted, authoritative source of digital materials. Quality assurance is a commitment that digital archives and libraries make to their patrons. Curators want their patrons to have confidence in the materials and to be certain of the authenticity. For digital materials, curators and patrons want to be assured of the quality, not only of the contents of the materials but also of the underlying binary data representation.

In this chapter, the concepts of quality will be discussed. Quality dimension, technologies to support quality, data profiling, and quality automation will be covered. While much of the research done in data quality comes from the business community, it can be easily adopted and adapted for digital libraries and archives to improve their curation services.

THEORETICAL OVERVIEW

The Nature of Quality

The definitions of data quality are quite ambiguous. Perhaps it comes from the problem describing anything of quality. Merriam-Webster defines *quality* as "how good or bad something is" (Quality, n.d.). Quality is a value judgment. "Contrary to popular belief, quality is not necessarily zero defects. Quality is conformance to valid requirements" (Geiger, 2004, p. 1). Other definitions also include the notion of requirements (Crosby, 1998; ISO 9000). Yet other definitions describe data quality as its ability to fulfill a function, its usefulness, and its fitness within a specific context (Redman, 2008; Wang & Strong, 1996). These vague definitions reflect the difficulty of defining value. It may be impossible to come up with a single, simple definition. Data quality is really a complex, multidimensional concept dependent on needs, situations, and circumstances. Data quality is often decomposed into a set of dimensions that ascribe and describe the elements of quality.

Quality Dimensions

Rather than fully and unambiguously defining data quality, researchers have concentrated on defining characteristics of quality data. These characteristics are usually described as dimensions, elements that can contribute to data quality. Quality dimensions are a combination of objective and subjective characteristics. Objective characteristics are measurable; subjective characteristics are perceptions that mirror the context of the stakeholders (Pipino, Lee, & Wang, 2002).

Table 5.1.

Matrix of Various Data Quality Dimensions (sorted alphabetically)

Redman, 2001	Batini & Scannapieco, 2016	SDM, 2016	DAMA, 2013
Accessibility	Accessibility	Accessibility	Accuracy
Accuracy	Completeness	Accuracy	Completeness
Complete	Consistency	Appropriate presentation	Consistency
Comprehensive	Currency	Completeness	Timeliness
Consistent with other	Integrity	Consistency across data	Uniqueness
sources	Timeliness	sources	Validity
Easy to read	Volatility	Relevance	
Easy to interpret		Reliability	
Proper level of detail		Update status	
Relevant			
Timely			
10^2	7	8	6

Beginning in the early 1990s, a number of data quality dimensions have been developed. Many of these describe similar, or even identical, characteristics (see Table 5.1). Researchers and business analysts have adopted and/or adapted various data quality dimension schemes. While there are a number of overlapping dimensions, these schemes vary in their level of granularity and number of characteristics. Some of the dimensions are at a very high level, for example, relevant and complete, while others are very specific, as in easy to read or easy to interpret. Some dimensions could be combined; those two "easy to . . . " dimensions could be combined into one entitled *usability*. In the four sets of quality dimensions in Table 5.1, the number of dimensions ranges from 6 to 10. By looking at a number of quality dimension schemes, some primary aspects of data quality emerge: accessibility, accuracy, completeness/comprehensive, consistency, and timeliness are the most common characteristics. Three of the sets of dimensions include a characteristic of validity, integrity, or reliability, trying to describe trustworthiness.

One of the early attempts at quantifying quality had two levels—a high-level dimension with underlying characteristics (see Table 5.2). Wang and Strong (1996) posited that data had intrinsic values; data needs to be believable, accurate, and objective in order to have a reputation of quality. Context, which digital curators call metadata, is a significant component of quality; context needs to be appropriate and adequate, timely, and relevant. Representational characteristics allow data to be understood and interpreted; data that is concise and consistent aids in representation. And quality requires accessibility; data must be available for those who need it and secured to protect it from those who do not need it.

In many ways, the high-level dimensions developed by Wang and Strong seem to be both relevant and well suited to digital curation. Libraries and archives have always been committed to the intrinsic dimension of data. Providing accurate, objective, and reputable data is the mission for most cultural heritage organizations. Accessibility is another time-honored value of libraries and archives. Accessibility of digital materials relies on the quality of the metadata and the ability of the patron to use the materials. Thus, accessibility relies on both context and representation.

Table 5.2.

Bi-level Dimensions of Data Quality

Intrinsic	Believable
	Accurate
	Objective
	Reputable
Contextual	Value-added
	Relevant
	Timely
	Complete
	Appropriate amount
Representational	Interpretable
	Easy to understand
	Consistent
	Concise
Accessibility	Available
	Secure

(Wang & Strong, 1996, p. 177)

As libraries and archives continue to increase their digital collection, context and representation will increase in importance. Context is a key component of digital archives and digital libraries. Libraries and archives can create quality contextual metadata that is relevant to the users, that is current and available when needed, and that is appropriate and usable. A major quality issue for digital archives is adequate representation of the digital object; being able to interpret the files for use in a variety of circumstances is a key goal that can be accomplished with the consistent use of standards.

In addition to thinking about the dimensions of quality, it can be helpful to think about the problems and errors in data and consider their impact on a digital collection. The taxonomy of imperfections can clarify the various dimensions of quality (see Figure 5.1). In the taxonomy developed by Smets (1997), the three primary imperfections are imprecision, inconsistency, and uncertainty; these are the inverse of common quality dimensions. Both imprecision and uncertainty have categories that provide a clearer picture about data problems. Imprecision can be problematic due to the very nature of the data either because of its vagueness or its deficiencies. Uncertainty can be objective or subjective. Subjective uncertainty can be more problematic as it involves perceptions; if the trustworthiness of the data is in doubt, patrons, funders, and the public will no longer support the organization.

Key Quality Dimensions for Preservation

For a digital archive, integrity, validity, and accessibility may be the most important quality factors. Ensuring integrity of the bitstream and the integrity of the entire logical object must be the primary of any digital library or archive. Integrity of the file is ensuring that the file today is the same as it was when it was created. As discussed in previous chapters, digital materials are fragile. Digital files can be changed either inadvertently or maliciously. Digital things are copied and moved

Figure 5.1.
Taxonomy of the Imperfections in Data

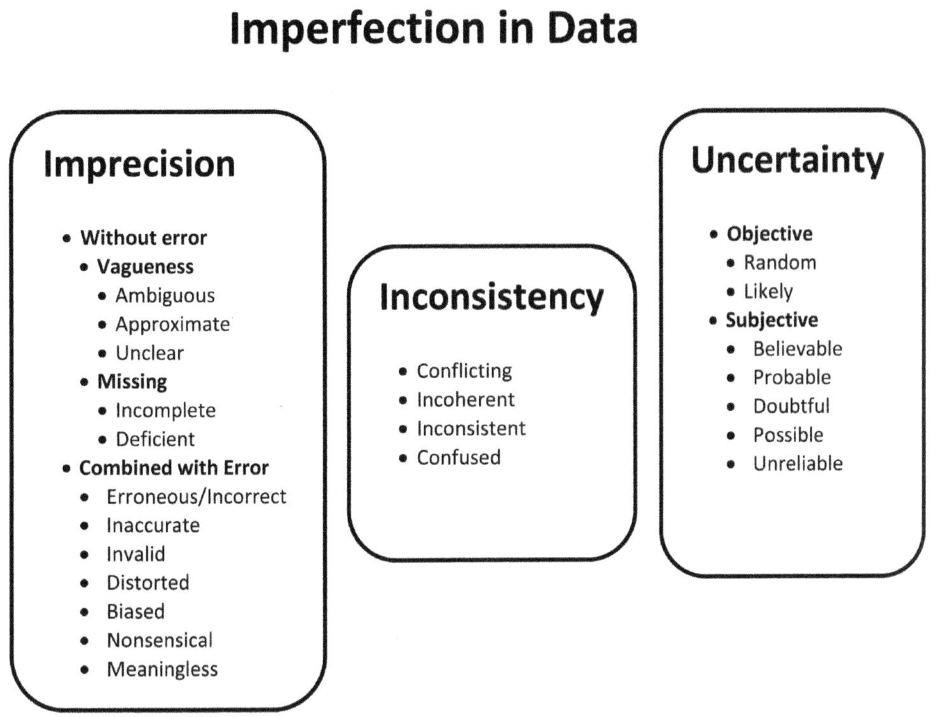

Imperfection in Data

Imprecision

- **Without error**
  - **Vagueness**
    - Ambiguous
    - Approximate
    - Unclear
  - **Missing**
    - Incomplete
    - Deficient
- **Combined with Error**
  - Erroneous/Incorrect
  - Inaccurate
  - Invalid
  - Distorted
  - Biased
  - Nonsensical
  - Meaningless

Inconsistency

- Conflicting
- Incoherent
- Inconsistent
- Confused

Uncertainty

- **Objective**
  - Random
  - Likely
- **Subjective**
  - Believable
  - Probable
  - Doubtful
  - Possible
  - Unreliable

via software over networks. During this process, data can be corrupted or lost. Digital files can be corrupted by an inadvertent error in software or by an embedded, intentional virus designed to do damage. Digital files can be corrupted by the hardware technologies, both computational and storage. This is a problem of fixity, which will be discussed in more depth later in this chapter. Digital objects are sets of files. Integrity of the object is ensuring that all of the component pieces are present and accounted for. Without the ability to ensure the integrity of the file and the object, a digital archive cannot really preserve or curate the materials.

Within the context of digital curation, validity means the ability to ensure that a file meets the requirements of a file format. Digital data is tied to a file format and a technology to render that file. Because data cannot be rendered without a valid file format and the requisite technologies, invalid files cannot be processed. This results in lost information. Validity, therefore, is very important.

Digital libraries and archives want to be able to provide accessibility to their content. In a web environment, access is through a URL. URLs are very unstable and can change when an object is moved. For digital libraries and archives, accessibility needs to be persistent; when an object in the digital archive is cited in a publication or embedded in another resource, the identification should not change. Persistence of identification is the quality indicator for accessibility.

As quality is important to the long-term preservation of digital content, libraries, archives, and other information-centric organizations managing digital data need to be able to assess their ability to consistently control for data quality. One well-established management tool for assessing an organization's ability is the maturity model.

Maturity Models

A maturity model is a tool to help an organization assess its methods, structure, and/or processes against a set of criteria. By using a maturity model, an organization can discover its strengths and weaknesses and find ways to improve. Maturity models abound with one (or more) for the different aspects of an organization. For example, an organization may want to understand its ability to successfully develop software. That organization would use the Capability Maturity Model to measure its ability to plan track, provide oversight for project as well as to manage subcontractors, ensure quality, and manage configuration options (Paulk, Curtis, Chrissis, & Weber, 1993). Other examples of various types of maturity models include organizational management, project management, program management, security, and so forth. The criteria used are specific to each domain being measured. However different, these criteria are often set in a framework with four to eight conceptual dimensions. To be useful, these dimensional criteria need to be specific and measureable. In addition to the criteria, maturity models have some number of rating levels or steps along which an organization maps itself. Models often have four or five of these levels that range from very low to very high.

Data Maturity Models

Data maturity models have been developed to help organizations understand and assess their ability to create, maintain, and exploit high-quality data. Data quality is always a component of a data maturity model. In many ways, quality is built into a number of dimensions: data management, policy, quantifying quality, and data governance among them. The model proposed by Dodds and Newman (2015), the data management dimension, specifically includes data quality as well as uses the standards for formats and metadata and formalized processes and workflows.

Policy is a very broad dimension and can include such quality issues as privacy, security, risk management, consistency, and accessibility. In the more granular model, metadata is specifically included as a measure of maturity; as metadata, context, is a component of quality, this is another indicator of the importance of data quality within an organization.

Quantifying and managing data usage and quality are included in a number of dimensions within the various data maturity models: strategic oversight, data management strategy, data operations, and auditing.

Data governance, the process of managing ownership and responsibility for data, is another dimension across all of the models, albeit with different terms: engagement, governance, awareness, and stewardship. Data governance will be discussed in the following section.

Table 5.3.

Data Maturity Models

Model	Open Data Maturity Model	Data Maturity Model	IBM Data Maturity Model
Dimensions	1. Data management processes 2. Knowledge and skills 3. Customer support and engagement 4. Investment and financial performance 5. Strategic oversight	1. Data management strategy 2. Data quality 3. Data governance 4. Data platforms and architecture 5. Data operations	1. Organizational structures and awareness 2. Stewardship 3. Policy 4. Value creation 5. Data risk management and compliance 6. Information security and privacy 7. Data architecture 8. Data quality management 9. Classification and metadata 10. Information lifecycle management 11. Audit information, logging, and reporting
Scale	1. Initial 2. Repeatable 3. Defined 4. Managed 5. Optimized	1. Ad hoc 2. Abbreviated 3. Organized 4. Managed 5. Optimized	1. Initial 2. Managed 3. Defined 4. Quantitatively managed 5. Optimizing
Citation	Dodds & Newman, 2015	CMMI, 2014	IBM, 2007

In a data maturity model, the dimensions are measured against a maturity scale. In the three examples listed in Table 5.3, each has a five-point scale. The scales are quite similar. The lowest scale point dictates a very immature process that is idiosyncratic and that is unique for each situation or in its earliest stages of being designed. The second stage of process maturity shows growth; the processes are no longer just random, not developed, and are becoming codified. In the third stage, processes are becoming well defined and used regularly. In the fourth stage of a maturity model, processes are being used consistently and throughout the organization; managers are responsible for the regular application of processes and may have their success measured against the application of the processes. The fifth level of the maturity scale, optimization, indicates a level of ongoing management and perfection of processes that rarely occurs. It is, however, the goal.

Metadata Maturity Models

The Metadata Management Maturity Model focuses on the quality of metadata (Zhao, 2005). The five maturity levels are ad hoc, discovered, managed, optimized, and automated. As with other maturity models, the scale moves from low to high competence and repeatability: ad hoc represents a random, hit-or-miss process; discovered is an intentional initial attempt at process; managed is a regular yet not universal adoption of the process; optimized is the regular and operationalized process; and automated represents the highest and completely regularized and automatic process.

In the Zhao model, the maturity dimensions are people, process, and technology. In this maturity model, the *people* dimension encapsulates awareness, usage, and motivation. Metadata begins with implicit knowledge within individuals; awareness begins with the codifying and sharing of metadata information. Awareness leads to metadata creation. Awareness also leads to understanding the need for quality metadata. People look for optimization opportunities, including data quality processes at data ingest. Finally, as people continue to see the positive impacts of quality, metadata becomes automated and ubiquitous.

In the process dimension of the Zhao model, metadata moves from localized conversations to fully automated with ontologies and seamless transformation between schemas. Within organizations, metadata often is initially created as a personal or localized unit's effort to solve a specific issue; access to data is a primary motivator. Once these initial metadata initiatives show positive results, others in the organization decide to begin creating metadata, which can start to actually cause problems, such as lack of consistency, inability to share metadata, and difficulty searching between units. These problems can help organizations realize the need to develop processes to improve the quality. These processes include manual processes to develop metadata policies, rules, vocabularies, and ontologies. As more people within the organization create, share, and use metadata, controlling access and modifications to the metadata becomes important; many organizations find a need to develop a metadata change management process to ensure quality.

The technology dimension of the Zhao model moves from local tools to their engines and finally to ontology and knowledge management. Local tools can include such ubiquitous software packages as Excel, Access, and other desktop database systems. These local technologies create some of the problems that cause organizations to develop processes. As the processes are developed, technology must either be modified or be reimplemented to support the process and policy requirements.

Digital Collection Maturity Model

Digital Collection Maturity Model is based on the quality of metadata. This model has six quality levels, including the following:

- Basic. Basic digital collections have metadata that is implicit, not encoded in using standard formats or vocabulary;
- Identified. Identified digital collections categorize the files into access by topic or file type;
- Curated digital collections Contain files that have been vetted and approved via quality control processes;
- Faceted. Faceted digital collections begin to optimize collections to allow asset reuse to meet the needs of a diverse and distributed community of users;
- Componentized. Componentized digital collections deconstruct objects into an atomized set of components that can be combined and used in multiple ways using standard metadata format and workflows to manage the processes; and

- Semantic. Semantic digital collections allow users to personalize and customize data access and presentation of media components to create new digital content using advanced search of semantic units (Digital Asset Management Foundation, 2015).

Data Governance

"Data Governance is a system of decision rights and accountabilities for information-related processes, executed according to agreed-upon models which describe who can take what actions with what information, and when, under what circumstances, using what methods" (DGI, 2015, para. 2). Data governance focuses on developing processes and policies about who can access data and the circumstances under which data is used. In addition to establishing rights and responsibilities for data management and stewardship, support and problem resolution, defining and specifying data quality requirements, is part of data governance (Thomas, 2006).

In many organizations, data governance can be problematic. The responsibilities for data are not specifically delineated and ownership is unclear or unknown. If the responsibilities are unclear, creating data quality objectives, rules, and processes becomes more difficult. Who will provide the motivation for quality and the support for quality? Who can define and monitor the quality rules and processes?

The Open Archival Information Systems (OAIS) conceptual model has considered data governance to be very important to the long-term preservation of data. The OAIS model has at its core the concept of a designated community, which is an "identified group of potential Consumers who should be able to understand a particular set of information" (CCSDS, 2012, p. 1–11). The archive defines the constituency of each designated community and can redefine communities as necessary as circumstances change. Designated communities are not static and can be combined or arranged to meet the needs of the data, the communities, and the archive.

The designated community helps the archive set the quality goals. The designated community has implicit knowledge that can contextualize the data objects to provide additional meaningful information that the formal technical metadata, descriptive metadata, and representational information may not provide. Providing avenues for the designated community to add their insights can improve the accessibility and reusability of the data.

Data quality needs to be a shared responsibility between the producers and the archive with a constant focus on the designated community. In digital libraries and archives, the producer can be the organization itself. But over time, it is likely that born-digital materials will become the predominate type of incoming data. The data producer is initially responsible for data, but responsibility needs to be transferred to the archive for long-term archiving and preservation (Lynch, 2008). In his work on preserving digital art, Grindley (2011) maps out the handoff of responsibility between the data creator (customer) and the archiving service (see Figure 5.2). In his model, verification, quality control, and data validation, among other tasks, are the responsibility of the repository service.

Figure 5.2.
Responsibility Matrix

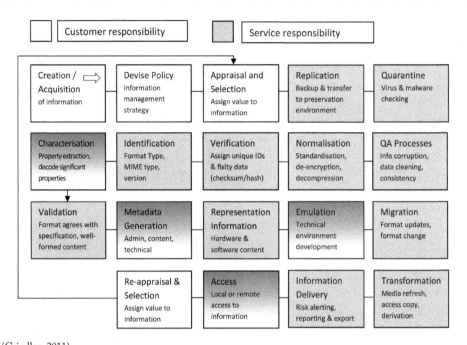

(Grindley, 2011)

Determining the standards, the metrics for quality, needs to be the responsibility of the archiving service. Understanding the quality needs of the materials, the data creators, and the designated community and translating these needs into specific technical specifications are key roles of the digital archive.

TECHNICAL IMPLICATIONS

Technology That Supports Key Quality Dimensions

For a digital archive, integrity, validity, and accessibility may be the most important quality factors. Over the years, librarians, archivists, and technologists have developed tools to help ensure the quality of the contents of the digital archive.

Checksums for Integrity

Integrity is a high-impact quality dimension. In digital curation, integrity of the file, knowing that the file has not changed, is very important. Digital files, unlike paper, are highly susceptible to change. *Fixity* is the term used to describe the problem that digital data is not set, not immutable, that it can be changed easily, either maliciously or inadvertently. Regardless of intention, data cannot be

Table 5.4.

Checksum Values Comparison

Checksum	Value
MD5	D02DCCDCAF8FB8C7564C8A2D7DFA2E40
SHA1	B07358197C48F645CC4B606855D3C263F4F48AA0
SHA256	1F26849A7503F9F36A25539E16222841FF365F26558760A02E324DDA1BF5724D

considered to be preserved if the digital repository cannot guarantee fixity—that the data has not been changed since it was archived. Errors can be introduced into the data via hardware; bits can be "flipped," that is, changed from a 0 to a 1, often referred to as "data rot"—software errors when the program that writes the software incorrectly calculates the length of the file or network errors such as when one of the file packets is lost or truncated.

Technically, assuring the fixity of a file is a simple task. Each archived object needs to have a checksum. A checksum is an established error detection mechanism that uses a mathematical algorithm to calculate a numerical value based on the sequence of 0s and 1s in the file. Any number of checksum algorithms is available for a wide variety of functions. These algorithms can be used to uniquely identify a file (a fingerprint function) and secure data by generating a unique and irreversible key (cryptographic hash) or randomizer function (random number generator). The more secure and unbreakable the checksum, the more complex the calculations, the longer the process takes, and the larger the number (see Table 5.4).

Since digital archives are not encrypting their data and are looking for data integrity, the more complex functions, such as the Secure Hash Algorithms, are not necessary. Because it is both simple and effective, many digital libraries use a simple MD5 checksum. An MD5 checksum generator will create a unique number that should be stored in metadata. But a checksum is only useful if it is validated by a process that calculates the checksum for each digital file and compares it to the saved checksum. Any change to the file will cause the MD5 generator to create a different number.

Verifying Files for Validity

In previous chapters, it has been established that the technical format of a digital file is a key component in digital preservation. Software requires valid files in order to read, render, and process data. Ensuring that the digital archive knows with certainty that the file is what it purports to be and that the file conforms to all of the specifications of the format is vital. With the volume of objects that organizations need to process at ingest, an automated process to both identify and validate the format is required.

Identification is the first step. Most files self-identify via the file extension—.txt indicates a text file; .doc indicates a Microsoft Word file, .tif indicates a TIFF file;

.jpg indicates a JPEG file; and the list could continue for pages. But self-identification is unreliable and insufficient for a digital repository. Files are not always in the format that they claim to be. "Invalid objects can arise through the use of poor-quality software tools or as the result of accidental or deliberate corruption" (A. Brown, 2006, p. 4). Not only does the repository needs to know with certainty that the file is a TIFF file, but it also needs to know that the file was created using the TIFF 6.0 specification.

Validation is the process of determining the level of conformance to the encoding specification of a specific format. This process has two steps. The first step is to determine if the object is well formed. Well-formed objects conform to the syntactic requirements for its format. In other words, it follows the grammar of the format. The second step is to determine its validity. Valid objects must conform to the semantic requirements of the format—that is, does the object contain the meaningful content that is required? If a TIFF file has an 8-byte header followed by a series of Image File Directories (IFDs) made up of a 2-byte entry count and a set of 8-byte tagged entries, it can be considered to be well formed. But to be considered valid, it must conform to additional rules that enforce more complex semantic rules: if the value of the tag PhotometricInterpretation = 2, 6, or 8, then the tag SamplesPerPixel must equal 3 (OPF, 2015).

While it might be possible to identify many file types via the UNIX file command using the "magic number" (G. Brown, 2006), many feel that this is insufficient (Abrams & Seaman, 2003). Harvard University Library and JSTOR, a not-for-profit organization that creates and maintains a trusted archive of important scholarly journals, have collaborated through a Mellon-funded project to create a tool set to automate format-specific validation of digital objects. The software is named JHOVE—the JSTOR/Harvard Object Validation Environment (OPF, 2016). In addition to identification and validation, JHOVE allows for characterization, the processes of determining the format-specific significant properties of an object. These actions are performed by modules, which plug into a layered architecture that can be configured at the time of its invocation to include specific format modules and output handlers. JHOVE includes modules for arbitrary byte streams, ASCII and UTF-8 encoded text; GIF, JPEG2000, JPEG, and TIFF images; AIFF and WAV audio; PDF, HTML, and XML; and text and XML output handlers. JHOVE has been used by a number of digital libraries and archives.

Persistent Identifiers for Accessibility

Persistence of identification is the quality indicator for accessibility. A persistent identifier (PID) is a unique, permanent, location-independent identifier for a network-accessible resource. A URL cannot be a PID because it conflates two important but separate functions: item location and item identification. By separating location from identification, PIDs help avoid the problem of broken links that is often referred to in the digital library community as the "404—not found problem." Persistent identification is especially crucial for important resources that are referenced from scores of web pages or cited scholarly works. Basically, PIDs are

Figure 5.3.
Harvard University's Name Resolution Service

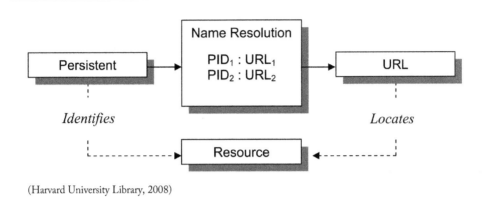

(Harvard University Library, 2008)

URLs that require a multiphased resolution process. This provides a level of indirection that separates the location from the resource identifier. The first-level resolution is to find the right resolution server. Once the resolution server is located, the second-level resolution finds the resource. The second phase of the resolution is relatively simple. A database has both the PID and a location of the object usually in the form of a URL. Using the PID as a key, the resolution service reads the database and redirects the http transaction using the location URL. As the problem of persistent identification of digital resources has become more prominent, a number of competing PIDs have been developed (see Figure 5.3).

The Harvard University Library developed an implementation of a PID system called the Name Resolution Service (NRS). This service is based on the Universal Resource Name (URN) syntax (WC3, 2001) with the expectation that web browsers would ultimately support URNs as specified. But unfortunately, most web browsers do not yet support URNs, so the URN system used the URL syntax (Harvard University Library, 2008). The Online Computer Library Center (OCLC) uses a PURL—persistent URL, a technology similar to the Harvard method but with a different syntax (OCLC, 2013). The Corporation for National Research Initiatives (CNRI) created another resolution system for its unique PID syntax named Handles. The Handle system is an open source, downloadable system with a set of open protocols and a namespace (CNRI, 2015). The International DOI Foundation developed the Digital Object Identifier (DOI) naming semantics that has been implemented using the Handle syntax and resolution system (IDF, 2016). DOIs are used predominantly by publishers of electronic information to provide persistent and controlled access to journal articles. The California Digital Library has developed the Archival Resource Key (ARK), which provides access to a digital information resource. ARKs are widely used because there is no service fee to use, the software is freely available, and the system is easy to maintain (CDL, 2015).

PRACTICAL APPLICATION

Virtuous Cycle of Quality

Data quality can be defined as a state of being, a measurable condition of data. Data quality can also be defined as an action or process. Data quality is not a single step or a single event; it is the outcome of decisions and practices. Bad decisions lead to lower quality; good decisions lead to higher quality. In some organizations, data quality has become a vicious cycle: a bad decision creates inadequate data that leads to more bad decisions and further reduction of data quality. However, the goal of data quality is to create a virtuous cycle in which assessment leads to continuous improvement. In a virtuous cycle, good decisions help create high-quality data, which helps in creating more good outcomes and decisions.

A continuous cycle of improvement, a virtuous cycle, has steps that require assessment, measurement, integration, operationalizing, and management (Loshin, 2009). *Assessment* is the process by which problems are identified. If a library or an archive receives complaints from the patrons that files are unreadable or are missing, the library must assess the situation. Is this a singular incident or the result of its systematic failure? Will the ongoing presence of this failure cause harm to our organization and our patrons? How the library responds to these and other questions will determine whether they began a vicious or a virtuous cycle. Ignoring the problem or considering it to be important could be the beginning of a vicious cycle. Investing resources to investigate and solve the problem could be the beginning of the virtuous cycle. Assessment also includes determining which quality factors are important to the organization.

Measurement is a process or set of processes that quantify those quality factors determined in the assessment process. Determining that files are well formed, well described, appropriately accessible, and renderable, in other words usable, can be systematically addressed by determining rules, creating standards of practice, and setting thresholds for quality. A digital archive may determine that integrity is a primary quality factor; integrity means that all digital objects must be complete and have an inventory of all components. In addition to the integrity of the digital object, the digital archive wants to ensure the integrity of the file by requiring that all files must be well formed and in an archival quality file format as well as regular fixity checks. The digital archive may determine that completeness is a priority quality factor. Completeness may require all digital objects have a MODS descriptive metadata record with the title field, a minimum of two subject fields, a creation date, and a creator field.

Integration is the process of addressing quality systematically. Scripts and programs can be written that ensure the quality of the data prior to its acceptance into the archival system. In addition, scripts and programs can be written that scan the digital collection, testing for various conditions, and notifying responsible departments of potential problems. Working in partnership, the information technology staff and the digital archivist would develop algorithms for determining the quality factors, write the programs and scripts that implement the algorithms, and test the programs and scripts for completeness and accuracy.

Operationalize is the process by which quality becomes institutionalized. Workflows across the organization implement quality standards, use the systems—both human and computer—that have been developed, and prioritize quality. All of the contributors to the digital archive would implement the quality assurance programs and scripts into their workflows. Digital archive and information technology staff would create a regular and automated schedule to monitor integrity checks and have processes to remediate any problems detected.

Management is an ongoing process that reviews quality standards and processes, monitors the quantitative measurements, and looks to improve quality of the data throughout the organization. Digital archivists, information technology staff, and other stakeholders would regularly review reports and implement changes to improve quality as required.

Quality Assurance for Curation

Data Profiling

Data quality is contextual and specific to an organization. An organization may create its own matrix of quality attributes based on its needs. Assessing the needs for quality data for long-term curation of digital objects may seem daunting. The problem can be approached from three angles: the file, the object, and the context. This approach considers the individual components of a complex digital object that is set within its context. In general, digital objects are hierarchical: individual files have properties and contain content that contribute to the properties and content of the object. In digital curation, quality factors compound; the quality requirements for individual files are the baseline for quality factors of the object, which sets the specification for the quality factors of the contextual information.

File Quality

Quality factors for files include integrity, validity, and, for many archives, consistency. Integrity includes ensuring fixity, making sure the bitstream does not change either inadvertently or maliciously. Digital archives want to ensure the integrity of the file format, ensuring that the file is well formed and accurate. The archive needs to know the exact precise format for each file and must ensure that the file follows all the rules of the format standard. Files must be valid. Every TIFF file must conform to the rules of the TIFF format. Many digital archives also want to ensure consistency among files within a collection or type of material. An archive might want all of the images for a book to have the same dimensions or all of the audio files for a collection to have the same sampling rate.

Object Quality

As digital objects are composed from individual files, the digital object must assure that all of the component files are of sufficient quality. Once the files have been confirmed, issues of the object can be addressed. Quality factors for digital objects include integrity, completeness, consistency, and accessibility.

Because digital objects are comprised of multiple individual data files, perhaps the most important quality factor for a digital object is its integrity; that is, all of its component pieces are known, documented, and available. An inventory of objects must be available in a standard metadata format such as METS, in a database, a spreadsheet, or in some other data store. The digital archives can check that all of the components files documented in the inventory are available; all of the files should be in the location indicated by the inventory.

Ensuring integrity of the object assumes the inventory to be complete; therefore, completeness is another very important quality factor for digital objects. Completeness relies on curators' thorough documentation. Many digital archives require consistency within a genre of digital objects. For example, a digital archive could require that all book objects have a TIF master file, a large JPEG for screen reading, and a text file for each page, a PDF file for each chapter, and a MARC record for each volume. A photographic image will have a different set of required components: a TIF master file, a large JPEG for screen viewing, a 200 × 100 pixel thumbnail JPEG for the delivery systems light table view. Each genre of material would have its own set of criteria. But the archive would want to ensure consistency within a genre to allow its discovery and delivery systems to provide a good user experience for its patrons.

Within the context of digital curation, accessibility generally means persistent identification; links to an object should not break or lead to all older personal information. Identifiers for digital objects should provide not only the digital content but also the content displayed in a renderable and usable interface. The digital object should have sufficient information to be able to provide access to all of the components.

Metadata Quality

Contextual data, also known as metadata, has its own quality requirements, including accuracy, completeness, consistency, and accessibility. Quality requirements do not vary regardless of the type of metadata: descriptive, technical, administrative, or structural. Metadata must be accurate. For example, the title in the descriptive metadata must be the title of the object; the date the object was created must be the date it was created; and the structure map of a digital object must be correct. It is certainly reasonable to expect that metadata must be complete; it must be sufficient to fulfill its mission. Completeness may depend on the source of the metadata. Metadata harvested from external systems may not be as complete as the digital archive would like. Archives may need to enhance metadata retrieved from other sources. Requirements for completeness may change over time; technical metadata that was once thought to be sufficient may not be in the future. As technology standards change, technical metadata will change; digital archives must monitor requirements for completeness and accuracy based on these changes. Consistency is another important quality factor for metadata. Metadata standards provide codified and structured templates for metadata. However, it is possible to interpret and use standards that make interoperability, even within a single system, difficult. Consistently encoded data will make searching more fruitful, objects more accessible, and data easier to manage. Metadata can be made more consistent by the use of controlled vocabularies and automated default values in data management systems. Accessibility as a quality factor of metadata indicates persistent identification and excellent indexing in quality access systems.

Implementing Quality Assurance

Many libraries and archives are familiar with workflows, which are a set of steps or processes to complete a specific task. In digital libraries and archives, workflows are often a combination of manual and automated process to digitize content, ingest data into a system, verify data within a system, analyze metadata, and so forth. Workflows are an efficient way for a digital archive to implement quality assurance program.

Most quality assurance processes can be automated. Automation can simplify repetitive and mundane activities while facilitating and enforcing best practice. Of course, an error in an automated process can replicate across thousands of digital objects. However, carefully crafted automated processes can greatly increase the quality of data. While some repository systems (see Chapter 6) have integrated workflow features, many libraries and archives create scripts using a combination of open source, commercial, and *homegrown* software components. Scripts are highly customizable and can be configured specifically to meet quality needs of the digital archive. Workflow systems, software that allows multiple components to be prioritized and configured, are also available and can be used for quality assurance. A number of workflow systems were developed for scientific research, but they can be easily implemented for quality assurance and ongoing curation activities.

Workflow Components for Quality Assurance

A digital archive could develop a number of components to assure the quality of their digital contents. The archive could use these components for preprocessing data prior to intake into their archival system, their digital repository, as well as for ongoing, regular monitoring and curation activities. These components can help ensure multiple quality dimensions: integrity, completeness, consistency, and accessibility.

Components to ensure integrity could include the following:

- File fixity—this component could have multiple subcomponents. Once a component would calculate the fixity hash and store it for future use, then another subcomponent would recalculate the hash and compare it to the stored hash. Email or other notification of failure would be generated.
- File format verification—this component would incorporate software such as JHOVE to ensure that files are what they purport to be.
- File format validation—this incorporates software such as JHOVE to ensure that files conform to standards.

Components to ensure object completeness could include the following:

- Object completeness—this component would verify the contents of the directory against an inventory. Missing or extra files would be noted as errors. Depending on the need of the archive, the process could either terminate or continue on as provisional. The provisional data will be segregated until it could be verified by the curatorial staff.

- Metadata creation—this could be implemented as a number of separate components, one component for metadata standard. Descriptive metadata could be created from information in a spreadsheet, from an EAD finding aid, harvested from a separate system, taken from the contents of the digital file itself, or inferred from file and directory names. Technical metadata can be created by extracting information from file headers or extracted from reports from software packages, such as JHOVE. Structural metadata can be created from the implicit metadata in directory structures, keyword data in file names, or spreadsheets or other inventory documents. Metadata creation components can verify accuracy, completeness, and consistency, or these components could allow a separate component in the workflow to make those verifications.

- Metadata completeness—this verifies that metadata is complete and ensures that all of the necessary metadata is present. This is especially important for metadata that comes from external systems. The component would review all of the tags within the metadata file and compare them to a list of required elements. Records without required elements could be flagged with appropriate reporting.

- Derivative creation—this occurs when many file types are inappropriate for screen delivery and use. Creating derivative files from archival master files is a common practice. A component could create multiple derivative files of different sizes needs in type of materials. Derivative file formats include JPEG, PDF, MP3, and so on.

Components to ensure consistency could include the following:

- Metadata consistency—this component would verify use of controlled vocabularies and other semantic tools.

- File quality and consistency—these two components verify style quality and consistency. They need to be unique to each file format. One component should be created for the image file to ensure that all of the images within one logical object have the same pixel dimensions, image orientation, pixels per inch, embedded color profiles, and so on. Audio files would have different quality inconsistency requirements that could also be enforced. Again, file that fails quality checks would be rejected or segregated until a new file is submitted.

- Object consistency—this component could be either part of an object completeness module or an individual stand-alone component. Object consistency would verify that all appropriate derivative files have been created and recorded in metadata and had been stored appropriately.

Quality assurance is most effectively applied at the data creation and system intake. When digital libraries and archives acquire data whether through analog to digital conversion or born-digital materials, they must ensure data and metadata quality before taking it into their systems. Digital archives can use these various components to build workflows based on the specific needs of the materials at hand. Digital archives generally have a set of reoccurring ingest scenarios. Single part objects, such as individual images or sound files, are very common. The process for multipart objects, such as a book, journal, or diary, is another common scenario. Digital archives often deal with multiple multipart objects, such as a journal run or a set of letters. There are as many scenarios as there are types of materials.

As the quality control workflow is being designed, the digital curator has a number of decisions to make. The curator needs to decide if the material needs to be processed as an entire batch or if subset of the records can be set aside for errors. This decision is based on the nature of the materials. It would be reasonable to require all of the items in a book as the batch that needs to be processed together and that a set of single item photographs is not a batch and can be processed independently. The curator would need to decide on error handling issues, such as responsibility for managing and resolving errors, feedback mechanisms, and processing updates when necessary.

Quality Control for Single Part Objects

Libraries and archives often have a large collection of photographs. Digitizing the photographs has been high priority for many cultural organizations. While there are many ways to organize the project, for many libraries and archives, this is a relatively simple process. An inventory of the photographs to be digitized is created with information such as collection name and number, item control number, item title, item date, and so forth. As the photographs are digitized, the files are named with the item control number and stored in a directory named for the collection. Both the directory of images and the inventory spreadsheet are input into the quality control workflow for single part objects (see Figure 5.4).

Figure 5.4.
Workflow for Single Part Objects

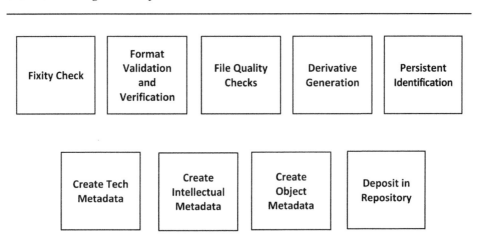

It is reasonable to start workflow with a fixity check. The hash can be used in future steps. Format validation and verification are often done in one set of software, such as (OPF, 2016). Once the object has been validated, format and project specific quality checks can be made. Generating derivative files is relatively simple to automate. The nature, number, and size of derivatives are often determined by the type of collection. The component can be designed to use the collection-specific rules. The next step would be to create persistent identification. The component for technical metadata can use the output of the JHOVE process to create a MIX file for each master file. The component for descriptive or descriptive metadata can extract data from the spreadsheet: title, creator, dates, and other fields as available. Again, based on configurations, specific standards could be created, such as MODS or Dublin Core. Structural metadata for the entire object is created when all of the component elements are available. A METS file is created that contains the master file, derivative files, MODS and/or Dublin Core records, and the MIX file. All of the files would be then uploaded to the digital archive.

Throughout the process, files are being produced. Some of the files are considered to be the final product, while others are temporary and are used to share information between workflow components. The process for single part objects as seen in Figure 5.4 would produce the following files for preservation:

- For each original image
  - Fixity hash, such as an MD5 checksum
  - JHOVE validation and verification report
  - File quality report
  - MIX file
  - Derivative files as specified
  - PIDs for each
- For each logical object
  - MODS or Dublin Core record
  - METS record

Multipart Objects

For this discussion, multipart objects are defined as a set of like files that have logical subgroupings; an example is a book that has multiple page files that are gathered into chapters or sections. Book-like objects include materials such as a journal, a newspaper, a magazine, a diary, and so on. The principles are the same.

Because a multipart object is comprised of individual files, the first step is to ensure their quality. The multipart object workflow (see Figure 5.5) uses the same components as the single part workflow as seen in Figure 5.4. But for the multipart object, a new component is added. Prior to processing the individual files, a step to ensure the integrity of the entire object is inserted. The object integrity component

Figure 5.5.
Workflow for Multi-Part Objects

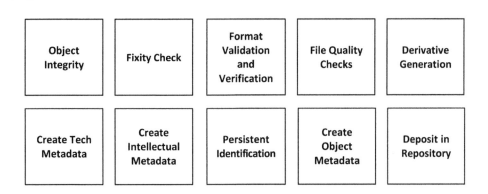

ensures that all of the necessary files are present. The process requires a thorough and accurate inventory of files. The process reads the inventory and compares the content of the input file directory. If files are missing, the process should be stopped. It is generally considered best practice to force all files to be present before processing any.

The multipart object workflow needs a robust metadata component. The metadata requirement will change based on the nature of the material. Many books have existing descriptive metadata. Generally, books have MARC records stored in a bibliographic control system, often called an Integrated Library System (ILS). The metadata component could extract the MARC record from the ILS and incorporate it into the digital archive. Other types of material, a diary or a letter, generally would not have an existing metadata record. In this case, the component would need to take information from the inventory or other input file to create a standard metadata record, such as MODS or Dublin Core.

The object metadata component could be configured to provide more functionality than is required for the single part object workflow. With a single item, there are no decisions to be made about the structure of the object. But with the multipart object, a curator could make a number of different decisions about structure. For a book, it would be possible to create a METS file that reflects the structure of the book with chapters, front matter, back matter, and so forth. A diary could reflect individual entries. A journal could reflect individual articles. In order for the component to build the structure, the information must be available either through the inventory or through directory structure and file names. This information is often captured during the digitizing process; the digitizers will create a new subdirectory for each chapter with an appropriate name (i.e., Book-number_Chapter2 or Diary-number_Entry_10-12-1920). The object metadata component will read the directory name, use that name within the METS file, and assume all files within that directory are pages within that chapter or entry.

The output of this process will include the following files:

- For each individual image file
  - MD5 checksum
  - JHOVE validation and verification report
  - File quality report
  - MIX file
- For each derivative file
  - MD5 Checksum
- For the whole object
  - DOI
  - MARC and/or MODS and/or DC record
  - METS record

Multiple Multipart Object Workflow

Not all objects in digital collections are single intellectual entities; many objects are more clearly understood within the context of a collection. Many archives and libraries have large set of letters, diaries, and other artifacts whose impact and importance and meaning are enhanced by their collectiveness. For example, a collection of correspondence has a number of individual letters, each of which has multiple pages. A run of journals has multiple objects: each journal has multiple articles, each journal is part of a volume, and a run has multiple volumes. Another example would be record albums; albums, whether analog or digital, often have multiple sound tracks. These types of materials can be described as multiple multipart objects.

The workflow for multiple multipart objects builds on the previous workflows (see Figure 5.6). Integrity and completeness verified is the beginning of the process. Individual files are then run through the various quality checks. In this workflow, multiple structural object metadata files and one collection level structural object metadata file are created.

Figure 5.6.
Workflow for Multiple Multi-Part Objects

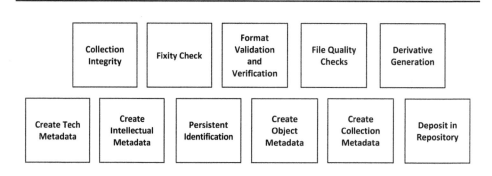

As with the other workflows, the structural metadata is created through inventory and/or implicit directory structure and filenames. Once the object integrity and file quality is assured, the structural metadata can be created. Nested directories can indicate the structure to the components:

Collection Directory

    Object 1 Directory

        Object 1 / subcomponent 1 Directory

        Object1 / subcomponent 1 / file 1

        Object1 / subcomponent 1 / file 2

        Object1 / subcomponent 1 / file 3

      Object 1 / subcomponent 2 Directory

        Object1 / subcomponent 2 / file 1 . . . .

    Object 2 Directory . . .

Nesting can model most objects. Two levels of nesting could model a set of letters: collection and letter. Four levels of nesting could model a journal: run, volume, issue, and article. The lowest level of the hierarchy would hold the files. In the journal example, the article level would contain the files. The other levels of hierarchy would indicate the relationships. The METS file for the article would map the files. The METS file for the issues would map the METS files for the articles. The METS file for the volume would map the METS files for the issues. The METS file for the run would map the METS files for the volumes.

The output for this workflow would consist of the following:

- For each file
  - MD5 checksum
  - JHOVE report
  - MIX file
  - File quality report
  - Derivative files
- For each logical object
  - Derivative object
  - MARC and/or MODS and/or Dublin Core record
  - METS file
  - DOIs
- For the whole collection
  - METS file
  - DC record

Ongoing Curation Scenarios

While quality assurance and control is most effective during ingest, regular quality assessment of the digital collections is also very important. Workflows can be created for a number of scenarios, including ensuring fixity, updating metadata, and creating new or additional derivative files. One of the most important ongoing quality checks is for file integrity. Ensuring fixity over time, making sure that all of the bits are exactly the same, is an essential component of a quality program. Many digital libraries and archives run a fixity check on a regular basis. A fixity process would generally involve reading each digital file, calculating the fixity hash, and comparing it to the existing hash that has been stored in metadata. If the hash is identical, the file is considered to be unchanged. The bit level integrity has been confirmed. This process can be expensive in terms of computational resources. For some files, the process is very quick. But for large image files, many of which are half a gigabyte, the process takes time and resources. However, ensuring level integrity is important.

Workflows and quality components can also be used during media migration. When new storage hardware is purchased, files need to be moved to the new equipment. Ensuring the quality of the transfer, including bit-level integrity, file path updates to metadata and other files, and URL updates for PIDs can be programmatically completed with workflows.

SUMMARY

Data quality is often decomposed into a set of dimensions that ascribe and describe the elements of quality. These dimensions include accessibility, completeness, consistency, currency, integrity, timeliness, uniqueness, and others. Some of the dimensions address intrinsic values of worth, others address contextual aspects of metadata, while still others address representational and accessibility. Quality can also be viewed through its absence by imperfections such as imprecision, inconsistency, and uncertainty. Quality dimensions can be applied to both the digital data and its metadata.

Maturity models can help organizations assess their methods, structure, and/or processes against a set of criteria. Quality is an important component in many data maturity models. Scales to rank processes range from ad hoc to well-established institutionalized ones. Digital libraries and archives can use these models to review and improve their processes.

Technologies for quality can help digital libraries and archives preserve their digital materials. Integrity of the file can be ensured by verifying fixity. Accessibility can be enhanced with persistent identification. Verifying that the data follows the structural and semantic rules of its format ensures the validity of quality dimension.

Data profiling is the process of determining the essential quality dimensions for a collection. Organizations need to prioritize their quality needs and create measurable quality criteria. Viewing the collection first as files, then as objects, and finally as metadata can help clarify the quality requirements.

Workflows can help digital libraries and archives automate their quality processes. Automation can help organizations increase the quality of their data. Each aspect of quality can be implemented as a component, a small program, that can be combined with others to create a set of processes for any type of file or object.

Questions for Discussion

1. Data quality has many dimensions. Which dimensions seem most important to you? Why?
2. Which data imperfection seems most serious to you? Why?
3. How can automated workflows increase quality of digital content?
4. What new tools could be developed to support quality in digital content?
5. What types of materials and ingest scenarios can you think of that could benefit from a quality workflow?

NOTES

1. http://www.searchquotes.com/search/Data_Quality/
2. Redman (2001) has 51 quality dimensions in 8 categories—availability/delivery, quality of content, quality of values, presentation quality, flexibility, architecture, privacy, and improvement. However, he states that these dimensions are the most important and lead to data fitness.

REFERENCES

Abrams, S. L., & Seaman, D. (2003). Towards a global digital format registry. In *World Library and Information Congress: 69th IFLA General Conference and Council.*

Batini, C., & Scannapieco, M. (2016). Data quality dimensions. In *Data and information quality* (pp. 21–51). New York, NY: Springer International Publishing.

Brown, A. (2003). Selecting storage media for long-term preservation. *Digital preservation guidance note 2, Issue 1* (Vol. 2). London. Found at http://www.nationalarchives.gov.uk/documents/selecting_storage_media.pdf

Brown, A. (2006). Automatic format identification using PRONOM and DROID. *Digital preservation technical paper 1, Issue 2*. London: National Archives of the United Kingdom. Found at http://www.nationalarchives.gov.uk/aboutapps/fileformat/pdf/automatic_format_identification.pdf

Brown, G. (2006). Virtualizing the CIC floppy disk project. Fall Depository Library Conference.

California Digital Library (CDL). (2015). *ARK*. Found at https://wiki.ucop.edu/display/Curation/ARK

CMMI Institute. (2014). *Data management maturity model v1.0*. Found at http://cmmiinstitute.com/resources/data-management-maturity-model-v10

Consultative Committee for Space Data Systems (CCSDS). (2012). *Reference model for an Open Archival Information System (OAIS)*. Issue 2. Recommendation for Space Data System Standards (Magenta Book), CCSDS 650.0-M-2. Washington, DC: ISO 14721:2012. Found at http://public.ccsds.org/publications/archive/650x0m2.pdf

Corporation for National Research Initiatives (CNRI). (2015). *HDL.NET® Information Services*. Found at https://www.handle.net/

Crosby, P. B. (1988). *Quality is free: The art of making quality certain*. New York, NY: McGraw-Hill.

DAMA UK Working Group on "Data Quality Dimensions." (2013). The six primary dimensions for data quality assessment: Defining data quality dimensions. Found at https://www.whitepapers.em360tech.com/wp-content/files_mf/1407250286DAMAUKDQDimensionsWhitePaperR37.pdf

The Data Governance Institute [DGI]. (2015). *Definitions of data governance*. Found at http://www.datagovernance.com/adg_data_governance_definition/

Digital Asset Management Foundation. (2015). Metadata and taxonomy maturities as they relate to digital asset management. In *DAM Knowledge*. Found at http://damfoundation.org/2011/08/05/metadata-and-taxonomy-maturities-as-they-relate-to-digital-asset-management/

Dodds, L., & Newman, A. (2015). *Data maturity model*. Open Data Institute. Found at http://www.opendata.institute/guides/maturity-model

Geiger, J. G. (2004). Data quality management: The most critical initiative you can implement. *Data Warehousing, Management and Quality*, *Paper* 098-29. Found at http://www2.sas.com/proceedings/sugi29/098-29.pdf

Grindley, N. (2011). What to curate? Preserving and curating software-based art. Presented at the Computers and the History of Art 27th Annual Conference, November 17–18, London. Found at http://www.slideshare.net/neilgrindley/grindley-what-to-curate-software-based-art-ch-art-2011

Harvard University Library. (2008). *Name resolution service user guide*. Found at https://wiki.harvard.edu/confluence/display/LibraryStaffDoc/Name+Resolution+Service+User+Guide?preview=/195497351/195658739/nrs-userguide.pdf

IBM. (2007). *The IBM data governance council maturity model: Building a roadmap for effective data governance*. Found at https://www-935.ibm.com/services/uk/cio/pdf/leverage_wp_data_gov_council_maturity_model.pdf

International DOI Foundation (IDF). (2016). *The DOI® System*. Found at https://www.doi.org/

Karr, A. F., Sanil, A. P., Sacks, J., & Elmagarmid, A. (2001). *Workshop report: Affiliates workshop on data quality*. Research Triangle Park, NC: NISS.

Loshin, D. (2009). Five fundamental data quality practices: White paper. In *Pitney Bows*. Found at http://www.pbinsight.com/files/resource-library/resource-files/five_fundamental_data_quality_practices_WP.pdf

Lynch, C. (2008). Big data: How do your data grow? *Nature*, *455*(7209), 28–29. Nature Publishing Group. Found at http://www.nature.com/nature/journal/v455/n7209/full/455028a.html

OCLC. (2013). *PURLS*. Found at http://www.oclc.org/research/themes/data-science/purl.html

Open Preservation Foundation (OPF). (2015). JHOVE TIFF-hul module. In *An introduction to JHOVE*. Found at http://jhove.openpreservation.org/modules/tiff/

Open Preservation Foundation (OPF). (2016). *Products*. Found at http://openpreservation.org/technology/products/

Paulk, M. C., Curtis, B., Chrissis, M. B., & Weber, C. V. (1993). Capability maturity model, version 1.1. *IEEE Software*, *10*(4), 18–27.

Pipino, L. L., Lee, Y. W., & Wang, R. Y. (2002). Data quality assessment. *Communications of the ACM*, *45*(4), 211–218.

Quality. (n.d.). In *Merriam-Webster.com*. Found at https://www.merriam-webster.com/dictionary/quality

Redman, T. C. (2001). *Data quality: The field guide*. Woburn, MA: Digital Press.

Redman, T. C. (2008). Data driven: profiting from your most important business asset. Harvard Business Press.

Search Data Management (SDM). (2016). Data quality. In *Guide to Managing a Data Quality Assurance Program*. TechTarget. Found at http://searchdatamanagement.techtarget.com/definition/data-quality

Smets, P. (1997). Imperfect information: Imprecision and uncertainty. In *Uncertainty management in information systems* (pp. 225–254). New York, NY: Springer.

Termens, M., Ribera, M., & Locher, A. (2015). An analysis of file format control in institutional repositories. *Library Hi Tech*, *33*(2), 162–174.

Thomas, G. (2006). The DGI Data Governance Framework. The Data Governance Institute. Found at http://www.datagovernance.com/wp-content/uploads/2014/11/dgi_framework.pdf

Wang, R. Y., & Strong, D. M. (1996). Beyond accuracy: What data quality means to data consumers. *Journal of Management Information Systems*, *12*(4), 5–33.

World Wide Web Consortium (WC3). (2001). URIs, URLs, and URNs: Clarifications and recommendations 1.0. *W3C uriclarification*, September.

Zhao, X. (2005). Meta data management maturity model. *Information Management*, October. Found at https://www.information-management.com/news/meta-data-management-maturity-model

Chapter 6

REPOSITORIES

I can't predict how reading habits will change. But I will say that the greatest loss is the paper archive—no more a great stack of manuscripts, letters, and notebooks from a writer's life, but only a tiny pile of disks, little plastic cookies where once were calligraphic marvels.
—Paul Theroux[1]

It's a great thing to live in a digital age. It's convenient; it's fast.

—Loretta Lynch[2]

INTRODUCTION

People view libraries and archives as repositories of knowledge. Photographs of beautiful libraries abound. Facebook memes of spectacular bookshelves filled with leather-bound, gold-leaf editions are commonplace as is nostalgia for paper, physical books, cinema on film, music on vinyl, and audio on tape. But in reality, very few people currently create data without using digital technologies. The tremendous convenience of writing using a word processing program on a powerful computer greatly outweighs the romantic notion of beautifully handwritten manuscripts. However, the convenience of digital data creates problems for libraries and archives; those piles of discs and stacks of hard drives produced through computational composition are barriers to preservation. Digital data needs to be managed in a system that understands its bits as well as its context.

Libraries and archives *are* the keepers of knowledge whether it is analog or digital. They have been dealing with digital information since the 1980s and have been leaders in developing systems to manage large quantities of digital data. Just as bibliographic information has been managed using an Integrated Library System (ILS), digital content is managed in digital repository systems. Many digital repository systems are available for libraries and archives. Libraries and archives have contributed to developing these repository systems (ARL, 2009). In this chapter, the theoretical, technical, and practical aspects of digital repository systems will be explored.

THEORETICAL OVERVIEW

Merriam-Webster defines a repository as a place where something is stored or deposited or a "place that contains or stores something nonmaterial *considered the book a repository of knowledge*," or "a [place where] something is entrusted" (Repository, n.d.). As libraries and archives considered themselves to be repositories of knowledge, it seemed logical to create repositories for their digital content.

Repository systems have been developed to solve the problems managing the vast amount of information generated by digitizing and the collection of born-digital materials, including describing the materials, providing access to the materials, and preserving the materials. Before digital repository systems, each digital collection had a website for discovery, and the digital content was stored on a file system. Each new collection had a new website, different descriptive metadata scheme, and a new set of directories on the file system. A new collection meant a new system. To find materials, patrons needed to search multiple systems. It did not take long for digital libraries and archives to find that this model was unsustainable. The time and money to develop these systems were too high, the amount of effort to maintain the system was not sustainable, and the inconvenience for end users trying to find material for their need was unacceptable.

Digital repositories can leverage economies of scale by providing a core set of functionality for accessing, indexing, describing, and managing digital content in a single software system. Applying curatorial functions such as file integrity checking, storage management, and so on could be centralized. Functionality can be enhanced and applied to multiple collections. A digital repository system can more easily tie into other institutional systems such as large storage arrays and organizational identity systems that manage log-in and passwords for enterprise systems. Digital repository systems can provide uniformity to user interfaces that help patrons remember functionality. Digital repository systems can provide application programming interfaces (APIs) that allow integrated services across systems, such as embedding a page turning system within the integrated library management system's online public catalog or a universal search function across all digital and analog library collections.

Libraries and archives have the Open Archival Information System (OAIS) reference model heavily influenced the development of digital repository systems. The OAIS defines many of the functions of a digital repository. Libraries and archives used the OAIS as a basis for their repository systems. In fact, many digital repository systems claim to be "OAIS Compliant."

OAIS and Repositories

The OAIS provides a good overview of the high-level functions for a digital repository. As seen in Figure 6.1, the primary functions include ingest, data management, archival storage, and access. Preservation planning and management are actions taken by people within the organization and are not considered to be system functions. This image is slightly different from the OAIS overview image seen in Chapter 1. In this version, the transformations of the data are included. The data

Figure 6.1.
OAIS Overview

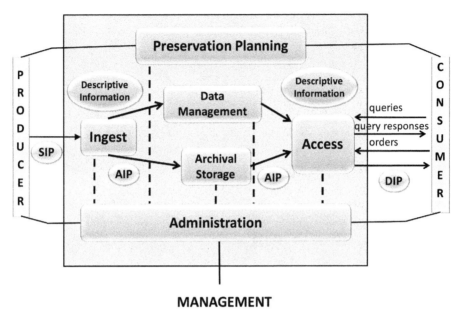

(CCSDS, 2012, p. 4–1. Reprinted with permission of the Consultative Committee for Space Data Systems.)

is enhanced and perhaps modified as it moves through the system from ingest to storage and the end user.

Repository Functions

Ingest

Ingest is a set of functions to prepare to bring data into the repository system. The data comes to the repository as a Submission Information Package (SIP). This SIP comes from the data producer and contains the files that comprise the digital object and information such as the relationships between the files and some type of description of the logical object. The data provided by the producer is rarely sufficient for curating the data over time. The data must be enhanced. During ingest, the data is evaluated and processed. The descriptive information is transformed into metadata. Files are validated and verified. Files are examined in order to create structural and technical metadata (see Chapter 5 for a fuller discussion of automated processes to evaluate quality and create metadata).

Data Management

After the ingest process, the data and metadata are ready to be accepted into the repository system. The digital repository's data management functions provide services that store the files, generate indexes researching and retrieving data, populate database tables, and create relationships between files and objects. The digital repository must ensure that it has sufficient data that is technical, structural, and descriptive metadata before it can fully commit to archiving the object. All of the component data files and elements are considered to be an Archival Information Package (AIP).

The data management functions extend beyond the initial deposit of objects. Data management is an ongoing process. Management reports, ongoing data integrity checks, and referential integrity monitoring are ongoing data management functions that the repository can provide. The repository also needs ongoing maintenance in order to ensure its ongoing data management functions. The repository's database needs to be maintained. Schemas need to be maintained. Software needs to be updated. Indexes need to be regenerated. Hardware must be maintained and upgraded as needed.

Archival Storage

Archival storage is more than just hardware. A repository needs to monitor hardware for capacity, use, and integrity. The repository needs to warn administrators when errors are detected, when reading or writing files, when fixity checks fail, and when a capacity threshold is passed. Repositories need to provide services for migrating data to new storage hardware that would include efficient and fast transfer, efficient use of storage, and integrity checks of the files as they are moved. The archival storage function would also need to maintain an inventory of files and objects and both detect and report any problems or errors. Archival storage functions can include disaster recovery planning. See Chapter 8 for a fuller discussion of disaster recovery planning.

Access

Throughout the literature, access to digital content is a key objective of digital curation. Thus, the OAIS emphasizes access as one of the primary functions of a digital repository system. The access function requires one final data transformation from the AIP to a Dissemination Information Package (DIP). The descriptive metadata that has been stored within the system needs to be searchable by end users. Objects and their contextual information need to be delivered to the end user's computer. Certainly, one would expect the descriptive metadata to be delivered to the end user, but additional information is often needed. Many access systems need structural metadata in order to support the behavior users need, such as turning a page in a book-like object, or picking between different sizes of a photograph, or choosing the best version of the document for reading. And rendering information may also be necessary; a system may want to present two options to a user for a JPEG2000 file, either the fully interactive version that allows panning and zooming or a straight JPEG version. To provide access to digital content, a digital repository system needs an interface to format and render the results of queries.

Trust in Repositories

From the earliest days of the digital age, librarians and archivists were concerned about preserving data. A significant component of their concern was in their ability to create repository systems that could be trustworthy (Waters & Garrett, 1996). They were concerned that people, their patrons, would not be able to trust that the digital object was the same as the physical object and that the object was not authentic. From the earliest days, librarians and archivists were concerned about creating a trusted digital repository. "A trusted digital repository is one whose mission is to provide reliable, long term access to managed digital resources to its designated community, now and in the future" (Beagrie et al., 2002, p. i). In order to be trustworthy, a repository needs more than just a sound technological infrastructure; it needs to have organizational support to sustain it over time so that it is able to accept responsibility for long-term maintenance of digital materials on behalf of the depositors. A trusted repository needs to develop policies and practices as well as metrics that measure its success.

Developing metrics to judge the trustworthiness of digital repositories has been an ongoing process in digital libraries. These metrics would be used to certify that a digital repository could be trusted (Waters & Garrett, 1996). The Trustworthy Repositories Audit and Certification (TRAC) checklist was published in 2007 and gained acceptance among libraries (Houghton, 2015) and is now an International Organization of Standardization (ISO) standard named the Audit and Certification of Trustworthy Digital Repositories: Recommended practice CCSDS 652.0-M-1 (CCSDS, 2011). The goal of a certification audit is to determine the institutional fitness to commit to manage and maintain digital objects for the community that needs them. The certification process evaluates the infrastructure of the organization, the technology infrastructure and its ability to manage risk, and the management of digital content. Evaluating the infrastructure of the organization involves reviewing its governance or organizational structure and management. It involves quantifying the organization's long-term viability or financial sustainability as well as infrastructure for developing and maintaining a suitable preservation policy. Evaluating the technology infrastructure and its ability to manage risk involves auditing the technology, including hardware and software replacement schedules, data backup processes, and monitoring processes. Evaluating the management of digital content includes a review of internal processes for acquiring content, preservation planning, and access management, as well as an audit of what OAIS refers to as the AIP.

Types of Repositories

In the years since the publication of the OAIS, a number of digital repository systems have been developed. These systems have been developed to meet a specific set of needs with a functional and technical model. Some of these systems have a very specific functional scope while others have a broader focus. Some of these systems are commercial products while others are open source. Some of these systems are applications while others are set of components and tools to be assembled by programmers. Some of these systems have integrated user interfaces for search, discovery, and retrieval while others are intended to be used as a back end system. There is no formally recognized categorization scheme. Several ways of categorizing repositories include the following:

- Subject-based repositories
- Research repositories
- National repository systems
- Institutional repositories (Armbruster & Romary, 2009)
- Digital repositories
- Open access repositories (JISC, 2009)

The existing categorizations seem to be insufficient to describe the wide variety of repository systems available today. It can be useful to think about digital repository systems as the functional roles they play in a preservation-focused organization. In the current environment, digital repository software can be categorized as useful for the following types of repositories:

- Institutional repositories
- Preprint services
- Digital library management systems
- Digital archives management systems
- Digital repository software infrastructure
- Federated repositories
- Dark archives
- Digital asset management systems

Broadly, the types of repositories are based on function and/or architecture. Any given real-life repository may fit into one or more of these types.

Institutional Repository

Institutional repositories are systems designed to be used to collect, manage, and disseminate the intellectual output of an institution. In a university that could include material such as publications of faculty, the research data for those faculty publications, and course materials, such as syllabi, lecture notes, PowerPoint slides, old tests and quizzes, and assignment descriptions, it could also include course catalogs, recruitment materials, and meeting minutes from boards of trustees, faculty senates, and other public groups. In libraries, institutional materials could be handouts and promotional materials from programs, strategic plans, superseded policies for collection development, privacy, and other types of policies.

In many organizations, the library has been the organizational owner of the institutional repository. Libraries have the experience managing and maintaining materials for long periods of time, have an infrastructure for supporting digital technologies, and have a knowledgeable staff who are able to design policies and work with others. Self-deposit is an underlying assumption of institutional repositories; that is, members of the institution are expected to submit their materials and enter sufficient metadata for access. In the early years of institutional repositories, librarians developed outreach campaigns to find key supporters within the organization. Even with these outreach efforts, the institutional repositories were not used among the rank and file of the organization as hoped. Librarians would find the data and create the metadata for the submissions. They often queried journal databases to find the publications of their faculty and sought the rights to get copies for their institutional repositories. Institutional repositories need to be able to take in a variety of different types of materials, organize them in a way that is intuitive to the people trying to find the materials, and provide robust search and retrieval functionality.

Preprint Services

In scholarly publishing, a preprint refers to "an issue of a technical paper often in preliminary form before its publication in a journal" (Preprint, n.d.). In digital repositories, the preprint service is designed to accept and provide public access to research papers prior to their publication. Preprint services act as an open access resource for emerging research. Many preprint services are organized as community data collections; that is, they are created, managed, and used by the specific community within a specific research domain. In a number of research domains, such as physics, ecology, and biology depositing, preprint is an important process for researchers.

As a community resource, preprint services have a specific set of requirements, the primary of which is ease of use. Preprint services are generally run as a community project with volunteers, so an easy data submission processes good error checking, metadata, and full text indexing, and a public search and retrieval interface are critical.

Digital Library Management Systems

Many libraries, regardless of size, want the equivalent of an ILS for their digital materials. Digital library management systems fill that need. Many of these systems are turnkey; they can be ready to implement and use with minimal configuration. Digital library management systems generally have a user-friendly search and discovery interface, an easy-to-use system for metadata creation and editing, a batch upload interface to ingest multiple objects in a single process, and some preservation functions such as managing relationships between files, validating fixity, persistent identification creation and resolution, and format validation and verification.

Most digital library management systems deal with a variety of media formats. They provide a consistent front end for both patrons and staff. However, their consistency does not allow for customization for unusual materials or special projects. Digital library management systems work well for library and archives that have rather traditional holdings. These systems also work well for organizations without a significant software development staff or who choose to use that staff in other ways.

Digital Archives Management Systems

In many ways, archives and libraries are similar in their missions and needs for digital curation. One significant difference between libraries and archives is in the manner in which they process their collections. Libraries generally require item-level access to objects, which implies metadata record for each object. Archives often process data at a higher level using a more collective description technique, so rather than creating a descriptive metadata record for each object, the collection is well documented, and the objects within that collection are organized and described as genre, such as correspondence, ephemera, photographs, or described as by its physical description, such as by box or folder. Archival description has its own standard known as the Encoded Archival Descript (EAD). Archivists used tools especially designed to support unique workflow preprocessing in describing archival collections. Some of the early versions of these systems focused on the process of physically organizing the collection and EAD creation. Now, however, digital archives management systems have implemented many of the features required of an OAIS repository and support born-digital and analog-to-digital conversion workflows, rights management, and preservation functions, such as fixity checks and format normalization.

Digital Repository Software Infrastructure

Unlike digital library management systems that are generally usable right *out-of-the-box*, the digital repository infrastructure category of digital repository has a set of software components set in a technical architecture that allows an organization to build a digital repository. These software packages are generally a set of tools that can be combined in a variety of ways to create a highly customized repository to meet very specific requirements. These components or tools are generally at a very low level; that is, they address a very specific technical function, such as building an index, creating a unique identifier, or running a fixity check.

These systems generally do not have a user interface for patrons or a management interface for staff. These must be built using a combination of the components and original code developed by the individual library or archive. Communities of technologists and software developers have arisen to support these systems. New functions are created and contributed to the community. For many large digital libraries and archives, these highly customizable systems are the only viable option. The turnkey systems are too restrictive and will not support the number of objects, the type of digital objects, and the number of collections that these institutions own.

The systems are generally open source, meaning that the code is available at no cost; these systems are not, however, free. The amount of effort in both time and resources to create an effective and usable system is significant. The flexibility and customization come with the substantial cost. In addition to the original investment in time and resource, ongoing maintenance to implement new features and upgrade to new version is required.

Federated Repository Systems

Federated repository systems use a network of interconnected computers to share information, objects, and management responsibilities. Each computer repository is a system in and of itself, but it is able to share and replicate its data on other servers. This model is very powerful in that it allows libraries and archives to distribute their data across a wide geographic area so as to minimize risk from a major software, hardware, or infrastructure failure.

A federated repository system can be structured in several ways. A system can be designed, or architected, as a federated system; that is, from its inception, the system was created to be distributed between multiple computers in multiple locations. That would allow each repository to check in with the other servers, verify its data, and distribute its data to multiple servers based on a set of criteria that can be configured to meet the needs of the various archives.

As an alternative for creating a federated archive, organizations could implement whichever repository meets their needs. They then would create software and a communication protocol to exchange data with their set of partners. This model would be an organizational federation with loosely coupled repositories.

Dark Archives

The dark archive model for a digital repository is significantly different. In all of the other models, the repository is used for both preservation and access; they have a user interface for researchers to find, review, and perhaps download objects for further use. A dark archive is used exclusively for preservation functions. It is specifically and purposefully not used for access. Some organizations use a dark archive as a "just in case" repository to be used in the event of catastrophic failure. The data from the dark archive can be used to recover from a disaster. Other organizations use a dark archive as the *back end* of their access system; the dark archive stores and manages the archival master files while another system manages access and delivery for derived files created for patron use.

Digital Asset Management Systems

Digital asset management (DAM) is the process of controlling access to and dissemination of digital materials for use in brand management and advertising. DAM systems are similar to digital library systems in that they have an interface for metadata creation, batch ingest for mass uploads of digital content, a repository back with file management, and perhaps some preservation functions. However, there are significant differences in the functionality for both end users and DAM staff. A DAM system provides a function that allows multiple users, often called clients, to view and approve content, to search for content based on advertising and marketing campaigns, and to track the number of times an object has been used. Objects can be versioned—that is, slightly modified—and tracked. Think of an ad campaign where a photo of the product has multiple, different text boxes about it; one photo has the first campaign message, the second photo has the next campaign message, and so forth. Digital assets are intended to be monetized, that is, to make money or save money for the organization by judicious reuse.

Many large academic institutions, cultural heritage organizations, and other not-for-profits use DAM systems for their marketing and branding digital contents because of the content management features, which are specific to the business side of the organization. Their digital library or archive systems do not meet their marketing needs. Many corporate archives use DAM systems for all of their content as the mission of the archive includes brand management as well as more traditional archival requirements of historical artifact preservation.

TECHNICAL IMPLICATIONS

Digital repositories are software applications that require computational and storage infrastructure. They can be implemented in any number of ways. Some digital library systems are open source while others are produced and distributed commercially. Some digital library systems are vertical turnkey applications while others are a set of components that provide repository services. Digital repositories can be licensed to run on the library or archive's hardware or can be a hosted service.

Licensing Models

Licensing models include both open source and commercial. *Open source* is a model of software distribution in which the source code, the program instructions, is made freely available. Open source allows *customers* to modify code to meet their needs. Open source software, by definition, does not require a licensing fee; however, open source software is not free. Organizations that use open source software must commit significant resources to implement the software. Some open source software is well documented and has a strong community for peer support. Other open source software packages are not well documented and not well supported and may be difficult to implement, modify, and support. Implementing a well-supported open source system can be less expensive, but it will still require a substantial investment in personnel.

Commercial software assumes a for-profit model. A software vendor develops a product and sells a license to use that software to organizations. In addition to the software license, they also offer services for additional cost, including software installation, hardware installation, data conversion, and training. Many software vendors charge an annual fee of between 10 and 25 percent of the initial software license for ongoing maintenance and support. The support costs are used to develop enhancements for the system based on customer input and feedback as well as to provide direct support for problems via email, telephone, or other communication methods. ILS vendors provide digital repository systems that can be closely the

ILS or used stand-alone. Other vendors include bibliographic service vendors and small start-up companies as well as large software organizations.

Application Models

Turnkey vertical application and software tool kits are application models. *Turnkey vertical applications* describe software that is ready to implement immediately with little effort to install and configure a turnkey product. It meets the needs and requirements of a single, specific market. A turnkey vertical application is generally an integrated system, which implies a smooth transition between major functions. Most commercial ILS systems are turnkey vertical applications. Turnkey vertical digital repository systems can be either open source or commercially licensed. Because they are vertically integrated—that is, the components and major functions of the system are tightly coupled—it can be difficult for libraries or archives to modify the system even if the code is open source. Turnkey vertical digital repository systems can provide a great deal of functionality with the significantly lower personnel investment.

Software tool kits model describes a set of software components that can be customized and combined to meet very specific needs and requirements. This model is nearly an exact opposite to a turnkey vertical application. This model requires a significant investment in both time and personnel. Software developers are required to build an integrated system from the component pieces. This model can produce incredibly powerful and highly customized systems that work very well for the organization. There is, however, a major commitment of time and resources. This model of software is almost always open source. Due to the high level of investment in time and resources, these systems generally have a very strong community of developers for support.

Implementation Models

A software package can be implemented using any number of ways. Some software has been designed to work across multiple computers in a variety of configurations: as a single computer located on-site for one institution, as a shared resource for a consortium, or hosted by a vendor. Each option is viable and reasonable. Libraries and archives can choose an implementation model that meets their needs.

On-site servers can be the simplest implementation. An institution purchases sufficient hardware, including servers in storage, to support the amount of data that currently exists, the amount of new data anticipated, and the access requirements of patrons. Software is loaded on the server, data is migrated to the storage devices, and systems are configured and deployed. With this implementation model, the institution assumes all responsibilities for system accessibility. One or more people need to monitor the system to ensure that it is functional, that data is properly managed and stored, and that the data is accessible. Four large institutions with established information technology (IT) infrastructure and on-site servers are a reasonable and often cost-effective option. With established procedures, robust network, and trained staff, the incremental cost of one new server is relatively low. For organizations without established IT infrastructure, the cost is significantly more. The overhead to develop a robust infrastructure can be more than the institution can bear.

Participating in a *consortium* can help institutions share the cost of the software and hardware infrastructure. Each member contributes to the consortium for the initial cost as well as ongoing support. Consortia often have pricing based on volume of materials and number of patrons because these are often the most significant cost drivers (see Chapter 2 for more about cost drivers). Consortia often provide small communities of practice for libraries and archives to share expertise, develop best practice, and provide advice. While consortia provide many benefits, including cost savings and community, consortia can also require significant compromise. Customizations to meet the needs of one institution can be very difficult to implement. While some customizing is usually supported, such as logos, colors, and splash page text, often institutions need to compromise on a common look and feel, a common metadata schema, and a common set of indexing options.

A wide variety of *hosted services* is provided by vendors and can include hardware, software, and other services. In current technology jargon, these are often referred to as cloud services. The two most common services offered are Software as a Service (SaaS) and Infrastructure as a Service (IaaS). Vendors offer services at a variety of levels. Some repository software vendors will offer a turnkey solution that provide hardware, software, configuration support, data management, and so forth. Other vendors offer only infrastructure support (IasS), which allows libraries and archives to implement their own software on a hosted computational platform using shared storage. This option offers flexibility to libraries and archives. However, there is significant concern about using cloud resources. Commercial organizations have their own needs that may conflict with the needs of libraries and archives: securing data, protecting the privacy of patrons, and ongoing financial viability are issues that need to be addressed when developing contracts. Developing a robust exit strategy is crucial for libraries and archives that choose to use hosted services. An exit strategy involves documenting the process of leaving the vendor and can include determining which organization is responsible for extracting data, what format will be used to transfer data, the process by which all of the data is transferred, and other issues. The cost of an exit strategy needs to be included when determining the overall cost of using a hosted service.

Repository Software Market

Libraries and archives have many repository options. The market for repository systems is surprisingly strong and includes both open source and vended options. Most of the software packages can be implemented in multiple ways. The options may seem overwhelming. Describing each repository system in detail is beyond the scope of this chapter; however, a brief look at some popular packages within their market segments follows.

Institutional Repositories

Libraries and archives have a number of software options for their institutional repository. There are three packages that are the most common. Of the 3,238 repositories listed in the Directory of Open Access Repositories (*Open*DOAR[3]), the most popular institutional repository software systems are DSpace[4] (44%), EPrints[5] (14%), and Digital Commons[6] (5%). DSpace, the most common of the packages, is an open source system supported by an active, committed, and well-funded foundation and user community. The software is nearly turnkey and easy to install and configure. The functionality is straightforward for patrons with traditional features such as search, display, and access; the staff functions allow for customized ingest and approval workflows. EPrints was developed as a preprint repository but is also used as an institutional repository (EPrints, 2011). Digital Commons is a hosted service that uses the BePress platform.

Digital Library Management Systems

One of the most popular digital library management systems is CONTENTdm, a product developed, maintained, and sold by OCLC. CONTENTdm is a stand-alone system and can be implemented in either the OCLC cloud or the library or archive's infrastructure. CONTENTdm supports a number of file formats and media types, uses commonly accepted metadata standards, and provides interfaces for both content administration and public access by patrons. The system is relatively flexible and allows libraries and archives some measure of customization. ILS vendors also offer digital library management systems. These can be stand-alone or fully integrated with the bibliographic application. There are advantages to using a single vendor such as a long-term investment and relationship with the support staff and an integrated interface for researchers and patrons. An example is Rosetta from ExLibris.

Digital Archives Management Systems

The digital archives management systems market has a wide range of tools. The two most complete and preservation quality systems are ArchiveSpace[7] and Archivematica.[8] Both of these systems are open source, both have multiple implementation options, including on-site and hosted services, and both support the OAIS reference model. Both systems have good governance structures, active user communities, and significant install bases.

Digital Repository Software Infrastructure

The Integrated Rule-Oriented Data System (iRODS) and the Flexible Extensible Digital Object Repository Architecture (Fedora) are the two major digital repository software infrastructure systems. Both are open source projects with robust governance organizations and committed and active development communities. Each of these systems requires programmer support for implementation and ongoing support. They both scale well to support very large digital collections.

iRODS is used by pharmaceutical and chemical companies, federal agencies with large research data sets, and academic institutions. Fedora is used by many large academic libraries, research centers, and national libraries to manage their digital contents. Fedora has a number of add-on applications to extend its functionality: Islandora provides a Drupal front to a Fedora repository; Hydra provides workflows and user front ends to a Fedora repository.

Dark Archives

Virtually, any of the digital repository systems can be implemented as a dark archive. However, two systems were developed specifically as such: Lots of Copies Keep Stuff Safe (LOCKSS) and DAITSS Digital Preservation Repository Software. LOCKSS was developed as a project from Stanford University libraries in 1999 through 2000 with the goal of providing a globally distributed network of dark repositories for electronic journals and other digital scholarly materials (Dobson, 2003). While intended to be a public network of hundreds of libraries, LOCKSS has been used as a private network that has a back-end storage repository for archives and libraries (Stanford University Libraries, n.d.). DAITSS was developed by the Florida Center for Library Automation (FCLA) is a back-end system for all of the libraries in the consortium. The original goal was to have a preservation quality repository that could be shared among others. After it was implemented in Florida, the software was released as open source and made available to other institutions interested in a dark archive (FCLA, 2011).

Digital Asset Management Systems

As more commercial entities begin to manage their digital content, the marketplace for digital asset management system marketplace expands. One of the digital asset management consulting companies estimates that this market has over 100 vendors producing software products.[9] Among the leaders are Media Bin/ Open Text, NorthPlains, and Adobe Experience Manager. These systems are large, complex, enterprise-scaled applications to manage the ingest, metadata capture, and preservation functions. Workflows for different media types are common. Unlike the systems developed for libraries and archives, DAM systems have sophisticated access controls with various levels of permissions for targeted distribution of digital content in order to control who can see what content under specific conditions.

PRACTICAL APPLICATION

Choosing a Repository System

Before choosing a repository, an organization must assess its current infrastructure and future needs. A review of current infrastructure could include network, computational, and storage capacity and an inventory of current digital materials to be archived. Organizations need to understand the depth of their technical personnel, such as programmers, systems administrators, and management. An infrastructure review may find that the organization needs to increase its capacity in one or more areas, or the organization may determine its capacity is sufficient. In addition to evaluating their current situation, organizations need to plan for their future. This often includes a strategic plan for digital content and curation. What types of materials will the organization archive? What is the current rate of acquisition in both number of files and bits? What is the expected rate of acquisition; will the rate increase, decrease, or remain stable? What initiatives will be instituted and what will their impact be on the repository infrastructure?

Once the infrastructure and capacity needs have been assessed, the organization can begin to assess its requirements for a repository system. The typical process is to develop a checklist of functions against which to evaluate various repository systems. Some checklists focus on functionality elements while others focus on software quality issues. Others focus on software development organization issues. The following checklist is an amalgam from the documented digital repository implementation experiences of various knowledge-keeping organizations (Austin et al, 2015; Goh et al., 2006; Kaczmarek, Hswe, Eke, & Habing, 2006; Marill & Luczak, 2009; Masrek & Hakimjavadi, 2012; NLM, 2008).

1. **Functionality**—the features required to make the system usable
   a. **User Interface customization**
   b. **Systems administration**
      i. **Ingest**
      ii. **Item description with standard metadata support**
      iii. **Export**
      iv. **Persistent identification**
      v. **Fixity**
2. **Software quality features**
   a. **Scalability**—the ability of the system to expand as needed based on the number of objects, the size of objects, and types of objects
   b. **Extensibility**—the ability to enhance the functions of the system
   c. **Interoperability**—the ability of the system to exchange data with other systems
   d. **System security**—the ability of the system to protect the data from both technology failures and unwanted intrusions
3. **Implementation issues**
   a. **Ease of deployment**—the level of complexity in implementing the system
   b. **System performance**—the ability of the system to support users with adequate response times and system availability
   c. **Implementation options**—ability to deploy the system to meet availability needs, disaster recovery needs, and infrastructure needs
4. **Software organization strength**
   a. **Demonstrated successful deployments**—number of satisfied users or organizations with production software installations

b. **System support**—the ability to receive help when necessary, which includes the effectiveness of the support personnel of a company or the user community of open source community and the level of system and user documentation

c. **Stability of development organization**—financial and organizational viability of the company or open source development community

d. **Strength of vision**—strategic plan for ongoing improvements and innovation of the system

While lists of functional requirement are useful, they should be a guide and not prescriptive. "Providing an objective measure of functional requirements is useful; though, in reality an institution must judge carefully the system that best matches their individual needs" (Wiseman & Matthews, 2016). Functionality is a moving target. Systems add features, remove features, and redesign features on a regular basis. The business model, the stability of the software provider, and the customer satisfaction with the provider may prove to be more important than any individual feature or function.

Multiple Repositories

Many large academic libraries have found that a single repository is insufficient to meet their needs. An institutional repository works really well for collecting and sharing traditional document-like materials with similar and limited metadata needs. While the systems work really well for documents, their support for multimedia data and complex metadata is limited. These libraries find that in addition to their institutional repository, a large and robust digital repository software infrastructure system, such as Fedora, is required to manage and preserve their more complex materials. In many large academic institutions, digital libraries work with archives to support their digital archives management systems. It is not uncommon for a digital library in a large academic institution to support and maintain three or four different digital repository systems.

Relationships between various repository systems can be quite complex. The Atlanta University Center Robert W. Woodruff Library, the library of a midsized academic institution, is a good example (see Figure 6.2). The library has developed a three-layer architecture: public access, data management, and archival backup.

The public access layer has three different repository interfaces: Hydra (a Fedora add-on that provides a number of functions including a front end) and CONTENTdm and Omeka, both digital library management systems. In addition, the public access layer also has a search interface for the archival EAD finding aids. The middle layer, for data management, uses two repository software packages: ArchiveSpace and Fedora. ArchiveSpace is specifically for managing all of the components for archival EAD finding aids. The Fedora system manages the entire data archive. The lowest level of the architecture manages the off-site redundant backup versions using various technologies, including cloud storage and the federated LOCKSS system (Wiseman & Matthews, 2016).

Figure 6.2.
An Architecture with Multiple Repositories

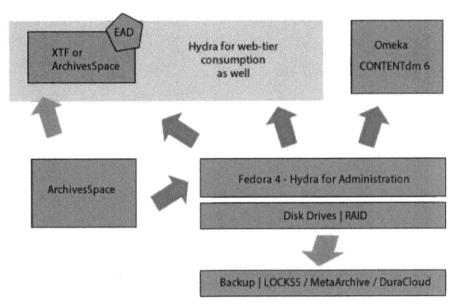

(Wiseman & Matthews, 2016, p. 51)

SUMMARY

Digital repositories are systems to manage large quantities of digital content. Central repository systems can leverage economies of scale by providing a core set of functionality for accessing, indexing, describing, managing, and preserving digital content in a single software package.

Digital repositories, as described by the OAIS, have four primary functions: ingest, data management, archival storage, and access. Managing a digital repository includes preservation planning to ensure the authenticity, quality, and persistence of the data.

Trust in the authenticity, quality, and persistence of the data is very important. In order to be trustworthy, a repository needs more than just a sound technological infrastructure; it needs to have organizational support to sustain it over time so that it is able to accept responsibility for long-term maintenance of digital materials on behalf of the depositors. A trusted repository needs to develop policies and practices as well as metrics that measure its success.

In a large and dynamic digital repository market, it can be useful to categorize the various types of repository systems. Think about digital repository systems as the functional roles within a preservation-focused organization; digital repository software can be categorized as institutional repositories, preprint services, digital library management systems, digital archives management systems, digital repository software infrastructure, federated repositories, dark archives, and digital asset management systems.

Digital repository systems can be deployed in a number of ways: via a hosted service, through a consortium, or installed on an on-site server. These systems can be licensed as open source or commercial. The systems can be a turnkey or tool kit.

Choosing a digital repository system is a complicated process that takes time and effort. Before choosing a repository, an organization must assess its current infrastructure and future needs. Developing an inclusive process can improve the probability of success. A first step is to create a list of functional and technical requirements to help narrow the scope of the search.

Each repository system has a specific functional focus. Many large libraries find that a single repository system does not meet all of their needs. Libraries can have multiple instances of a single repository software package or have several different repository systems.

Questions for Discussion

1. Why is trust such an important factor in digital repositories?
2. Which implement/deployment options seem most sustainable? Why?
3. What significant problem could you anticipate when choosing a repository system?
4. What functionality would be the most important when choosing a repository system?

NOTES

1. http://www.brainyquote.com/quotes/quotes/p/paultherou466020.html
2. http://www.brainyquote.com/quotes/quotes/l/lorettalyn676300.html
3. Data found at Usage of Open Access Repository Software-Worldwide © 2016, University of Nottingham, UK. Last updated: October 13, 2016. Found at http://www.opendoar.org/onechart.php?cID=&ctID=&rtID=&clID=&lID=&potID=&rSoftWareName=&search=&groupby=r.rSoftWareName&orderby=Tally%20DESC&charttype=pie&width=600&height=300&caption=Usage%20of%20Open%20Access%20Repository%20Software%20-%20Worldwide
4. http://dspace.org/
5. http://www.eprints.org/uk/
6. http://digitalcommons.bepress.com/
7. http://www.archivesspace.org/
8. https://www.archivematica.org/en/
9. https://www.realstorygroup.com/Vendors-Evaluated/

REFERENCES

Armbruster, C., & Romary, L. (2009, November 23). Comparing repository types: Challenges and barriers for subject-based repositories, research repositories, national repository systems and institutional repositories in serving scholarly communication.

In *Research repositories, national repository systems and institutional repositories in serving scholarly communication*. Found at http://arxiv.org/ftp/arxiv/papers/1003/1003.4187.pdf

Association of Research Libraries (ARL). 2009. *The research library's role in digital repository services: Final report of the ARL Digital Repository Issues Task Force*. Washington, DC. Found at http://www.arl.org/storage/documents/publications/repository-services -report-jan09.pdf

Austin, C., Brown, S., Fong, N., Humphrey, C., Leahey, A., & Webster, P. (2015, June). Research data repositories: Review of current features, gap analysis, and recommendations for minimum requirements. In *IASSIST Annual Conference*, Minneapolis, MN (pp. 2–5).

Beagrie, N., Bellinger, M., Dale, R., Doerr, M., Hedstrom, M., Jones, M., … Woodyard, D. (2002). Trusted digital repositories: Attributes and responsibilities. *Research libraries group and online computer library center, Report*.

Consultative Committee for Space Data Systems (CCSDS). (2011). *Audit and certification of trustworthy digital repositories*. Recommended Practice (Magenta Book), CCSDS 652.0-M-1. Found at http://public.ccsds.org/publications/archive/652x0m1.pdf

Consultative Committee for Space Data Systems (CCSDS). (2012). *Reference model for an Open Archival Information System (OAIS)*. Issue 2. Recommendation for Space Data System Standards (Magenta Book), CCSDS 650.0-M-2. Washington, DC: ISO 14721:2012.

Dobson, C. (2003). From bright idea to beta test: The story of LOCKSS. *Searcher, 11*(2), 50–53.

EPrints. (2011). *A brief history of EPrints*. Found at http://wiki.eprints.org/w/History

The Florida Center for Library Automation (FCLA). (2011). *DAITSS digital preservation repository software*. Found at https://daitss.fcla.edu/content/welcome-daitss-website-0

Goh, D. H., Chua, A., Khoo, D. A., Khoo, E. B., Mak, E. B., & Ng, M. W. (2006). A checklist for evaluating open source digital library software. *Online Information Review, 30*(4), 360–379.

Houghton, B. (2015). Trustworthiness: Self-assessment of an institutional repository against ISO 16363-2012. *D-Lib Magazine, 21*(3), 5. Found at http://mirror.dlib.org/ dlib/march15/houghton/03houghton.html

JISC. (2009). *Digital Repositories InfoKit*. http://tools.jiscinfonet.ac.uk/downloads/ repositories/digital-repositories.pdf

Kaczmarek, J., Hswe, P., Eke, J., & Habing, T. G. (2006). Using the audit checklist for the certification of a trusted digital repository as a framework for evaluating repository software applications: A progress report. *D-lib Magazine, 12*(12). ISSN 1082-9873.

Marill, J. L., & Luczak, E. C. (2009). Evaluation of digital repository software at the national library of medicine. *D-Lib Magazine, 15*(5/6). ISSN 1082-9873. Found at http://www.dlib.org/dlib/may09/marill/05marill.html

Masrek, M. N., & Hakimjavadi, H. (2012). Evaluation of three open source software in terms of managing repositories of electronic theses and dissertations: A comparison study. *Journal of Basic and Applied Scientific Research, 2*(11), 10843–10852.

National Library of Medicine Digital Repository Evaluation and Selection Working Group (NLM). (2008). Recommendations on NLM digital repository software. In *National library of medicine*. Found at https://www.nlm.nih.gov/digitalrepository/DRESWG -Report.pdf

Preprint. (n.d.). In *Merriam-Webster*. Found at http://www.merriam-webster.com/dictionary/ preprint

Repository. (n.d.). In *Merriam-Webster*. Found at http://www.merriam-webster.com/dictionary/repository

Stanford University Libraries. (n.d.). *Global and private LOCKSS networks*. Found at https://www.lockss.org/community/networks/

Waters, D., & Garrett, J. (1996). *Preserving digital information. Report of the task force on archiving of digital information*. Washington, DC: The Commission on Preservation and Access.

Wiseman, C., & Matthews, A. (2016). *Time, money, and effort: A practical approach to digital content management*. AUC Robert W. Woodruff Library Staff Publications. Paper 8. Found at http://digitalcommons.auctr.edu/libpubs/8/?utm_source=digitalcommons.auctr.edu%2Flibpubs%2F8&utm_medium=PDF&utm_campaign=PDFCoverPages

Section III

Planning for Preservation

Chapter 7

DATA MANAGEMENT

When we have all data online it will be great for humanity. It is a prerequisite to solving many problems that humankind faces.

—Robert Cailliau[1]

Data is a precious thing and will last longer than the systems themselves.

—Tim Berners-Lee[2]

INTRODUCTION

Most digital curators would agree with the quote from Tim Berners-Lee that data in all its various forms—including documents, images, sound recordings, video recordings, and so on—is precious; this is a motivating factor for the digital curation movement. However, many digital curators would disagree with an implication of the second phrase of this quote that all data is supported by and managed with a system. A great deal of data exists outside of a formal information system. In order to fulfill the great promise of data, its use and reuse to solve humanity's problems, the data must be managed; it must exist, it must be findable, and it must be understandable. This is the systematic effort of curation.

Managing data is key to long-term curation of data. Defining data management is difficult. *Data management* is a very broad and imprecise term that has many meanings and is context dependent. In some contexts, data management is a catchall phrase for an information technology (IT) infrastructure. In other contexts, data management refers to the lifecycle of data: acquisitions, storage, description, use, reuse, and disposal of data. In yet other contexts, data management refers to the storage of and physical access to the data. In still further contexts, data management can imply database management: indexing, defragmenting, and other performance enhancing functions. In other words, data management means whatever the speaker intends.

Data management can be defined as "administrative process by which the required data is acquired, validated, stored, protected, and processed, and by which its accessibility, reliability, and timeliness is ensured to satisfy the needs of the data users" (Data Management, 2016) or the "development and execution of architectures, policies, practices and procedures in order to manage the information lifecycle needs of an enterprise in an effective manner" (TechTarget, 2016).

Within the context of digital curation and digital repository systems, data management refers to the functions needed for "populating, maintaining, and accessing" metadata, archival files, and administrative data (CCSDS, 2012, p. 4-2). However, this definition neglects all of that data outside of information systems. This chapter looks at the issues of data management within an archive as well as the issues of data management before data arrives at the archive.

THEORETICAL OVERVIEW

Data management is difficult to define because it is complex; it is what researchers call a multifaceted construct, a concept with many components. Data management includes issues of data access, data publishing, data quality, data governance, data integrity, data security, and data monitoring.

To add to the complexity, data management is a multilevel construct as well. Data is managed at many levels: the micro level, the intermediate level, and the macro level (see Figure 7.1). The micro level represents individuals managing their own files whether for their job or personal use. The intermediate level represents mid-level institutions, including businesses, research institutions, not-for-profits, and so on.

Figure 7.1.
Data Management Levels

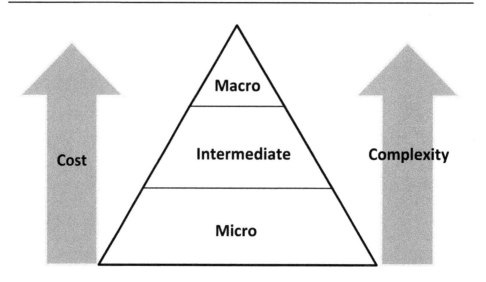

At each of these levels, data is created, used, organized, accessed, and perhaps deleted. How *good data management* is defined depends on the level. What is acceptable data management practice for an individual can be very different than what is best practice for a large data-centric organization.

The majority of data created currently is managed at the micro level. Most data is stored outside of formal information systems; most digital information, photographs, documents, and data are created, stored, and managed by individuals on personal computing devices. This is true whether the individual is acting as an independent entity or as an agent of a larger organization. When working as an independent entity, an individual can create and be responsible for managing digital content, such as photographs, budget spreadsheets, tax returns, and various types of documents. For this individual, the two primary data management tasks are to organize the files for *findability* and make sure that the storage is sound.

That same person may have very similar types of digital content on his/her desktop computer at work: photos of a job site, images of a product design, preliminary project budget spreadsheets, documents in various stages of completion, and final project documentation. While this work is owned by a larger organization, in many ways, it is still data that is managed at the micro level. The individual, this time acting as an agent of the larger organization, is responsible for organizing the data.

The intermediate level of data management occurs at the work group level. Many work groups, such as units, departments and teams, have policies and procedures for organizing and storing digital work products. The policies may define acceptable file types and specific file naming and directory structure standards. Some work groups have policies that prescribe software settings, such as the Preferences in Microsoft Word, which embed metadata, such as title, subject author, manager, company, category, keywords, and comments, and with customization allow additional fields to record information about editors, clients, departments, publishers, projects, purpose, and status. Policies may also include required formatting specification, such as fonts, font size, document headers with title and date, and documents footers with page number and file name. The work group may have server space to collect and organize work products. Depending on the nature of the work and the nature of the organization, files may need to be saved to the server when they are complete and ready for review or saved only when the project is complete. In a security-minded group, all files may need to be created, maintained, and stored exclusively on the server. Work groups may develop procedures to enforce the policies. These procedures may be either manual or automatic. In some work groups, management or quality control personnel may review, edit, modify, approve, and/or publish files. Automated processes can include verifying file types, verify settings, and so on. (For a fuller discussion, see Chapter 5).

The macro level of data management happens at the organizational level. At this level, data management involves providing policy, procedures, and infrastructure for the individual as well as workgroups. The data management policy for the organization needs to be able to be rigorous enough to ensure the data and flexible enough to accommodate the needs of its various work groups. Infrastructure for data management includes sufficient and secured storage, effective networking, and automatic backups at the server and desktop level (for fuller discussion of data backup in business resumption, please see Chapter 8). Some organizations feel that a robust server architecture is sufficient to maintain their data. But for long-term preservation, many libraries and digital archives rely on repositories.

Data Management in Open Archival Information Systems

Data management is vital to the ongoing archiving operations of an Open Archival Information System (OAIS) repository (see Figure 7.2). Data management in OAIS often resides at the organizational level. The OAIS defines data management "as the services and functions for populating, maintaining, and accessing a wide variety of information including processing algorithms that may be run on retrieved data, access statistics, billing, security controls, and preservation activities, schedules, policies, and procedures" (CCSDS, 2012, pp. 4–10). In OAIS, data management includes such functions as creating, maintaining, and accessing descriptive metadata and administrative metadata, as well as monitoring policy compliance and tracking activities, such as item access and preservation provenance.

Maintaining the repository database system is a significant component of data management within OAIS. Database management includes maintaining the database schema, that is, the database organization and the definition of the tables, rows, and columns. In addition, database management includes defining and maintaining the data views, which are subsets of the data arranged for different functional needs. Insuring the referential integrity of the database is another significant component of database management. Referential integrity refers to the process by which the database enforces internal consistency. For example, if a metadata table refers to a value stored in another table, the database will not allow that value to be deleted.

Data management often requires repeated actions that can be referred to as *events*. Events can include such activities as billing, accounting, database and file system maintenance and optimization, data and metadata loading, systematic metadata updates, preservation process history and provenance data logging, and administrative reporting. These events require administrative metadata, such as billing information, accounting information, customer information, authorization information, access policy, retention policy, and so forth.

Managing Research Data

Over the past 15 years, preserving research data has become a major initiative at many digital libraries and archives in academic and other research organizations. However, only a small percentage of research data is submitted to repositories for long-term preservation. Thus, good data management in research labs becomes an important and necessary prerequisite for preservation. Rusbridge (2007) claims that data management is a discipline that requires the necessary context information and associated documentation to ensure successful use and reuse of data. It is a dynamic process that needs to be mindful of the entire data lifecycle.

Figure 7.2.
OAIS Data Management Function

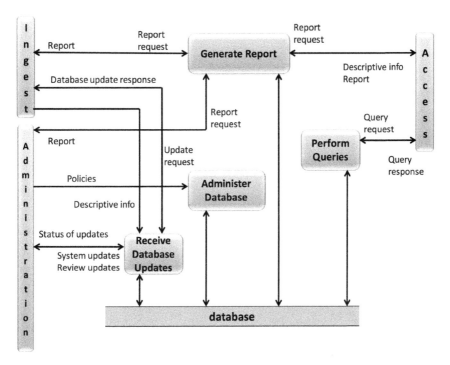

(CCSDS, 2012, p. 4–10. Reprinted with permission of the Consultative Committee for Space Data System.)

"Good data management is not a goal in itself, but rather is the key conduit leading to knowledge discovery and innovation, and to subsequent data and knowledge integration and reuse by the community after the data publication process" (Wilkinson et al., 2016, p. 1). The goal of good data management is data reuse. Wilkinson et al. (2016) reported on the outcome of a workshop held in the Netherlands in 2014 that developed a set of principles for measuring the outcome of good data management for data sharing. The goal is for data to be Findable, Accessible, Interoperable, Reusable (FAIR). Each of these attributes is defined as

To be Findable:
    F1. (meta)data are assigned a globally unique and persistent identifier
    F2. data are described with rich metadata (defined by R1 below)
    F3. metadata clearly and explicitly include the identifier of the data it describes
    F4. (meta)data are registered or indexed in a searchable resource

To be Accessible:
    A1. (meta)data are retrievable by their identifier using a standardized communications protocol
    A1.1 the protocol is open, free, and universally implementable

A1.2 the protocol allows for an authentication and authorization procedure, where necessary

A2. metadata are accessible, even when the data are no longer available

To be Interoperable:

I1. (meta)data use a formal, accessible, shared, and broadly applicable language for knowledge representation

I2. (meta)data use vocabularies that follow FAIR principles

I3. (meta)data include qualified references to other (meta)data

To be Reusable:

R1. meta(data) are richly described with a plurality of accurate and relevant attributes

R1.1. (meta)data are released with a clear and accessible data usage license

R1.2. (meta)data are associated with detailed provenance

R1.3. (meta)data meet domain-relevant community standards

(Wilkinson et al., 2016, p. 2)

Data Management Plans

Funding agencies—organizations that provide money as grants for scientific and humanities research, digitization, and collection development—have developed policies, procedures, and practices to encourage their grant recipients to manage their data so that it can be findable, accessible, interoperable, and reusable. In 2013, the U.S. Federal Office of Science and Technology Policy issued an executive order requiring all data and papers produced with government[3] funding must be shared with the public. This includes National Science Foundation, National Institutes of Health, National Oceanographic and Atmospheric Research, the National Endowment for the Humanities, the National Endowment for the Arts, the Institute of Museum and Library Services, and others. Due to the great cost of creating research data, the initiatives to require grant applications to require a data management plan were first implemented in the sciences, but the humanities organizations followed quickly. Currently, each of the federal funding agencies has instituted a requirement for a data management plan (DMP) in all of their grant applications. The National Science Foundation, one of the largest U.S. funding agencies, states:

> Investigators are expected to share with other researchers, at no more than incremental cost and within a reasonable time, the primary data, samples, physical collections and other supporting materials created or gathered in the course of work under NSF grants. Grantees are expected to encourage and facilitate such sharing. (NSF, 2017, 4b)

In 2015, Canada implemented a similar requirement (Austin et al., 2015).

In addition to the U.S. federal funding agencies, many private funding organizations are requiring researchers to develop and submit plans for the long-term management of their data as part of the grant application process. Funding organizations want to ensure that their investment in data can be reused. DMPs require researchers and their organizations to think, plan, and commit resources to the ongoing preservation of the research data. The DMPs need to include information about the nature of the data to be created and/or collected: the type format and volume of data, methodologies and standards used, quality assurance processes, and naming conventions and directory structure to be used. DMPs often require the answers to questions about documentation and metadata: what information is needed to be able to find, access, and reuse the data; what standards will be used; and what are the conditions for access and reuse (DCC, 2013). Ethical and legal compliance issues need to be addressed as well including such areas as informed consent, anonymization, secure storage of sensitive data, and intellectual property rights, including ownership, access restrictions, and licensing. Some funders require specific details about data storage and backup (for a full or discussion of backup and recovery, see Chapter 8).

Other issues that need to be addressed in DMPs include data sharing policies and data retention policies. Many funders require organizations to commit long-term resources to manage and preserve the data generated out of the grant sponsored projects. In many organizations, libraries and archives partner with researchers and the IT department to develop DMPs.

Research Data Collections

When describing research data, the National Science Board (NSB, 2005) developed a three-layer typology that is organized by size and scope: research data collections, community data collections, and reference data collections. The NSB defines data collections as the infrastructure, organizations, and individuals needed to provide persistent access to stored data. While this ideal of a research collection was developed in the sciences, it is equally applicable to humanities research. Research data collections refer to the output of a single researcher or lab during the course of a specific research project. This collection may use the data standards of its community and may have use beyond its own original purpose. Community data collections generally serve a well-defined area of research. Often, standards are developed by the community, a specific research domain, to support the collection. At the highest level, reference data collections are broad in scope, widely disseminated, and well-funded collections that support the research needs of many communities (NSB, 2005). The three-tiered data collections typology interacts with the data management hierarchy. Research collections are managed by the individual. The community collections are managed by a group or team. The reference collections are managed by large organizations.

While established and well-funded data collections often have dedicated data management staff and large data centers to manage the petabyte datasets, it is the individual researcher's responsibility to manage their data (Lyon, 2007). Researchers expect to manage their data and understand the importance of good data management but often are unsure of how best to implement good data management practices. As discussed in Chapter 2, decisions made at one stage of the research lifecycle affect the range of options available at a later stage. Thus, decisions made as data is created are of the utmost importance because they influence all subsequent decisions.

For researchers, data management can be a low priority, can require skills and expertise not readily available, and can cost more than its perceived value. With all academic incentives rewarding new work, it is counterintuitive for scientists to invest time, effort, and money to care for older data. Data management is frequently considered to be overhead and not research and can be a burden for researchers. Data management is expensive in terms of both personnel and equipment. Frequently, researchers lack the necessary funding that would allow them to develop a robust data management infrastructure (ARL, 2006). So in the absence of data management as a project is in progress, data is too frequently abandoned, transferring any data recovery costs to the future with significant risks of both loss of data and loss of context.

Recent research indicates researchers are aware of their responsibilities, that they understand the importance of data management, and believe that they follow best practice. However, the researchers do think that they could improve their data management practices. If funds were not a constraint, researchers would save more data, use different storage systems, back up their data more frequently, and would hire professional staff to manage their data. This could indicate that while researchers understand their responsibilities as data managers, they would rather find someone else to take on the responsibility and do the work (Kowalczyk, 2015).

Lost Research Data

Research on lost data is sparse. Holzner, Igo-Kemenes, and Mele (2009) found that approximately 40 percent of the high-energy physicists surveyed think that they have lost important data in the past. But few of the specific losses are documented.

A recent study reports that 51 percent of researchers who have received National Science Foundation grants have lost data. The researchers in the study were from hard sciences, social sciences, and education. Most of the data loss was attributed to inadvertent human error and equipment malfunction. This study had one really interesting, almost counterintuitive, finding. Researchers who worked in large labs (more than five researchers) were more likely to report problems and want to change their data management practices than small labs or individual researchers. One would expect that a large lab would have more resources to manage their data. However, it seems that more people cause more complexity and result in more problems. Large labs were more likely to report data loss due to human error than small labs or individual researchers. It is likely that these human errors are due to communication failures; explaining which files are *good* and should be kept and which files should be deleted can be complicated. Large labs are also more likely to have lost data due to equipment failures. As large labs are generally associated with hard sciences, it is more likely that they would have more equipment than an individual researcher. Researchers in large labs were also more likely to report implementing data management early in the research process; with multiple people and multiple pieces of equipment generating data, it is reasonable that the researchers would see the need to manage data as soon as it is created. Researchers in large labs were more likely to want to change their data management practices; again, this is a reasonable response if they have lost data and/or struggled with managing their data (Kowalczyk, 2015).

Two of the most famous, or perhaps infamous, examples of lost data are from National Aeronautics and Space Administration (NASA). The first of these is data collected during the Apollo 11, 12, and 14 moon missions from instrumentation for collecting lunar surface environmental information. The 173 tapes of that data were misplaced by the University of Sydney's data center before they were archived or documented by NASA. In 2008, researchers realized that the data on lunar atmospheric dust could be useful for future lunar exploration research. The tapes were located but the tape drives needed to read the data were no longer available (MacBean, 2008). The second example is a similar story. The tapes of Neil Armstrong's first walk on the moon, along with approximately 700 other data tapes of Apollo data, were withdrawn from the National Archives in 1984 by NASA's Goddard Space Center in Maryland. These tapes are now missing (Macey, 2006). Significant data, both historical and scientific, was lost. These two losses of valuable data can be attributed to human error. As Baker, Keeton, & Martin (2005) described, multiple, cascading, and compounding errors occurred: data was not managed, technology was not monitored, and policies were ignored.

A Model for Data Management Responsibility

The Digital Curation Centre (DCC) works with research organizations in the United Kingdom and the world to develop policies and practices for preserving data. They have developed a set of responsibilities and skills needed to manage data (see Figure 7.3). While this is specifically for research data, it would be applicable to many data-centric organizations.

In the DCC model, responsibilities for data management are shared among four roles: the data manager, the data creator, the data librarian, and the data scientist. The data manager is responsible for security, including access control, authentication and authorization, and data security. The data manager also needs to assess risk, prepare for disasters, and have contingency plans prepared and tested. The data creator is responsible for data integrity, metadata, and context. The data librarian works with departments within the institution to coordinate best practice, negotiate for resources, and promote and market the repository and data management services. The data scientist develops tools to make the data accessible for others, including modeling the data to provide a consistent view for search and retrieval and data extraction for specific needs. There are points of intersection between the different actors. The data creator needs to submit the data and the metadata to the data manager in a way that is acceptable to both. The data manager and the data library work together to develop preservation strategies as well as to determine and articulate the preservation value proposition. The data librarians and the data scientist develop and/or adopt standards for their data and metadata, for the transmission of data, and for the access of data. And at the center is facilitation and communication; as with all organizational endeavors, good communication is the key to success.

Figure 7.3.
Data Management Roles and Skills

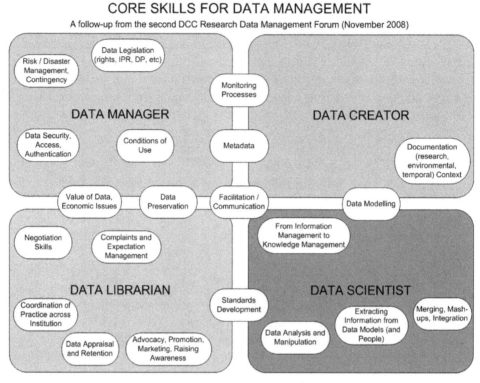

(DCC, 2017)

TECHNICAL IMPLICATIONS

"With cheap computing and storage, it is easier to create files . . . than it is to keep track of them" (Long, 2009, p. xxv). The sheer volume of data that organizations, groups, and individuals create is the big problem with which data management is concerned. From a technical perspective, data management is a set of tasks and activities to avert problems. In the context of digital curation, data management includes organizing, accessing, and sharing data.

In large corporations, millions of dollars are spent on various initiatives to bring order to their data. Data warehousing software, enterprise resource plan initiatives, data sharing, and worker collaboration platforms are but some of the efforts undertaken to get control of data. Various best practices advice can be found on consulting company websites. In general, the advice follows a general format of creating and enforcing data standards, finding and fixing data inconsistencies, consolidating data streams for efficiency and findability, and instituting change control over the data descriptions and standards to ensure ongoing compliance (Oracle, 2012). These are surprising similar to the best practices for researchers and the general public.

A number of academic libraries, including Stanford, Boston College, University of Cambridge, the University of California, and many others, and organizations that support digital curation efforts, such as the DCC and the National Center for Ecological Analysis and Synthesis, provide advice and support for individuals trying to keep their data viable over time. While there is some variation in detail, the overarching advice is to be consistent, descriptive, open, and diligent.

Organizing Data

Directories, also called folders, are the primary organizing structure in most computer file systems. Directories are very analogous to a manila folder in that they allow data to be grouped by any organizing principle. Data can be grouped by topic, project, experiment, file type, date, and virtually any data point that makes sense to the owner.

Naming of both directories and individual files is of primary importance for organization (Borer, Seabloom, Jones, & Schildhauer, 2009). Directory and file names are the primary source of metadata for the data. Some domain specific data management guidelines advise readers to create a "data map" in a text document that describes each folder and the files within them; while this makes sense for complex scientific research, it is impractical for most. Directory and file names should be descriptive and informative; that is, name should describe the contents of the directory/file and provide context. Directory and file names should be meaningful in order to aid in access. For example, a descriptive name for a directory with a set of photographs would include the word *photographs,* the time frame as either a single date or a range of dates, and a subject. A directory name of "Photos_2017-09_Fall_Festival" would be helpful. Naming each file with the event, date, and subject could further enhance accessibility. The file name of "Fall_Festival_Pumpkins _2017-09-10" would help the owner identify the photograph without opening it. In a work group situation, it is best to avoid naming files after people as staff members and/or students leave. Project names, departments, and other work-related topics make for better directory names.

Consistency is required for file naming to be useful in organizing data. Consistency in vocabulary, punctuation, date formatting, and order are essential (UC, 2017; SUL, n.d. a.). When developing a directory or file naming convention, choosing a complete vocabulary is useful so that everyone who needs to access the files can share a common language. Determining appropriate punctuation for file names also helps with consistency. Some of the punctuation marks that are appropriate for directory file names are hyphens, dashes, underscores, and spaces, as well as capital letters. In the aforementioned example, the convention for punctuation was initial capital letters, words separated by underscores, and date elements separated by dashes. Choose a standard way to record the date the file was made; yyyy-mm-dd is widely used because it sorts well and is easy to remember.

Most work is more complex than personal photos. In general, photos are static; they are not changed and modified. However, other types of data are dynamic; they can be changed often. Documents, papers, research data, and many other types of files can have multiple versions over time. Managing these many files can be difficult. It is important to manage the versions. Tracking different iterations of a file is called version control. Best practice calls for implementing a version control number system that encodes file names with sequential number that indicates the version. For example, the first major version of a document adds "v01" to the file name. The next version with minor changes uses the version "v01_01." Each new minor version increments the number. When the file has a major change, the version number can change—"v02_01." While some best practice sources recommend that the final version be marked with the word "final" (UC, 2017), others are concerned that a final version is not really final and confusing file names like "final_revised," "final_v2," or "final_final" will complicate version control (SUL, n.d. b).

Complex projects with multiple people making changes to data and document may require more version control than a number scheme. It may be useful to include a version control table that documents the versions and their changes along with the name of the person who made the change (UC, 2017).

Using the hierarchy of directories and folders can simplify the organizing process. Start with the highest level, the project, add subdirectories for subcomponents of the project and additional subdirectories for individual deliverables, and so forth. It can be useful to separate current work from past, completed work. Having a directory entitled "Completed Projects" can help minimize clutter by removing nonrelevant material from the daily workflow. The primary issue with this type of organization is maintaining it. Developing policies and practices to move finished work to the "Completed Projects" may be necessary.

Consistency is the key to data management. An organizing scheme is only as good as the practice of the data creators and users. Again, developing policies and practices to enforce the naming scheme is necessary.

Accessing Data

Accessing data is more than just finding it in the file system; it includes being able to open and use the data. The best way to ensure the long-term access of data is to choose file formats that are open, nonproprietary, and widely used (Borer et al., 2009). Proprietary formats are often typed to specific commercial software applications, such as Microsoft Excel, SPSS, and so on. It can be difficult to avoid using proprietary formats. Many of them are ubiquitous, that is, they are everywhere. But as the software changes, the format could change making the data inaccessible. In addition, software licenses can expire again preventing ongoing access. Good data management practice includes converting proprietary formats into nonproprietary formats. For example, converting an Excel spreadsheet from a .xlsx into a .csv (comma separated values) file would be considered best practice.

Sharing Data

One of the primary goals of digital curation is to ensure that data can be reused and shared. Data sharing assumes that the data is usable, so data needs to be in usable, nonproprietary, and open formats. Data also needs to be described, so metadata is a prerequisite of data sharing (Kowalczyk & Shankar, 2011). Metadata about the data and the data creation process should be included with the archived data (BCL, 2017).

Not all data can be shared without additional effort. There are circumstances, when sensitive or private data is involved, when the data needs to be *cleaned* before it can be shared. Sensitive information that can identify individuals involved in the research needs to be redacted (BCL, 2017). Anonymizing data can be more difficult than just removing some data elements and obscuring personal details. It is incumbent upon both the data owner and the digital repository to ensure that the data does not contain inappropriate data.

Keeping Data

In order to preserve data, it must be managed well. Good data management needs to be consistent in order to be effective and reproducible. Thus, once a management plan has been developed with an organizing scheme, meditator, version tracking, and other best practices, it is important for both individuals and organizations to document their processes, procedures, and policies. For work groups and organizations, using the collaboration tools, such as a wiki or a Google doc, can provide easy access to the documented processes. Delegating responsibility for maintaining the best practices documentation and enforcing policies, processes, and procedures is also very important (SUL, n.d. a).

PRACTICAL APPLICATION

Libraries in research and academic settings have been active partners in data management. When the DMP mandate was implemented in 2013, many academic and research institution administrators were concerned about their ability to meet the requirements. Many reached out to their libraries to join in the planning process. This inclusion was due to the legacy of trust that librarians know how to preserve information as they are in the business of storing, organizing, and preserving data. Libraries also had existing infrastructure for the preservation of their digitized content making the repository a natural home for research data. Administrators, librarians, and technologists worked together on policies for their communities.

The California Digital Library developed a tool to make DMPs easier for researchers and more sustainable for libraries and research organizations to support. They made the tool available for institutions to implement in their own environment and also provide a subscription-based model for shared implementation. The tool, called DMPTool, supports almost all of the funding agencies' requirements for DMPs. Researchers can create the DMP specifically for their grant. As time has passed, some researchers have become proficient in developing DMPs. However, for many researchers, the DMP remains a difficult process. Librarians can help these researchers describe the products of their research, data formats, both data and metadata, access and sharing policies, and the archiving infrastructure.

In addition to one-on-one support, some libraries have special services designed to help researchers write and fulfill their DMPs. A typical set of data management services would include:

- DMP review support;
- DMPTool access;
- descriptions and help for the elements of a DMP;
- funding agency guidelines;
- data storage services, including work spaces and repositories;
- consulting services for formats and data organization;
- metadata for data, and intellectual property and copyright;
- data citation tools; and
- data sharing.

Many libraries offer a variety of workshops and training opportunities for their various services.

Libraries in research organization are very active in helping to develop the DMP. But beyond the very excellent websites with data management advice, neither the libraries nor the parent research institution has provided infrastructure for data management for researchers prior to deposit in the repository (Kowalczyk, 2015). Recent research has shown that researchers are concerned with their ability to manage their data. If funding were not an issue, researchers would make different choices about the amount of data they stored, the technologies used to store that data and the processes, and staff by which they managed their data. If funding were not an issue, researchers would hire professional staff to manage their data (Kowalczyk, 2015). The current data management infrastructure is insufficient to meet the current needs.

Public libraries are beginning to implement data management workshops and other educational outreach activities to the public. These workshops discuss the best practices for managing personal photos, papers, documents, and social media. Along with digital literacy, personal information data management is a growth area for public libraries.

SUMMARY

- Managing data is key to long-term curation of data. Within the context of digital curation and digital repository systems, data management refers to the functions needed for "populating, maintaining, and accessing" metadata, archival files, and administrative data (CCSDS, 2012, p. 4-2).
- Not all data that could be important to preserve is managed in an information system.
- Data management is a multilevel process. Data is managed at many levels: the micro level, the intermediate level, and the macro level. The micro level represents individuals managing their own files whether for their job or personal use.

The intermediate level represents a mid-level organization, such as work group, team, or department. The macro level represents the institution, including businesses, research institutions, not-for-profits, and so on.

- In OAIS, data management includes such functions as creating, maintaining, and accessing descriptive metadata and administrative metadata, monitoring policy compliance, and tracking activities, such as item access and preservation provenance.
- Responsibilities for data management are shared among four roles: the data manager, the data creator, the data librarian, and the data scientist. There are points of intersection between the different actors.
- Data management best practice includes organizing data, accessing data, sharing data, and keeping data.
- Academic libraries are very active in helping researchers in their organizations prepare DMPs for research grant projects.

Questions for Discussion

1. How would you define data management for a repository? For a workshop for researchers? For a workshop for the general public?
2. What data management policies and procedures have you encountered in your professional life?
3. What data management policies and procedures do you practice with your personal data? Do you have a special set of procedures for your academic work?
4. Have you lost data? What happened?
5. Is it important for libraries to support outreach and educational efforts on data management?

NOTES

1. https://www.brainyquote.com/quotes/quotes/r/robertcail409512.html
2. https://www.brainyquote.com/search_results.html?q=data+is+a+precious+thing
3. For funding agencies with budgets of over $100 million.

REFERENCES

Association of Research Libraries (ARL). (2006). *To stand the test of time: Long-term stewardship of digital data sets in science and engineering.* Arlington, VA: Association of Research Libraries.

Austin, C., Brown, S., Fong, N., Humphrey, C., Leahey, A., & Webster, P. (2015, June). Research data repositories: Review of current features, gap analysis, and recommendations for minimum requirements. In *IASSIST Annual Conference*, Minneapolis, MN (pp. 2–5).

Baker, M., Keeton, K., & Martin, S. (2005, June). Why traditional storage systems don't help us save stuff forever. In *Proceedings of 1st IEEE Workshop on Hot Topics in System Dependability* (pp. 2005–2120).

Borer, E. T., Seabloom, E. W., Jones, M. B., & Schildhauer, M. (2009). Some simple guidelines for effective data management. *The Bulletin of the Ecological Society of America, 90*(2), 205–214.

Boston College Libraries (BCL). (2017). *Data management: Best practices in data management*. Found at http://libguides.bc.edu/dataplan/best_practices

Consultative Committee for Space Data Systems (CCSDS). (2012). *Reference model for an Open Archival Information System (OAIS)*. Issue 2. Recommendation for Space Data System Standards (Magenta Book), CCSDS 650.0-M-2. Washington, DC: ISO 14721:2012.

Data Management. (2016). In *Business dictionary*. Found at http://www.businessdictionary.com/definition/data-management.html

Digital Curation Centre (DCC). (2013). *Checklist for a data management plan. v.4.0*. Edinburgh: Digital Curation Centre. Found at http://www.dcc.ac.uk/resources/data-management-plans

Digital Curation Centre (DCC). (2017). *Roles*. Found at http://www.dcc.ac.uk/resources/roles

Henry, G. (2012). *Core infrastructure considerations for large digital libraries*. Council on Library and Information Resources, Digital Library Federation. Found at https://www.clir.org/pubs/reports/pub153/pub153.pdf

Holzner, A., Igo-Kemenes, P., & Mele, S. (2009). *Data preservation, reuse and (open) access in high-energy physics. CERN-OPEN-2008-028* (Vol. CERN-OPEN-). Geneva, Switzerland: CERN. Found at http://cdsweb.cern.ch/record/1152295/files/CERN-OPEN-2008-028.pdf?version=1

Kowalczyk, S. T. (2015, June). Before the repository: defining the preservation threats to research data in the lab. In *Proceedings of the 15th ACM/IEEE-CS Joint Conference on Digital Libraries* (pp. 215–222). ACM.

Kowalczyk, S. T., & Shankar, K. (2011). Data sharing in the sciences. In B. Cronin (Ed.), *Annual Review of Information Science and Technology* (Vol. 45, pp. 247–294). Medford, NJ: Information Today, Inc.

Long, J. S. (2009). *The workflow of data analysis using Stata*. College Station: Stata Press. Found at https://www.surveydesign.com.au/preview/wdaus-preview.pdf

Lyon, L. (2007). *Dealing with data: Roles, rights, responsibilities and relationships. Consultancy report*. Bath, UK: UKOLN and Joint Information Systems Committee (JISC) Committee for the Support of Research. Found at http://ie-repository.jisc.ac.uk/171/1/13ealing_with_data_report-final.pdf

MacBean, N. (2008, November 10). Fridge-sized tape recorder could crack lunar mysteries. *Australian Broadcast Corporation News*. Sydney, Australia. Found at http://www.abc.net.au/news/stories/2008/11/10/2415393.htm

Macey, R. (2006, August 5). One giant blunder for mankind: How NASA lost moon pictures. *The Sydney Morning Herald*. Sydney, Australia. Found at http://www.smh.com.au/news/national/one-giant-blunder-for-mankind-how-nasa-lost-moon-pictures/2006/08/04/1154198328978.html

National Science Board. (2005). *Long-lived digital data collections Enabling research and education in the 21st century*. Arlington, VA: National Science Board Committee on Programs and Plans, NSB-05-40. Found at http://www.nsf.gov/pubs/2005/nsb0540/nsb0540_1.pdf

National Science Foundation (NSF). (2017). *Chapter XI—Other post award requirements and considerations*. Found at https://www.nsf.gov/pubs/policydocs/pappg17_1/pappg_11.jsp#XID4

Oracle. (2012). Spend management best practices: A call for data management accelerators. *An Oracle white paper.* Found at http://www.oracle.com/us/industries/industrial -manufacturing/spend-management-best-practices-1621437.pdf

Rusbridge, C. (2007). Create, curate, re-use: The expanding life course of digital research data. *EDUCAUSE Australasia 2007.* Melbourne, Australia: EDUCAUSE. Found at http://hdl.handle.net/1842/1731

Stanford University Library (SUL). (n.d. a). *Data best practices.* Found at https://library .stanford.edu/research/data-management-services/data-best-practices

Stanford University Library (SUL). (n.d. b). *Data versioning.* Found at https://library .stanford.edu/research/data-management-services/data-best-practices/data-versioning

TechTarget. (2016). Glossary. In *Enterprise records management strategy guide for GRC professionals.* Found at http://searchdatamanagement.techtarget.com/definition/ data-management

University of Cambridge (UC). (2017). *Organising your data.* Found at https://www.data .cam.ac.uk/data-management-guide/organising-your-data

Wilkinson, M. D., Dumontier, M., Aalbersberg, I. J., Appleton, G., Axton, M., Baak, A., ... Bouwman, J. (2016). The FAIR Guiding Principles for scientific data management and stewardship. *Scientific Data, 3*(1).

Chapter 8

DISASTER PLANNING

It wasn't raining when Noah built the ark.

—Howard Ruff[1]

A prudent person foresees the danger ahead and takes precautions. The simpleton goes blindly on and suffers the consequences.

—Proverbs 27:12

INTRODUCTION

Contemplating disaster often brings about biblical visions of floods, droughts, pestilence, and plagues. And occasionally disasters are exactly that. However, more frequently, disasters that impact computer systems and cause data loss are much more mundane: a broken pipe, an electrical surge, or human error. But whether pestilence, accident, or stupidity, data loss can be catastrophic for an organization, particularly libraries and archives whose goal is to preserve in perpetuity. Librarians and archivists often see themselves as stewards of the information entrusted to their care. Lynch (2003) posits that "stewardship is easy and inexpensive to claim; it is expensive and difficult to honor, and perhaps it will prove to be all too easy to later abdicate" (p. 334).

Librarians and archivists can be better stewards of their digital content by understanding the threats to preservation, assessing the risks those threats entail, and planning to mitigate the threats and risks. Plans to mitigate risk are often called disaster recovery plans. A disaster is "any event that can cause a significant disruption in operational and/or computer processing capabilities for a period of time, which affects the operations of the business" (Martin, 2002, p. 3). Disruptions of service are interruptions or outages in access to systems and data. Business operations can be resumed when systems and data have been restored.

A central tenet of preservation is mitigating risks to the well-being of the content. This is true whether preserving digital or physical materials. Some of the threats are similar—floods and other natural disasters. But digital materials have some additional threats that need to be addressed. This chapter will review the literature on threats to digital materials, risk assessment issues, and recovery planning.

THEORETICAL OVERVIEW

Disaster planning can seem ghoulish; thinking about everything that could go wrong can be a bit depressing. Major disasters can be categorized as natural disasters, human disasters, and infrastructure disasters. Natural disasters are primarily weather related and include such phenomena as flood, ice, heat wave, and storms: lightening, hurricane, tornado, and blizzard. Additional natural disasters include wildfire, earthquake, tsunami, avalanche, and landslide. Human disasters include acts of war and terror with bombs and other destruction or criminal acts for financial or political gain. Infrastructure disasters include prolonged power failures, water main breaks that cause flooding, and hazardous materials mismanagement. These types of disasters have caused damage to organizations, some of their employees, and their digital content. However, these types of disasters are not the only problems that can negatively impact preservation. There are many other threats to the long-term preservation of digital materials.

Threats

Defining and categorizing the threats to digital preservation have been a significant theme in the literature. Assessing, describing, and managing risk are significant components of preservation infrastructure management. The risks associated with preservation infrastructures have been defined through the literature as threats to preservation. These threats have been categorized in a number of ways: component failures, management failures, disasters, and attacks (Barateiro, Antunes, Cabral, Borbinha, & Rodrigues, 2008); physical threats, technology threats, human threats, and institutional threats (Altman et al., 2009); and economic threat, human error, disasters, and attacks (Rosenthal, Roussopoulos, Giuli, Maniatis, & Baker, 2004). But at the most elemental level, threats to reliable preservation are either technology-based or human-based. Table 8.1 provides a summary of relevant issues raised in the literature about various technology-based threats to digital preservation.

Technology-based threats are defined as failures where the hardware, software, or storage media did not perform as expected. Hardware failures can interrupt processes that leave data incomplete, resulting in inconsistent or corrupted files. Hardware failures can also lead to failures in other hardware components such as storage devices.

Storage failures are particularly devastating for preservation; missing, corrupt, or erroneous data undermines preservation. In general, storage has two primary points of failure: the mechanical elements required for reading and writing and the storage media itself. When the mechanical elements that write the data fail, data can be corrupted; bits may be changed or omitted. The errors may not be discovered for some period of time. If the error occurred during the creation of the data, the fixity

Table 8.1.

Technology-Based Threats to Preservation

Threat	Authors
Hardware failures	Altman et al., 2009; Baker et al., 2005; Barateiro et al., 2008; Rosenthal et al., 2005
Media flaws	Barateiro et al., 2008
Massive storage failure	Altman et al., 2009; Baker et al., 2005; Rosenthal et al., 2005
Intermittent failures ("bit rot")	Baker et al., 2005
Network services failures	Barateiro et al., 2008; Rosenthal et al., 2005
Software failures	Altman et al., 2009; Baker et al., 2005; Barateiro et al., 2008; Rosenthal et al., 2005

checksum created might *verify* the bad file. Threats to storage also include flaws inherent in the media itself. These flaws often occur during the manufacturing process. These may not be detected by operating system software or the hardware's firmware. The media itself may also fail intermittently; that is, individual magnetic grains on hard drives or tapes may fail or the dye or bond on optical media.

Software failures often include data errors and/or corruption. Data errors are often due to insufficient programming; that is, the programs do not verify the data for valid values, accuracy, or reasonability. For example, the applications should not allow a record creation date to be in the future; it does not pass a reasonability test. In a digital repository, a format type that is not supported should not be allowed. Software can also introduce corruption, again by programming errors. In a project to preserve and make more accessible U.S. government data published via the Government Printing Office (GPO) on floppy disks, researchers found that the copy operation in some operating systems did not read the entire file; hundreds of bytes of data were ignored producing corrupt files (Woods & Brown, 2009).

Threats as Management Failures

Many of the threats to preservation have been previously categorized as technology faults when, in practice, many of these threats are really human failures: failures of attention, failures of management, and failures of planning. Table 8.2 provides a summary of relevant issues raised in the literature about various human-based threats to digital preservation.

Organizational issues are human issues. The humans who manage organizations make decisions that impact and sometimes threaten their ability to preserve their digital content. Changing priorities and the attending financial choices can pose a threat to preservation. Without a mission-driven mandate, resources to support preservation activities will not be allocated: staff will be reassigned, infrastructure will decay, and data will disappear. Because of the impact of the organization on its digital content, institutional commitment to preservation is a significant component of the certification for a trusted repository (see Chapter 5).

Table 8.2.

Human-Based Threats to Preservation

Threat	Authors
Erasure error	Baker et al., 2005
Loss of context	Baker et al., 2005
Operator error	Altman et al., 2009; Barateiro et al., 2008; Rosenthal et al., 2004, 2005
Lack of disaster preparedness	Barateiro et al., 2008; Rosenthal et al., 2004, 2005
Communication errors	Barateiro et al., 2008; Rosenthal et al., 2005
Media obsolescence	Baker et al., 2005; Barateiro et al., 2008; Hunter & Choudhury, 2004; Rosenthal et al., 2005
Format obsolescence	Altman et al., 2009; Baker et al., 2005; Barateiro et al., 2008
Software obsolescence	Baker et al., 2005; Barateiro et al., 2008; Hunter & Choudhury, 2004; Rosenthal et al., 2005
Hardware obsolescence	Hunter & Choudhury, 2004; Rosenthal et al., 2005
Funding/Economic failure	Altman et al., 2009; Baker et al., 2005; Barateiro et al., 2008; Hunter & Choudhury, 2004; Rosenthal et al., 2004, 2005
Institutional failure	Baker et al., 2005; Barateiro et al., 2008; Hunter & Choudhury, 2004; Rosenthal et al., 2005
Mission change	Altman et al., 2009
Legal regime change	Altman et al., 2009
Malicious attack—either internal or external	Altman et al., 2009; Baker et al., 2005; Barateiro et al., 2008; Rosenthal et al., 2004, 2005

Technology obsolescence is the enemy of preservation. Obsolescence of hardware, software, and media has been categorized as a technology risk (Altman et al., 2009; Barateiro et al., 2008; Rosenthal, Robertson, Lipkis, Reich, & Morabito, 2005). However, as obsolescence is inherent to technology, it cannot be considered some vague future threat but a surety. Planning for obsolescence is a specific management task. It is the lack of management that is the threat. Because management is a human activity, obsolescence must be considered a human risk. As discussed previously in this book, digital content is tightly coupled with its technical implementation; in order to use digital content, the software and hardware needed to access and render the material must be functional. Hardware becomes obsolete when it is no longer supported by its vendor. Organizations are often forced to buy new hardware because the operational risk of running on obsolete, unsupported hardware is too great. Software is often written for a specific hardware platform. When that platform changes, the software may become obsolete; it may no longer function with the new hardware. Therefore, managing hardware means managing software and understanding the relationship between the two.

Storage media is a specialized type of hardware for storing data that is also vulnerable to obsolescence. Like computing hardware, it becomes obsolete and is no longer supported by its vendor. In addition, storage media is vulnerable to failure;

that is, the media itself can just wear out. Storage media has a lifespan often based on the number of reads and writes. When storage media is replaced, the data must be transferred from the old device to the new device. Sometimes, this data transfer is referred to as data migration. The Open Archival Information System (OAIS) model refers to four types of data migration: refreshment, replication, repackaging, and transformation. Refreshing the storage media is the process of copying data to a new storage device to avoid media failures. Data migration is for refreshment.

Malicious attacks can be initiated by external or internal actors and can be either physical or cyber. External actors can include such groups as competitors or foreign governments acting as competitors who are looking for strategic advantages or to eliminate competition. They can be hackers looking for glory, information, or money. Internal attacks are often carried out by disgruntled employees, employees under financial stress, or employees who are spies or moles for other organizations. Attacks can be physical by disrupting infrastructure, such as electricity, water, and networks, as they can impact the normal course of business for any organization. Physical attacks can be violent with intent to destroy the infrastructure, including the buildings. Cyberattacks are designed to damage, disrupt, or infiltrate a system. Cyberattacks have become big business with syndicates of criminals holding the digital contents of organizations hostage.

Humans can make mistakes, and these errors constitute a significant threat to preservation. Data deletion, whether accidental or purposeful, and operator errors, such as overwriting tapes, misnaming files, and linking incorrect metadata are the all-too-frequent human failures that threaten preservation. Data deletion can be inadvertent by either hitting the wrong button or mistakenly thinking that the data was no longer needed. Humans can overwrite files by accident. Data storage disks, hard drives, and other removable media can be lost. Backup processes can be ignored or interrupted. Human error can occur due to a lack of oversight, a lack of policy, a lack of training, and a lack of fail-safe system design. The list could go on.

Lack of planning might be the most significant threat to long-term preservation of digital content. The OAIS conceptual model addresses preservation planning in general and disaster recovery planning specifically. In OAIS, the disaster recovery function is a way for libraries and archives to duplicate their digital content for storage in a remote location. The OAIS disaster recovery function focuses primarily on data management activities, such as system backups. Real disaster recovery planning requires developing contingencies for process resumption, hardware and network redundancy, automatic failover, and site mirroring.

Assessing the Risk by Threat

The various schemes for categorizing threats can help digital librarians and archivists identify issues. However, the categories are not organized to help identify the level of risk and priority. It does not seem reasonable to treat network service outage at the same level of risk as a natural disaster. Antunes, Barateiro, Cabral, Borbinha, and Rodrigues (2009) developed a risk assessment scale for the various established preservation threats. This relatively simple assessment uses three levels of risk: low, medium,

Table 8.3.

Risk Assessment of Preservation Threats

Risk	Threat
Low	Organizational failures Economic failures Media/hardware obsolescence Communication faults Network failures
Medium	Human operational errors Media faults Hardware faults Software faults Software obsolescence
High	External attacks Internal attacks Natural disasters

(Antunes et al., 2009)

and high. Table 8.3 shows the threats and risk levels. It would certainly be possible to quibble with any single assessment. For example, one could argue that human error could be rated as a high risk. However, the risk assessments seem sound.

Barateiro, Antunes, Freitas, and Borbinha (2010) developed a taxonomy of preservation threats that differentiates between the inherent risks of technologies, described as vulnerabilities, and real threats. This nuanced taxonomy provides a different view of risk assessment (see Table 8.4). Vulnerabilities include process, data, and infrastructure; threats include disasters, attacks, management, and legislation (Barateiro et al., 2010). Vulnerabilities are inherently lower risk than threats and can be monitored and managed as an ongoing business process, reducing their risk to near zero. Threats can be evaluated, and risks can be assessed on an ongoing basis. Resources can be deployed to minimize the risks.

Table 8.4.

Taxonomy of Vulnerabilities and Threats to Preservation

Vulnerabilities	Threats
• Process ○ Software faults ○ Software obsolescence • Data ○ Media faults ○ Media obsolescence • Infrastructure ○ Hardware faults ○ Hardware obsolescence ○ Communication faults ○ Network services failures	• Disasters ○ Natural disaster ○ Human operational errors • Attacks ○ Internal attacks ○ External attacks • Management ○ Economic failures ○ Organizational failures • Legislation ○ Legislative charges ○ Legal requirements

(Barateiro et al., 2010)

Vulnerabilities versus Threats

An example might illustrate the differences between vulnerabilities and threats. By looking at mitigating the vulnerability of media faults and the threat of malicious external attack, these differences will become clear.

Vulnerability

Media faults, whether manufacturing issues or deterioration over time due to use or environmental factors, can corrupt data. Data corruption negatively impacts digital curation; preserving *bad* data is hardly preservation. Digital curators mitigate the risk of data corruption via media faults by ensuring the fixity of the digital files. As was discussed in Chapter 5, fixity is a significant data preservation issue (Gladney, 2004; Hedstrom & Montgomery, 1998). While some storage devices have internal fixity functions, fixity is often the responsibility of the repository system. So many repository systems include a fixity function; that is, a checksum is generated when the object is created or ingested and verified on a regular schedule to ensure that the bytes have not changed. This vulnerability can be further mitigated by regular maintenance and monitoring of the storage technologies with replacements scheduled on the recommended timetable. Because media failures are predictable and preventable, they can be considered a vulnerability.

Threat

External malicious attacks can occur in any number of ways ranging from physical destruction to data theft. Because of the wide range of potential external malicious attacks, they are much more difficult to mitigate; they are difficult to predict, protect against, and recover from. Malicious external attacks are criminal activities planned and executed in secret to hide the identities of perpetrators. Cyberattacks can be particularly difficult to detect; it may be weeks before the break-in is discovered and even longer to determine the damage done. Digital libraries and archives are often part of a larger organization. In many cases, other departments, such as information technology (IT), have the responsibility for risk assessment and risk mitigation activities for cyberattacks. However, it is important for digital librarians and digital curators to participate in the cybersecurity planning. Many tools, both hardware and software, that detect cyber break-ins can be deployed; however, most of these tools are developed and maintained retroactively. That is, they fix problems once hackers have already exploited the system. Determined hackers are very difficult to stop. This discussion is not intended to frighten or deter digital library creation but is intended to illustrate the complexity of defending from unpredictable and complex threats.

Disaster Planning

Organizations assess threats and risks in order to develop plans to help them recover from disasters. Disaster recovery plans (DRPs), also known as business resumption plans (BRPs), document the impact of various disasters on critical systems and the various steps and resources required to repair and restart them within an acceptable timeframe. A disaster recovery plan should help an organization to do the following:

1. Limit the magnitude of any loss by minimizing the duration of a critical application service interruption.
2. Assess damage, repair the damage, and activate the repaired computer center.
3. Recover data and information imperative to the operation of critical applications.
4. Manage the recovery operation in an organized and effective manner.
5. Prepare technology personnel to respond effectively in disaster recovery situations (Martin, 2002).

Just as it is important to identify risk, identifying the impact—the damage—caused by a disaster is important. A five-tier level scheme for classifying disasters by impact was developed (Talon, 2005).

- Level 1 and 2 reflect minimal impact. These are often associated with benign hacking. The system has been compromised with unauthorized access. There is little evidence of incursion and no evidence of data loss, corruption, or theft. The incursion could cause damage due to public exposure. The organization could be embarrassed, or stakeholders could lose confidence in organization.
- Level 3 indicates minor damage. In this scenario, minor, noncritical systems are harmed. Some data could be lost or unrecoverable. While this is a high priority, it may not be an emergency requiring immediate response.
- Level 4 indicates major damage. Major systems have been compromised, and/or substantial amounts of data have been lost. Multiple critical systems have failed simultaneously. A level 4 major disaster is a high-priority and high-urgency emergency requiring an immediate response.
- Level 5 indicates the total loss scenario. This includes massive disruption in all systems and loss of all data. This could also include mass causalities, loss of buildings, and long-term psychological impact on personnel. Recovery in this scenario is very difficult.

A successful disaster planning process addresses each level of disaster. Data managers often hold assumptions that have been proven to be false. The first assumption is that all faults can be easily and quickly detected and repaired; the second assumption is that faults happen independently. Baker, Keeton, and Martin (2005) found that while some faults can be visible, detected, and fixed immediately, other faults are latent, undetected, and dormant. In addition, they found that failures are not independent but happen in multiple, cascading, and compounding occurrences. A *thorough* disaster planning process helps organizations deal with multiple disasters simultaneously.

DRPs focus on recovery, on the process of getting back to normal. Each system is assessed for its importance, its impact, to the organization. The importance and level of impact of a system determine its priority in the recovery plan. Recovery point objective (RPO) and recovery time objective (RTO) are metrics in the DRP to document how long the system can be unavailable and how much data (or work) must be recovered.

- RTO is the amount of time that an organization can be without a specific system; it is the time allowed to recover the system. This timeframe reflects the importance of the system. A system with an RTO of two seconds is a significantly higher priority than a system that has an RTO of 24 hours.

- RPO is the maximum time period in which data can be lost because of a disaster. This metric is another indicator of the significance of the system. While no organization wants to lose data, not all systems need to be recovered perfectly. Organizations may decide that the cost of total data recovery is too high and are willing to duplicate human effort to recreate data.

The RTO and the RPO impact the cost of recovery both in terms of money and personnel. The faster the recovery time and the higher the requirements for data recovery, the more equipment, storage, and people are required. A system that requires an RTO of one second would require significantly more equipment than a system that could be down for 24 hours. A system that could not tolerate any data loss would require more storage equipment and more processes than a system that could lose up to four hours of data. RPOs are particularly important in transaction-based, financial systems, such as bank ATMs and point-of-sale cash register applications. It is easy to see why banks and stores are not willing to lose any data; data is money in these applications. However, other applications do not have the same financial impact to both the organization and the customer and can tolerate some level of data loss. For example, a library or an archive may be willing to accept the loss of four hours of work in their metadata cataloging system.

DRP requires the entire organization to work together to determine priorities and strategies for surviving disasters. Planning for disaster recovery involves conducting a business impact analysis, determining recovery strategies, developing and documenting the plan, and, finally, testing the plan (see Figure 8.1). A successful DRP process relies on the cooperation of the business experts and the technologists. These experts, the librarians and archivists, need to analyze their operations and determine the recovery requirements, the RTOs and RPOs for each system. The technologists need to develop strategies and processes to ensure recovery within the parameters determined from the business impact analysis.

Recovery strategies include preventative measures, detective measures, and corrective measures. Preventative measures, as the name implies, are designed to mitigate risks. A number of threats can be prevented by implementing relatively simple measures, such as surge protectors to protect equipment from electrical grid issues and lightning as well as regular and routine inspections of wires, pipes, and other infrastructure that can fail. The most important preventative measure is to ensure that the organization's data has been appropriately stored and saved; there can be no recovery if the data has not been saved. Many disasters can be lessened when they are detected early. Detective measures include fire alarms, motion detectors,

Figure 8.1.
Disaster Recovery Planning Process

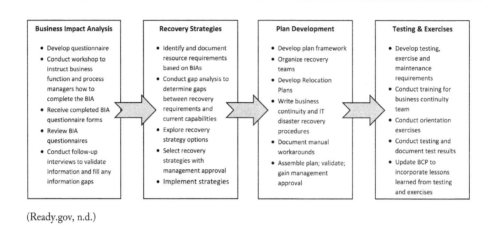

(Ready.gov, n.d.)

network intrusion software, and computer virus monitoring. Corrective measures include the detailed description of each step to take to restore the business operations; corrective measures are the core of the disaster recovery plan.

As with many other management processes, DRP—business continuity planning —requires ongoing attention. DRP has a lifecycle; the plan needs to be reviewed on a regular cycle. As new systems are developed and/or implemented, the plan needs to be revised to include these new applications.

TECHNICAL IMPLICATIONS

DRP does not just entail what happens after a disaster, but it carefully plans to ensure that the RTP and the RPO can be met. In this section, the technology options for restoring the operations and the data will be explored.

Operational Recovery Options

Depending on the nature of the disaster and the requirements of the recovery time objectives, organizations may need to have additional, reserve equipment to be able to continue their business operations. This can range from having spare parts on hand to having a fully operational remote data center at the ready. For an organization that needs continuous operation with zero interruptions, the only real option is the high-end solution of a spare data center. With substantial resources for personnel, network bandwidth, equipment, and automation, organizations can have immediate failover from their primary data center to the remote data center. Most *Fortune* 500 organizations, financial organizations, and others with no tolerance for downtime have implemented this type of solution. However, for many organizations, this is not financially feasible. The cost is simply too prohibitive.

Rather than building and maintaining a spare data center, many organizations have contracted with third-party data center vendors who provide access to computers and storage devices when necessary. Organizations can contract with these vendors for all of their systems or a subset of the most important. These third-party data center vendors offer a variety of services that can improve recovery time substantially. While substantially less expensive than a full duplicate data center, these services are still expensive.

Data Recovery Options

In order to be able to recover data, the data must be saved and in a location not impacted by the disaster; in other words, the data must be backed up. Technologists within most organizations have experience creating backups. Specialized software can generate and maintain the backup files so that the appropriate files can be found when recovery is required. Conceptually, backup is a simple process; however, the process can become quite complex depending on the number of storage technologies involved, the volume of data to be copied, the RPO, and the recovery time requirements. In order to recover data, it is important to determine the level of backups, the frequency of backups, and the distribution of the backups.

Types

In general, there are three types of backups: full backups, incremental backups, and partial backups. A full backup is very simple; it copies everything. An incremental backup is more complicated; it only backs up data that is changed since the previous backup. An incremental backup requires substantial data management infrastructure. A database is needed to record the file names, the date for the last backup, the names and locations of the backup files since the last full backup, and so forth. Incremental backups are used because they are faster and require less storage since only changed data is being copied. Partial backups are used under special circumstances when only specific directories or files need to be copied. Partial backups can be used prior to software upgrades or other unusual circumstances. Data recovery options mirror the backup options. A full backup replaces everything. An incremental backup applies specific transactions/changes, and a partial recovery replaces specific files.

Frequency

Frequency of backups depends on the nature of the data and the recovery point requirements. The volatility of the data, that is, the more the data changes or grows, and the tolerance of data loss impact the frequency of data backups. Very volatile data that had low tolerance of loss needs very frequent backups while very stable data with a higher tolerance for loss needs less infrequent backup.

Organizations that have the requirement for zero data loss often use a replication technology called mirroring where the data is copied immediately to additional storage devices. This is usually done to a combination of specific storage technologies and software. One of the most common technologies for mirroring is redundant arrays of independent disk (RAID). This technology is often used in financial systems. However, there are applications for archives and libraries. For example, if a library wanted to ensure that they never lost a circulation transaction, all circulation transactions would be mirrored; that is, when a book was checked out, the circulation system would write the transaction on the primary disk, and the replication technology would immediately copy the data. To be completely safe, the library or archive would have a third device at a remote location, which would also be updated.

Most of the data in libraries and archives is not particularly volatile. For digital libraries and archives, the repository ingest process is the most active. Large quantities of data are added in batches. Libraries and archives are often willing to strike a reasonable balance between cost and loss. Mirroring as a backup strategy would be very expensive due to large size of the data files. A weekly full backup with daily incremental backups for the repository is usually seen as sufficient. During a heavy digitizing project, some archives and libraries implement a partial backup strategy to secure the safety of the ongoing to digitization output.

In addition to the data, application software, software keys and licenses, systems software, and systems data, such as configuration files and user information, need to be backed up to be saved for disaster recovery. The software components need a weekly full backup. The systems data, the configuration files, and other similar data need a daily backup.

Distribution

Once data has been backed up, the media needs to be distributed so that it too is protected. Distribution of backup media is relatively straightforward. A set of best practices has been developed through the experience of the many organizations that have recovered from disasters. In general, best practice dictates three copies of the data: the primary data store, on-site backups, and an off-site copy. The on-site backup should include the most current full backup plus all of the incremental backups made since the full backup. The off-site backup should also have the most current full backup plus all of the incremental files. If the organization has a very low tolerance for downtime and data loss, they may, as mentioned earlier, have a remote data center for instant failover. For these organizations, the third copy would be stored there. For those organizations without a remote data center, the third copy should be stored in an environmentally appropriate remote site.

Levels of Recovery

The ability for an organization to recover from a disaster depends on the level of planning and the resources allocated. Without sufficient equipment, recovery cannot occur. However, there are many recovery options that can be expressed as levels of recovery. In the 1980s, the SHARE Technical Steering Committee, an IBM user group, developed a seven-tiered classification of business resumption/disaster recovery possibilities. There are several schemes to classify levels of recovery

(Alhazmi & Malaiya, 2014). The SHARE scheme has been widely used (Alhazmi & Malaiya, 2016).

- Tier 0 indicates that the organization has no backups available because either they did not make any or none are available after the disaster. There is no possibility of recovery at this level.
- Tier 1 indicates that the organization has backups in a remote location but does not have a hot site in which to deploy their systems. Tier 1 recovery could take weeks or months depending on the damage sustained to the primary data center.
- Tier 2 indicates that the organization has backups in a remote location and equipment on which to deploy their applications. The backups are generally on tape and need to be restored. Tier 2 recovery can be complete but may take substantial time, depending on the amount of data that must be copied and restored.
- Tier 3 indicates that the organization has backups in a remote location and equipment on which to deploy the applications. The backups have been electronically vaulted; that is, the data has been electronically sent to the remote site and is easier to load. Recovery time is much quicker than Tier 2.
- Tier 4 indicates that an organization electronically sends backups and transaction incremental backups to the remote site. The backups are stored on disk for immediate use. The data will be accurate to the most recent backups.
- Tier 5 indicates that the organization uses a transaction integrity strategy, which requires a high consistency between the primary and the recovery data center. The site transmits each transaction to the remote site.
- Tier 6 indicates that the organization requires virtual total data retention. The primary site implements mirroring with the remote site.
- Tier 7 indicates that the organization implements a fully automated disaster recovery process with mirroring of data and instant failover to the remote site when the primary site is unavailable (Kent, 2015).

Immediate and full operational resumption and data recovery are possible with time and money.

PRACTICAL APPLICATION

It is completely natural for librarians and archivists to feel slightly overwhelmed with the prospect of developing a disaster recovery plan. The list of threats seems daunting with so many problems to worry about. While all of the threat areas should be considered over time, it is possible to prioritize the list and address the most likely problems first.

Developing a Disaster Recovery Plan

Libraries and archives often exist within a larger organization: a university, a research organization, a corporation, a governmental agency, or city, county, state government. Often these larger entities have a disaster recovery or business

Table 8.5.

Sample Disaster Plan

Critical System	RTO/RPO	Threat	Prevention Strategy	Response Strategy	Recovery Strategy
Digital Repository	4 hours/ 2 hours	Server failure	Secure equipment room, backup server, UPS	Switch over to backup server, validate UPS functions	Fix/replace primary server; move back to primary server
Digital Repository	4 hours/ 2 hours	Storage failure	Secure equipment room, backup server, UPS; maintain store of spare disks	Swap out damaged hard drive with spares. Restore data	Obtain more spare disk drives
Building Security	2 hours/ 2 hours	Security system deployed	Locate system in secure area; UPS; install protective enclosure around sensor units	Deploy guards at strategic points	Obtain/install replacement unit/ sensors

continuation planning process. Librarians and archivists should understand these processes and become involved with their governance. The larger organization may be able to provide resources and technologies that the library archive would not be able to do on its own. The larger organization may also have a specific planning methodology that specifies the entire process.

Regardless of the specific methodology, the process is relatively straightforward although time-consuming and somewhat stressful: the business impact analysis, developing recovery strategies, developing the plan, and implementing and testing. But before any of these activities can happen, a team needs to be formed that includes senior management, business experts, and technologists. This team needs the given resources, primarily time and access to all areas of the organization, in order to be successful.

The first step is doing the business impact analysis. In many ways, this is the most important step. During the analysis phase, the planning team interviews business experts about their systems, both digital and physical, to determine the requirements for recovery: the impact on the customers and the organization, volatility of the data, level of data loss that is acceptable, and the amount of time the systems can be unavailable. From this data, strategies are developed; for each system, for each threat, a method of preventing and fixing problems. As seen in Table 8.5, the strategies can be rather simple.

Once the strategies have been determined, the full plan can be developed. The full plan concentrates on assigning responsibilities to real people with clear instructions for communicating to the organization, emergency personnel, and services as required; to customers; and to the media. Disaster recovery plans need to be tested to find errors, omissions, and problems. Unfortunately, testing the plan is expensive and time-consuming. This step is often overlooked.

Options for Implementing a Plan

In addition to building their own recovery infrastructure, libraries and archives have the option to partner with other organizations or purchase services designed specifically for their preservation means. Some digital libraries and archives have formed partnerships to support continuity of service and operation recovery. These organizations have agreements to share computing resources and store data in case of disaster. When the sites are geographically distant, the probability of both having a disaster simultaneously is rather low. The most public of these partnerships involves the University of Michigan, Indiana University, and the HathiTrust Digital Library. The HathiTrust Digital Library provides both access and preservation services to more than 700 terabytes of data.[2]

The HathiTrust is a very visible and important digital repository that serves dozens of major libraries. Uninterrupted access to this material is a high priority. The University of Michigan and Indiana University have designed a very robust infrastructure to ensure the continuity of service. The HathiTrust uses mirroring as its disaster recovery strategy. The primary data center is managed by the University of Michigan. The data is mirrored at Indiana University's data center in Indianapolis, Indiana. Both sites save data. With load balancing and failover, a user is unaware of which site they are searching. If one site fails, the other will be able to take the total load. In addition to the data synchronization, a tape backup is stored in a third site in Michigan (York, 2010).

Other digital libraries and archives do not have the same need for uninterrupted service. Developing other, perhaps less robust, options could be very helpful.

Services

Two organizations have developed services to support digital preservation, backup, and recovery. The two services use completely different business models; one is a subscription model, and the other is a membership model. Both organizations focus on libraries in archives and other cultural heritage organizations, and they are not-for-profit.

DuraCloud

DuraCloud is a service offered and run by DuraSpace, the organization that develops and maintains the DSpace and Fedora repository software packages. DuraCloud was first deployed in 2009. DuraCloud is a hosted repository and distributed data service for preserving and archiving digital content. It operates as a subscription service with pricing based on the amount of data stored, the number of copies, and access services used. DuraCloud provides support services that minimize the risk of using cloud storage, thus making it a viable option for digital libraries and archives. DuraCloud distributes, manages, and synchronizes digital content across various cloud storage services. By using different vendors, DuraCloud minimizes the risk of using a single vendor. DuraCloud simplifies cloudy dat management processes by providing a single interface, a single point of contact, and a single billing process.

DuraCloud can be used for online data backup. Rather than using tape drives or another storage device, a library or archive repository could use the DuraCloud services as its backup media. DuraCloud offers preservation services, such as checksum validation and other data insurance processes. In addition, DuraCloud offers access services, such as audio streaming.

The Digital Preservation Network

The Digital Preservation Network (DPN) is a membership organization that provides a technology infrastructure for distributed backup and long-term preservation of digital content. DPN members contribute to the development of the network. DPN uses best practices for digital curation and data management; data is distributed and replicated across three of the nodes. Content is synchronized and checked for fixity.

DPN is a federation of geographically separated repositories that are built upon technology platforms. These repositories act as nodes in the network. "The Nodes work in concert to ensure that the digital content is secure and that the objects are preserved" (DPN, 2017, para. 2). The five primary nodes are:

- Academic Preservation Trust (University of Virginia)
- DuraCloud Vault (University of California at San Diego and DuraSpace)
- Stanford Digital Repository
- Texas Preservation Node
- HathiTrust (University of Michigan; DPN, 2017, para. 4)

SUMMARY

- Disasters will happen. Librarians and archivists need to understand the threats to preservation and plan accordingly.
- Threats to reliable preservation are either technology-based or human-based. Technology-based threats include hardware failures, media flaws, massive storage failure, and software failures. Many of the threats to preservation are due to a lack of management planning. Lack of planning is a major threat to preservation. Not planning for disasters and not planning for economic and organizational issues are human failings. Since technology changes so quickly, obsolescence of storage media, hardware, and software must be understood as a management issue rather than a technology issue.
- Assessing the risk of threats helps librarians and archives identify and prioritize the mitigation efforts. Threats with a low risk of loss are organizational, network, and communication failures, and media and hardware obsolescence. Threats with a medium risk of loss are human error, software obsolescence, and faults in storage media, hardware, and software. Threats with a high risk of loss are attacks (both internal and external) and natural disasters (Antunes et al., 2009).

- Disaster recovery planning is a collaborative effort requiring technologists, librarians, and archivists to work together. Planning for disaster recovery involves conducting a business impact analysis, determining recovery strategies, developing and documenting the plan, and, finally, testing the plan.

- The disaster recovery plan is focused on restoring business processes as soon as possible. The two most important parameters within the disaster recovery plan are RPO and RTO, which document how long the system can be *down* and how much data (or work) must be recovered.

- The technical options for the operational recovery and data recovery are tied to the RTO and the RPO. The greater the need for fast operational and complete data recovery, the higher the cost in both money and personnel.

- Digital libraries and archives are collaborating to find technical platforms for high-level disaster recovery options. These collaborative efforts may provide real help for those organizations concerned with the long-term preservation of digital content.

Questions for Discussion

1. Do you see other threats to preservation?
2. Are there other ways to categorize the threats to preservation that could help libraries and archives as they plan?
3. Have you experienced data loss due to a disaster? Which types of disasters/threats? Was there a disaster recovery plan? How was the situation resolved?
4. What are the most likely disasters in your area?
5. Think about an important system in a library or archive that you know. How would you determine reasonable RPO and RTO values for this system? What would you need to do to make that happen?
6. What other types of collaborative solutions would be helpful for libraries and archives as they develop disaster recovery plans?

NOTES

1. http://www.dataweld.com/Data-Thoughts/it-wasnt-raining-when-noah-built-the-ark
2. https://www.hathitrust.org/about

REFERENCES

Alhazmi, O. H., & Malaiya, Y. K. (2014). Are the classical disaster recovery tiers still applicable today? In *Software Reliability Engineering Workshops (ISSREW), 2014 IEEE International Symposium* (pp. 144–145). IEEE.

Alhazmi, O. H., & Malaiya, Y. K. (2016). Discretization of disaster recovery choices: A survey of tiers schemes. In *31st International Conference on Computers and Their Applications*. CATA, Las Vegas, Nevada. Found at http://www.cs.colostate.edu/~malaiya/p/AlhazmiCATA_2016.pdf

Altman, M., Adams, M. O., Crabtree, J., Donakowski, D., Maynard, M. M., Pienta, A., & Young, C. H. (2009). Digital preservation through archival collaboration: The data preservation alliance for the social sciences. *American Archivist, 72*(1), 170–184. Found at http://archivists.metapress.com/content/EU7252LHNRP7H188

Antunes, G., Barateiro, J., Cabral, M., Borbinha, J., & Rodrigues, R. (2009). Preserving digital data in heterogeneous environments. *Proceedings of the 9th ACM/IEEE-CS joint conference on Digital Libraries* (pp. 345–348). ACM.

Baker, M., Keeton, K., & Martin, S. (2005). *Why traditional storage systems don't help us save stuff forever* (Technical Report 2005-120). Palo Alto, CA. Found at http://citeseerx.ist .psu.edu/viewdoc/download?doi=10.1.1.65.2375&rep=rep1&type=pdf

Barateiro, J., Antunes, G., Cabral, M., Borbinha, J., & Rodrigues, R. (2008). Using a grid for digital preservation. In G. Buchanan, M. Masoodian, & S. J. Cunningham (Eds.), *Digital libraries: Universal and ubiquitous access to information* (Vol. 5362, pp. 225–235). Berlin, Germany: Springer. Found at http://www.springerlink.com/content/ k71v8x6081738x18

Barateiro, J., Antunes, G., Freitas, F., & Borbinha, J. (2010). Designing digital preservation solutions: A risk management-based approach. *International Journal of Digital Curation, 5*(1), 4–17.

Digital Preservation Network (DPN). (2017). *Our work—Core nodes.* Found at https:// www.dpn.org/about

Hedstrom, M., & Montgomery, S. (1998). Digital preservation needs and requirements in RLG member institutions: A study commissioned by the Research Libraries Group. Mountain View, CA: Research Libraries Group.

Hunter, J., & Choudhury, S. (2004). A semi-automated digital preservation system based on semantic web services. *Proceedings of the 4th ACM/IEEE-CS Joint Conference on Digital Libraries (JCDL '04)* (pp. 269–278). Tucson, AZ, June 7–11: ACM & IEEE. doi:10.1145/996350.996415

Kent, T. (2015). *The seven tiers of BCP: On point.* Found at http://go.dewpoint.com/ onpoint/the-seven-tiers-of-bcp

Lynch, C. A. (2003). Institutional repositories: Essential infrastructure for scholarship in the digital age. *Portal: Libraries and the Academy, 3*(2), 327–336.

Martin, B. (2002). Disaster recovery plan strategies and processes. In *SANS Institute InfoSec reading room.* Found at https://www.sans.org/reading-room/whitepapers/recovery/ disaster-recovery-plan-strategies-processes-564

Ready. (n.d.). Business continuity planning. In *Ready: Official website of the Department of Homeland Security.* Found at https://www.ready.gov/business/implementation/continuity

Rosenthal, D. S. H., Robertson, T. S., Lipkis, T., Reich, V., & Morabito, S. (2005). Requirements for digital preservation systems: A bottom-up approach. *D-Lib Magazine, 11*(11). Found at www.dlib.org/dlib/november05/rosenthal/11rosenthal.html

Rosenthal, D. S. H., Roussopoulos, M., Giuli, T., Maniatis, P., & Baker, M. (2004). Using hard disks for digital preservation. *IS&T Archiving Conference Final Program and Proceedings (Archiving 2004)*, 249–253. Found at http://www.ingentaconnect.com/ content/ist/ac/2004/00002004/00000001/art00053

Talon, M. (2005). Classification system for disaster levels. In *TechRepublic.* Found at http:// www.techrepublic.com/article/classification-system-for-disaster-levels/

Woods, K., & Brown, G. (2009). Creating virtual CD-ROM collections. *International Journal of Digital Curation, 4*(2), 184–198.

York, J. (2010). Building a future by preserving our past: The preservation infrastructure of HathiTrust digital library. In *76th IFLA general congress and assembly* (pp. 10–15).

Chapter 9

DIGITAL CURATION
ASSESSMENT AND PLANNING

History is shaped by the people who seek to preserve it.

—Susanna Kearsley[1]

. . . everything has a past. Everything—a person, an object, a word, everything. If you don't know the past, you can't understand the present and plan properly for the future.

—Chaim Potok (Potok, 1983, p. 10)

INTRODUCTION

Assessing and planning for the curation needs of born-digital materials is indeed planning for the future. How born-digital materials are preserved will matter to history. Collection development policies, acquisition processes, and archival collection assessment for traditional materials are well established in both theory and practice. Libraries and archives have developed and implemented such policies for years. Since the early days of digitization, libraries and archives have developed criteria for selecting appropriate collections and materials for conversion in an effort to fairly and transparently allocate limited resources to meet a huge latent demand for digitization. While and archives have been collecting born-digital material, not many have had a formal collection policy for born-digital materials.

Assessing born-digital collections includes all of the traditional appraisal steps, such as evaluating the collection content within the collection strategy of an organization, assessing the content for research use, and an assessment of originality and authenticity. Sone of these steps, within the digital context, may seem daunting to archivists and librarians. With traditional materials, developing the plans for conservation and storage is relatively straightforward; the processes are well established and well known. However, developing plans for born-digital materials is often idiosyncratic, based on the specifics of the storage media, the file format, and the infrastructure of the accessing organization.

Decisions made at acquisition will impact the collection for its lifecycle. As discussed in detail in Chapter 2, the lifecycles of data are path dependent; the decisions made at each stage determine what is available at the next (Rumsey, 2010; Wallis, Borgman, Mayernik, & Pepe, 2008). It is unclear "how (or whether) traditional archival policies apply to digital collections, and how these policies can be applied in bulk. . . . As digital collections become larger and more complex, we must identify ways that such archival policies can be applied so that they do not compromise efficiency" (Rosin, 2013, para. 23).

THEORETICAL OVERVIEW

Collection development policy and collection preservation policy are both important components of a good archival and/or library collection. Explicit collection policies create coherent and usable collections for the patrons, and preservation ensures sustainability over time for ongoing access and use (NISO, 2007). Neither good collection development nor preservation can happen in a vacuum. Collection development policies are set within the context of the organization: its mission, its goals, and its priorities. For born-digital materials, preservation also must be planned.

Traditionally, preservation planning can be defined as the "process by which the general and specific needs for the care of collections are determined, priorities are established, and resources for implementation are identified" (Kumar, 2011, p. 94). Preservation planning is an action plan for the long-term maintenance of the collection. This planning "defines a course of action that will allow an institution to set its present and future preservation agendas . . . [and] identifies the actions an institution will take and those it probably will never take so that resources can be allocated appropriately" (Ogden, n.d., para. 2). This definition holds up well when considering digital materials. Preservation planning can be even more important with digital materials because "the underlying data stream and/or the hardware and software that renders it will sooner or later be subject to change" (Schrimpf & Keitel, 2014, p. 208).

Collection development policies and the preservation planning process interact. Curatorial assessments of digital collection content need to be integrated with preservation decisions so that technical activities support curatorial requirements for the collections (Day, 2015). Acquisition decisions should consider the long-term preservation requirements of the materials. The acquisition process should consider the current state of the objects, the condition, and the manner in which the objects have been stored (DPC, 2017a). The organization needs to weigh the value of the acquisitions against the cost of preservation; the outcome of this cost-benefit analysis may be to decline to acquire (Child, n.d. b). "[H]eritage institutions should carefully consider how (or whether) traditional archival policies apply to digital collections, and how these policies can be applied in bulk . . . As digital collections become larger and more complex, we must identify ways that such archival policies can be applied so that they do not compromise efficiency" (Rosin, 2013, para. 27).

Many organizations developed their own preservation survey and assessment methodologies that have been designed specifically for their own needs to navigate across the organization and the various collections. For many large organizations, there is no single organizational view of collection development, collection assessment, or preservation planning. Each unit has its own needs and requirements. For example, the preservation unit in the Harvard University Libraries developed a model using four types of assessments: an environmental assessment, preservation assessments, collection surveys and assessments, and a preservation review (HLPP, 2017; HLPS, 2016). These assessments and surveys can be completed individually or as a set with the goal of developing disaster plans and preservation plans with priorities.

The environmental assessment reviews the condition of the physical space in which collections reside with the goal of identifying preservation risks due to avoidable environmental conditions. The preservation assessment focuses on the collections themselves; preservation assessments are often done by material type, such as photographs, documents, and so on. The preservation assessment provides advice to the collection managers about storage, handling, and metadata options. The collection survey reviews the condition of individual items; each item is then assessed with its condition and recommendations for treatment recorded. The collection survey is often part of a digitizing project. This preservation review is similar to the collection survey that includes a determination of the future use of the object and may include a recommendation for reformatting. The preservation review may be "triggered by research use, acquisition, exhibition or loan, collection transfer, or emergency recovery. This service enables the strategic use of both preservation and repository resources" (HLPS, 2016, para. 4).

Levels of Preservation Assessment

Assessing for preservation readiness is a significant aspect of preservation planning. The various types of preservation assessments can be customized for each library and archive to meet the needs of the specific institution and the collection. The various types of assessments can be conducted at any level of an institution: the organizational level, the collection level, and the individual item level (Child, n.d. a). Some of the preservation assessment processes are designed for an external reviewer while others are designed as self-assessment tools.

Organizational preservation assessment generally focuses on the capability and capacity of the organization by examining the organization's policies, structures, and infrastructure. *Readiness assessments* can evaluate the nature of the organization by reviewing the mission, goals, policies, and procedures; the structure of the organization, including its management, staffing, and finances; and its infrastructure by reviewing its technology for supporting digital content, metadata, digital preservation, and rights management (Bishoff & Rhodes, 2007). *Needs assessment* processes focus on articulating the preservation requirements of an organization based on its specific collections. The needs assessment survey evaluates policies and collections in order to develop a preservation action plan. This survey reviews policies, practices, and conditions of an organization. It evaluates the condition of the collections and determines the changes needed to improve the condition. It develops an action plan to implement those changes to improve the condition of the collections for long-term preservation (Ogden, n.d.). As the needs assessment surveys examine the organization and the collections, these assessments can be implemented in a number of ways. An organization has several options for its needs assessment. The organization may conduct the assessment for the entire organization and all of its collections, or it could conduct needs assessments for each of its units as separate organizations within the larger one. Because of the complex nature of the collections themselves, the organization could conduct needs assessments for each individual collection that meets specific criteria, to name but a few options.

Another high-level type of survey examines the physical conditions in which the objects will be stored; these are generally called environmental surveys. As with the needs assessment, the environmental survey can be implemented for the entire organization or specific archival units, depending on the size and requirements of the organization. An environmental survey looks at these specific physical conditions, such as temperature, humidity, light exposure, and so on. Conditions that undermine the preservation of materials can be mitigated; new glasses or shades to block the sun, dehumidifiers for removing excess humidity, and air conditioners to control temperature can be installed. The conditions can be monitored on an ongoing basis to maintain optimal conditions (Child, n.d. a).

Condition surveys are, as the name implies, a systematic review of the collections' holdings. Representative samples of individual items are examined to document the overall condition of the collection. The needs of material types (images, documents, etc.) and perhaps of specific items are recorded for further action (Child, n.d. a).

Preservation Assessment in a Digital Environment

As with traditional collections, preservation assessment in the digital environment occurs at multiple levels—the organization, the collection, and the item. As noted earlier, readiness assessments evaluate the organization's ability to support preservation. In the digital domain, readiness must include a repository system (see Chapter 6). It is virtually impossible to preserve digital content without a fully functional digital preservation repository that was built on the concepts and principles of the Open Archival Information System (OAIS) model.

The OAIS model emphasizes preservation planning. The preservation planning functional entity is prominent in the overview diagram (see Figure 1.2). It is conceptualized as an overarching function of management and technology. Preservation planning in the OAIS is a set of services and functions for monitoring the technical environment of the repository to determine if and when functionality must be upgraded, format migrations are required, or standards and policy need revision (CCSDS, 2012). As evidence of preservation planning, the standard for trusted digital repositories (ISO 16363/TDR) looks for "[p]reservation planning policies tied to formal or information technology watch(es); preservation planning or processes that are timed to shorter intervals (e.g., not more than five years); proof of frequent preservation planning/policy updates" (CCSDS, 2011). In many ways, the OAIS preservation planning function acts as an ongoing environmental survey. By implementing a process that monitors the technology environment for changes to file formats, storage technologies, application changes, and other elements that can impact the digital collections, the repository can react quickly to mitigate any risks to its content.

Preservation Assessment for New Digital Collections

New digital collections generally come to the library or archive via via a donor, often the person who created and collected the content or that person's heir. Since their inception, libraries and archives have worked with donors, and most have developed sophisticated agreements to document the wishes of the donor and the commitments of the organization. These agreements describe the contents, which contents can be made available immediately, which contents must be embargoed and the timeframe of that embargo, intellectual property rights of the materials, and so on. Many libraries and archivists have developed strategies "to accommodate the personalities of creators and provide the best possibility of strong digital archives collections" (Thomas, 2007, p. 2). Donor agreements need to be flexible to be able to deal with the peculiarities of any given situation.

The Donor Agreement

The donor agreement is a document that outlines the expectations of both the donor and the organization accepting the materials. It should be detailed, with assumptions made explicit, and written in clear language. Donor agreements cover issues of transfer, the rules of access, and the ongoing maintenance of the materials. Archives and libraries have used the donor agreements for decades for traditional collections. However, "language used in existing donor agreements is rarely specific enough to resolve the ethical issues" for digital materials (Lee, 2010, p. 59).

Many of the components of a donor agreement for digital collection will mirror those of a traditional collection as the nature of the contents of the collections is similar. Many of the same issues arise—copyright issues, transfer of materials, access issues, and privacy issues. However, there are differences. While copyright is an issue in both traditional and digital collections, digital collections may have added complications. Due to the nature of digital technologies, it may be difficult to know the copyright holder for any given file in a digital collection. Files may be inadvertently downloaded when browsing. They may belong to family members. They may be attachments from emails or other electronic communication technologies. Working with the donor to document as many of these issues as possible will facilitate processing the collection.

The process of transferring digital contents is logically similar to traditional materials, but logistically it is very different. The process for prioritizing content and developing a schedule for transfer is very similar. The donor and the curator determine the timeline by which materials should be transferred. But the mechanisms are very different. While it may be that digital devices and media are boxed up and transported by various means the materials are not really transferred until the media has been read and the data saved in the new technical environment. This transfer requires many decisions, which are technical, tedious, exacting, and time-consuming. Determining exactly what data to transfer is a significant issue with digital collections and may be the most difficult to make. It is possible to transfer the entire image of a device, that is, all of the files, the operating system, and file system information, as well as deleted files. Transferring the entire device image is a more complete view of the collection. It captures all of the history of all files. However, it may provide more information than the donor expects. It is also possible to transfer individual files or directories. This requires much more planning by the curator and donor as well as for the technicians who will do the transfer. However, it does give more control to the donor. Explaining the issues, reaching consensus, and documenting the decisions are important for the donor agreement for digital collections.

Access and embargo issues have some additional considerations for digital collections. Determining if there are any access rights to the collection and the timeframe that certain materials should be withheld from the public is very common in archival collections. Preserving the privacy of the living can be very important to donors. With digital collections, the nature of embargo can be extended; in addition to delaying the exposure because of the contents, files may be excluded based on file format. For example, a donor may want to protect financial information; all spreadsheet files should be archived and preserved but only accessible by researchers after an embargo. In another example, a donor may be willing to allow access to a PDF version of a document but limit the access to the original word processing versions of that file. This may be due to concerns over fixity because the word processing file could be modified or due to the ability to see the change history of the document. The access restrictions could be temporary; the donor may wish these files to be accessible to researchers after an embargo period. Embargo and access issues need to be discussed with donor.

New issues specifically associated with digital collections also need to be addressed. It is likely that curators will need the log-in identifiers and passwords for various digital devices, computers, applications, and services in order to access and transfer data. The donor needs to provide the access information, and the curators need to document these in the donor agreements. The donor might need to be reminded to change the ids and passwords for data and applications that are not being donated. Donor permission to reformat and copy files for access and preservation should be made explicit in the donor agreement.

In addition to carefully documenting the agreement with the donor, it can be very helpful to "[record] an interview (audio or video) with the creator or donor about their use of technology and their 'digital life'" (AIMS, 2012, p. 12). Future curators and researchers will be able to use the recordings for guidance when encountering technical and ethical issues not covered in the document.

Costs of Donated Collection

Estimating the cost of processing, ingesting, managing, and preserving new digital collections is difficult. During initial donor discussions, it is important to assess the collection for any unusual technologies, content display issues, or processing concerns. Some special considerations are the file formats of the born-digital materials, the overlap between born-digital and analog materials, the nature of any access restrictions to content, any legal restrictions or conditions to access the material, and the rate and frequency of data transfers (AIMS, 2012). As more decisions about the collection are made, the estimates of cost become more realistic. However, unexpected issues can arise that impact the costs.

Documenting the Acquisition and Preservation Plan

During a new collection assessment, curators will determine which files to accession based on collection policies, the donors' needs and desires, and curatorial experience and discretion. These decisions must be documented. Other decisions will be made as additional curators, managers, and technologists become involved in the process, such as decisions about formats, technologies, staffing, and so on. These decisions need to be documented as well. The results of these decisions should result in a plan to acquire and preserve the data.

All curation activities are set within an institutional context. Curatorial decisions can be influenced by the institutional setting; the options available to an academic library may be different than those available to a special collections archive or museum. Curatorial decisions are also influenced by previous decisions. Technology choices, such as the type of repository, storage, and interfaces, can limit or expand the curator's options. For example, if the organization has a turnkey vendor repository system, the file types allowed, the metadata formats, and the functionality for embargo may be limited. If the organization has as open source, expandable repository system, adding new file types and customizing embargo and access requirements may be possible. Staffing and financial resources are similarly context dependent.

When assessing a new digital collection, the curator must be concerned with preserving the content as well as accessioning it. Because the digital content should be ingested into the repository system at collection transfer, decisions about the internal organization, metadata, file formats, and technology strategies need to be addressed. These decisions need to be documented in a collection assessment and preservation plan. This document is a communication device to explain the decision, the rationale for this decision, and the impact of the decision. A collection assessment and preservation document should

- set the context of the institution and the collection;
- inventory the collection;
- define the accession criteria;
- determine the preservation strategy;

- define the level of metadata required;
- determine the access requirements;
- set the staffing; and
- determine the technology required.

TECHNICAL IMPLICATIONS

The repository can facilitate ongoing collection- and item-level preservation assessment. The quality assurance processes discussed at length in Chapter 5 provide a roadmap for such continuous assessment. Collection-level assessment is concerned with the consistency of treatment across the entire repository. Item-level assessment is concerned with the integrity of the digital files and the integrity of the digital object. File integrity includes file fixity, file format verification, and file format validation. Object integrity includes object completeness, metadata creation, metadata completeness, and derivative creation. Different collections may need different preservation assessment procedures (HLDPS, 2016). Preservation planners develop assessment plan based on their evaluation of the collection, its setting, and the requirements (Becker et al., 2009). Preservation planning in the repository is an ongoing process.

Implementing Preservation Planning

Preservation planning can seem rather abstract. It may be easier to understand in terms of a specific situation. For example, a repository uses TIFF 6.0 as its archival format for images. If a new version of that format is released, perhaps TIFF 7.0, that repository needs to be aware of that change, to understand the impact of that change to its archival objects, and make decisions about how to proceed.

Planets,[2] one of the European digital preservation research projects, has produced a very interesting model of digital preservation planning. The Planets Functional Model identifies three key preservation functions: watching, planning, and action. Preservation Watch is the logical equivalent of the environment survey discussed earlier. However, the environment for digital preservation involves the entire technology spectrum. Changes in the technology environment can have an impact on digital preservation. In order to detect these changes, *monitoring* various trusted sources to collect and analyze the information is the first step. The data analysis must include a risk analysis to determine the impact of the changes to the repository, the digital contents, and the metadata. Information about changes to formats, tools, and other issues should be encoded and stored in a database that the Planets Functional Model entitles as the Knowledge Base. In addition, the watch process includes developing a test bed as a "controlled environment for studying the operation of tools and services on content in controlled experiments, thereby facilitating the assessment of the capability of the tools and services for preservation purposes. Results are stored in the KNOWLEDGE BASE and these will inform the Preservation Planning activities" (Sierman & Wheatly, 2010, p. 10).

Preservation planning is based on the information gathered from the Preservation Watch. Using information in the Knowledge Base and from testing, the people responsible for planning determine which solutions would be best for the situation. The planning function also considers technology impacts on the longevity of the repository. All of the watching and planning lead to preservation actions. Characterizing the data, that is, determining the specific characteristics or features of a digital object, is one of the steps before many preservation actions. One of the main preservation actions is migration—moving from one file format to another, from one storage device to another, and from one technology to another. Preservation actions are developed as programs or scripts, which are then deployed (Sierman & Wheatly, 2010).

The Preservation Watch, the key element of the Planets Functional Model, has been adopted and/or modified by other preservation organizations. For example, the Digital Preservation Coalition's preservation planning process highlights a Technology Watch that includes defining the precipitating events that will initiate preservation actions and developing and populating a knowledge base to inform preservation activities (DPC, 2017b).

Implementing a technology environment watch program needs automation (Faria et al., 2013). The Scout system is an automated technology watch service that detects preservation risks and creates a centralized database about those risks (DPC, 2017b). The Scout system characterizes the content of the repository and monitors external sources looking for any changes. The Scout system would know that TIFF 6.0 is the archival format for images and would find the new version of the TIFF specification from any one of a number of format registries through many other sources. The Scout system would notify the preservation planners about this change (Faria, 2013). The British Library uses the Scout system in its preservation planning process (Day, 2015).

Technical Preservation Assessment for New Collections

New digital collections need to be assessed to discover the technical issues that will impact preservation. As files are the base unit of preservation, file formats are the most important element in the technical preservation assessment process. The format analysis reviews the collection to determine the range of file formats, the number of files of each format, and the condition of the files. This analysis can be efficiently and accurately completed using many of the tools developed for quality assessment and repository ingest (see Chapter 5) and digital forensics (see Chapter 10).

Defining Types of Born-Digital Materials

It is very difficult to get a list of all available file formats. Attempts to list them are generally incomplete either because of the dynamic nature of file formats because they come and go with alarming frequency or because the list focuses on a domain or a type of data, either research data or audio files. Efforts to categorize types of born-digital data are also limited for very similar reasons. One categorization of born-digital data found in libraries and archives may help curators:

- Digital photographs
- Digital documents
- Digital manuscripts
- Harvested web content
- Electronic records
- Static data sets
- Dynamic data
- Digital art
- Digital media publications (Erway, 2010)

This list is a good start; however, it may be helpful to add several categories to make it more comprehensive. It is important to remember that any of these categories can incorporate many types of file, file formats, rendering software, relationships, and metadata. Rather than using the term "digital photographs," a broader and more inclusive term would be "digital images." While digital photographs are the most common forms of digital images as they are taken with cameras, cell phones, tablets, and other ubiquitous electronic devices, many other types of digital images are widely created and used. Medical imaging produces a huge amount of data, X-rays, CAT scans, MRI scans, and so on that may require archiving. Other research enterprises use digital imaging as well: astronomy, biology, geology, and so forth.

Digital documents, of which digital manuscripts are a subset, include the text output of word processing programs regardless of format. In addition to the traditional fully formatted documents, much of life's ephemera may be digital, including notes, receipts, to-do lists, calendars, and so on. These digital equivalents of what used to be called *personal papers* can be in a wide variety of formats and in various web and mobile apps. Digital correspondence could be added as a subcategory to digital documents. Letters are frequently emails, texts, or chats.

Dynamic data is an interesting issue for curators. It is not clear if dynamic data can be considered archived if it is continually being updated. The needs of data that is actively being used and modified regularly can be better serviced when maintained in a traditional data processing environment with staff who deal with the issues of security, systems maintenance, transactional backup, server availability, and other production issues. A *snapshot* of dynamic data, that is, a copy of the data at a specific point in time, may be necessary either by regulatory or policy requirements. A snapshot is a suitable data set to be archived. It can be maintained in the repository with appropriate metadata.

There is no single way to deal with any of these materials within an archive. The treatment of materials depends on its context: Is this email part of the personal correspondence or a business record? It depends on the nature of content, the situation of its creation and use, and the intent of the creator. And, of course, at their most basic level, all of these types of digital materials are files, and these files need to be processed.

Assessing Formats

Digital libraries and archives develop policies about the types and formats of data that they accept. Some policies have a binary choice—a format is acceptable or it is not. Others are more nuanced; formats may have multiple levels of acceptance, such as preferred or allowed, depending on the type of object. A format may be acceptable for a delivery version but unacceptable for an archival version. Looking at still images as an example, a repository may prefer JPEG files for delivery and accept JPEG for archival version if no other format is available; it may accept a GIF as a deliver version but reject a GIF for an archival version.

Using the automated tools and the repository policies, curators should review the file formats in the new collection. The various file formats should be tallied and saved as a format inventory. Determining the overlap and gaps between the preferred, acceptable, unacceptable, and unknown (or not implemented) formats and the new collection helps the curator know what materials will be able to be preserved, what materials will be at higher risk, and what materials cannot be ingested at all. It may be that the gap between the file formats of the new collection and what is accepted is small; however, if the gap is large, the curator may need to reevaluate the feasibility of accessioning the collection. Depending on the importance of the collection, the resources for accessioning the collection, and the technical constraints of the repository, the curator may want to modify the policy and enhance the repository software to be able to handle additional formats.

PRACTICAL APPLICATION

While libraries and archives have made progress in preserving the output of their analog to digital conversion projects, most do not adequately curate their born-digital acquisitions. Most libraries and archives are storing the data on its original media in boxes on shelves (Nelson et al., 2012). The actual implementation of assessing, processing, and curating born-digital materials is difficult and expensive in terms of technology, time, and staffing.

Staffing Issues

Many libraries and archives staff their digital curation efforts with the existing staff who are trained to deal with digital materials, and some are able to get funding to hire new staff. Most libraries and archives would like to double the amount of stuff that they have allocated to digital curation (Atkins, Goethals, Kussmann, Phillips, & Vardigan, 2013). Many organizations have a large backlog of curation work especially dealing with the born-digital materials on devices in boxes. Allocating and prioritizing the work can reduce stress on the curation staff.

In some organizations, digital curation staff are dispersed among different departments, while in other organizations, there is a centralized digital curation unit.

Some organizations—the British Library, Stanford, University of Virginia, and Yale —have developed special teams for accessing born-digital collections and extracting the data from old technologies (Nelson et al., 2012). Each of these models has benefits and drawbacks, but either will work with the appropriate organizational culture and management. The amount of staffing required depends on the amount of data to curate and manage. Assessing the staffing needs for a digital curation program requires the organization to answer some difficult questions:

- Do you have staff specifically assigned to the digital collection initiative? Is staff from other parts of your organization involved in the digital collection initiative? What are the roles of the different individuals?

- What technology staff are involved in your project? Are they part of your organization, your parent organization, or another organization? What are their responsibilities in the digital initiative?

- What staff are involved in digital preservation activities, both within your organization and parent organization? Is technology staff involved in digital preservation? Is preservation staff involved? What roles do they play?

- What training do you provide staff involved in the digital initiative? What staff attend this training?

- What training in digital preservation do staff attend?

- Do you participate in a digital collaborative? What role does the collaborative play? What role do members of the collaborative play? (Bishoff & Rhodes, 2007, p. 2).

Accessioning Activities

To determine the amount and type of staff required, it is helpful to understand the details of the tasks involved. For accessioning new collections, a simple list of tasks could include the following:

- Initial content survey
- Initial technical survey
- Research capture scenarios
- Interaction with donor—scope
- Draft terms of agreement
- Capture materials
- Create accession record
- Ingest materials
- Ongoing support/dialog with donor (Redwine et al., 2013)

The tasks in the list vary from traditional archival assessments to highly technical; thus, the members of the team must have management, archival, and technical skills. A team of people is often required as no one person will have sufficient skills to do all of the tasks. The number of people required for any specific accessioning project will depend on the amount, the complexity, and the sensitivity of data.

Staffing Roles

Roles for staffing include archival, management, and technical. These are expanded here.

Archival Staffing—In order to accession any type of archival collections, including born-digital, subject specialists and curators need to evaluate and survey the material. Subject specialists and curators interact with the donors, help draft the donor agreement, process the collection, create metadata, and document the entire process.

Management Staffing—Accessioning new collections requires project planning skills, such as determining steps and milestones, budgeting, and staffing (Agnew, 2006). Once the project has been established, the project must have ongoing management—review of the schedule, identification and resolution of issues, and control for quality of the work.

Technical Staffing—Technical staff need to provide advice to curators and managers about various issues providing information about the benefits and drawbacks of each. Technology staff conduct the initial technical survey and file assessment. When born-digital collections arrive at a library or archive, the materials are stored on a wide variety of technologies—so many different technologies that it is rare that the hardware configurations are similar. Because of this variety, it is a technical challenge to access and read this data. The technical staff work with the repository and manage the ingest process.

SUMMARY

- Collection development policy and collection preservation policy are both important components of a good archival and/or library collection. Neither good collection development nor preservation can happen in a vacuum. Collection development policies are set within the context of the organization: its mission, its goals, and its priorities. For born-digital materials, preservation also must be planned.

- Collection development policies and the preservation planning process interact. Acquisition decisions should consider the long-term preservation requirements of the materials. The organization needs to weigh the value of the acquisitions against the cost of preservation.

- The donor agreement is a document that outlines the expectations of both the donor and the organization accepting the materials. It should be detailed, with assumptions made explicit, and written in clear language. Donor agreements cover issues of transfer, the rules of access, and the ongoing maintenance of the materials. Archives and libraries have used the donor agreements for decades for traditional collections.

- The collection assessment and preservation planning documents are communication devices to explain all of the curatorial decisions, the rationale for these decisions, and the impact of the decisions. A collection assessment and preservation document should set the context of the institution and the collection, inventory the collection, define the accession criteria, determine the preservation strategy, define the level of metadata required, determine the access requirements, set the staffing, and determine the technology required.

- The technology assessment for each born-digital collection needs to account for the various types of equipment as well as the file formats found. Determining the overlap and gaps between the repository policies and the actual collection will help curators decide how to process the collection.

- The tasks required to accession a born-digital collection range from traditional archival assessments to highly technical; thus, the members of the team must have management, archival, and technical skills. No one person will have sufficient skills to do all of the tasks. The number of people required for any specific accessioning project will depend on the amount, the complexity, and the sensitivity of data.

Questions for Discussion

1. How are traditional collections assessments similar to digital collection assessments?

2. How are traditional collections assessments different than digital collection assessments?

3. What issues could you see arising when dealing with a collection donor?

4. What technical issues need to be assessed during the collection assessment process?

NOTES

1. https://www.brainyquote.com/quotes/quotes/s/susannakea728987.html

2. More information about Planets (Preservation and long-term access through networked services) found at http://www.planets-project.eu/

REFERENCES

Agnew, G. (2006). *Staffing roles for digital collection building*. Rutgers University Libraries.

AIMS Working Group (AIMS). (2012). *AIMS born-digital collections: An inter-institutional model for stewardship*. Found at https://dcs.library.virginia.edu/files/2013/02/AIMS _final_text.pdf

Atkins, W., Goethals, A., Kussmann, C., Phillips, M., & Vardigan, M. (2013). *Staffing for effective digital preservation: An NDSA report*. Found at http://www.digitalpreservation. gov/documents/NDSA-Staffing-Survey-Report-Final122013.pdf

Becker, C., Kulovits, H., Guttenbrunner, M., Strodl, S., Rauber, A., & Hofman, H. (2009). Systematic planning for digital preservation: Evaluating potential strategies and building preservation plans. *International Journal on Digital Libraries*, *10*(4), 133–157. Found at https://publik.tuwien.ac.at/files/PubDat_180752.pdf

Bishoff, L., & Rhodes, E. (2007). *Planning for digital preservation: A self-assessment tool questions*. Northeast Document Conservation Center. Found at https://www.nedcc.org/ assets/media/documents/DigitalPreservationSelfAssessmentfinal.pdf

Child, M. (n.d. a). 1.2 Preservation assessment and planning. In *Planning and Prioritizing*. Northeast Document Conservation Center. Found at https://www.nedcc.org/free

-resources/preservation-leaflets/1.-planning-and-prioritizing/1.2-preservation-assessment
-and-planning

Child, M. (n.d. b). 1.5 Collections policies and preservation. In *Planning and Prioritizing*.
North East Document Conservation Center. Found at https://www.nedcc.org/free
-resources/preservation-leaflets/1.-planning-and-prioritizing/1.5-collections-policies
-and-preservation

Consultative Committee for Space Data Systems (CCSDS). (2011). *Audit and certification
of trustworthy digital repositories: Recommended practice*. CCSDS 652.0-M-1 (Magenta
Book). Found at https://public.ccsds.org/pubs/652x0m1.pdf

Consultative Committee for Space Data Systems (CCSDS). (2012). *Reference model for an
Open Archival Information System (OAIS)*. Issue 2. Recommendation for Space Data
System Standards (Magenta Book), CCSDS 650.0-M-2. Washington, DC: ISO
14721:2012. Found at http://public.ccsds.org/publications/archive/650x0m2.pdf

Day, M. (2015). *Preservation planning at the British Library*. Presented at the ABD-BVD—
INFORUM 2015 Brussels, June 4. Found at https://www.slideshare.net/michaelday/
preservation-planning-at-the-bl

Digital Preservation Coalition (DPC). (2017a). *DPC 12-step questionnaire template*. Found
at http://www.dpconline.org/component/docman/?task=doc_download&gid=1493

Digital Preservation Coalition (DPC). (2017b). Preservation planning. In *Digital
Preservation Handbook*. Found at http://www.dpconline.org/handbook/organisational-
activities/preservation-planning

Erway, R. (2010). Defining "Born digital." *OCLC Research*. Found at https://www.oclc.org/
content/dam/research/activities/hiddencollections/borndigital.pdf

Faria, L. (2013). *Scout—A preservation watch system*. Found at http://openpreservation.org/
blog/2013/12/16/scout-preservation-watch-system

Faria, L., Akbik, A., Sierman, B., Ras, M., Ferreira, M., & Ramalho, J. C. (2013).
Automatic preservation watch using information extraction on the web: A case study
on semantic extraction of natural language for digital preservation. In *iPRES 2013—
10th International Conference on Preservation of Digital Objects* (pp. 215–224).
Biblioteca Nacional de Portugal.

Harvard Library Digital Preservation Services (HLDPS). (2016). Format assessments.
In *Harvard Library Digital Preservation Services Wiki*. Found at https://wiki.harvard.
edu/confluence/display/digitalpreservation/Format+Assessments

Harvard Library Preservation Services (HLPS). (2016). *Surveys and assessments*. Found at
http://library.harvard.edu/preservation/surveys-and-assessments

Harvard Library Preservation Program (HLPP). (2017). Digital preservation services. In
Harvard Library Digital Preservation Services Wiki. Found at https://wiki.harvard.edu/
confluence/display/digitalpreservation/Harvard+Library+Digital+Preservation+Services
+Wiki

Kumar, S. (2011). *Archives principles and practices*. Gyan Publishing House.

Lee, C. (2010). Donor agreements. In M. Kirschenbaum, R. Ovenden, G. Redwine, & R.
Donahue, *Digital forensics and born-digital content in cultural heritage collections*. Council
on Library and Information Resources: Washington, DC. Found at https://www.clir.
org/pubs/reports/pub149/

Nelson, N. L., Shaw, S., Deromedi, N., Shallcross, M., Ghering, C., Schmidt, L., . . . Pyatt,
T. (2012). *Managing born-digital special collections and archival materials*. SPEC Kit 329.
Association of Research Libraries. Found at http://publications.arl.org/Managing-Born
-Digital-Special-Collections-and-Archival-Materials-SPEC-Kit-329

NISO Framework Working Group (NISO). (2007). *A framework of guidance for building good digital collections.* Found at http://www.niso.org/publications/rp/framer work3.pdf

Ogden, S. (n.d.). 1.1 What is preservation planning? In *Planning and Prioritizing.* Northeast Document Conservation Center. Found at https://www.nedcc.org/free -resources/preservation-leaflets/1.-planning-and-prioritizing/1.1-what-is-preservation -planning

Potok, C. (1983). *Davita's harp.* New York: Random House.

Redwine, G., Barnard, M., Donovan, K. M., Farr, E., Forstrom, M., Hansen, W. M., . . . Thomas, S. E. (2013). *Born digital: Guidance for donors, dealers, and archival repositories.* Washington, DC: Council on Library and Information Resources. Found at https://www.clir.org/wp-content/uploads/sites/9/pub159.pdf

Rosin, L. (2013). Applying theoretical archival principles and policies to actual born-digital collections. *National Library of New Zealand.* Found at http://www.archivejournal.net/ notes/applying-theoretical-archival-principles-and-policies-to-actual-born-digital -collections/

Rumsey, A. S. (2010). *Sustainable economics for a digital planet: Ensuring long-term access to digital information. Final report of the Blue Ribbon Task Force on Sustainable Digital Preservation and Access.* Washington, DC: National Science Foundation (NSF Award No. OCI 0737721). Found at http://brtf.sdsc.edu/biblio/BRTF_Final_Report.pdf

Schrimpf, S., & Keitel, C. (2014). Nestor guideline for preservation planning—A process model. *Liber Quarterly, 23*(3), 201–213. Found at http://doi.org/10.18352/lq.9166

Sierman, B., & Wheatly, P. (2010). *Evaluation of preservation planning within OAIS, based on the Planets Functional Model* (Report IST-2006-033789). Found at http://www .planets-project.eu/docs/reports/Planets_PP7-D6_EvaluationOfPPWithinOAIS.pdf

Thomas, S. (2007). *PARADIGM: A practical approach to the preservation of personal digital archives.* Bodleian Library. Found at http://www.paradigm.ac.uk/projectdocs/ jiscreports/ParadigmFinalReportv1.pdf

Wallis, J., Borgman, C., Mayernik, M., & Pepe, A. (2008). Moving archival practices upstream: An exploration of the life cycle of ecological sensing data in collaborative field research. *International Journal of Digital Curation, 1*(3), 114–126. Found at citeulike -article-id: 6338125

Section IV

Preservation in Practice

Chapter 10

CONSIDERATIONS IN
ARCHIVING PERSONAL DATA

Our technologised [sic] *society is becoming opaque. As technology becomes more ubiquitous and our relationship with digital devices ever more seamless, our technical infrastructure seems to be increasingly intangible.*

—Honor Harger[1]

INTRODUCTION

"Our photo albums, letters, home movies and paper documents are a vital link to the past. Personal information we create today has the same value. The only difference is that much of it is now digital. Chances are that you want to keep some digital photos, email and other files so that you—and your family—can look at them in the future" (LOC, n.d.).

Personal archiving is the process of preserving an individual's family life, personal life, and professional life as a legacy for future generations. This includes both physical objects and digital materials, both born digital and reformatted to digital, such as photographs, old records, financial records, and personal correspondence. Boxes of papers and photos tucked in the corner of the attic, a ledger book found on the shelf in the basement, an envelope caught in the back of a drawer in old desk: these accidents of happenstance have preserved some of our history. A pack rat relative who could not throw things away provided a window into the past. Because nothing bad happened—no flooding, no fires—the content of this material was saved.[2] As our history is recorded digitally via electronic documents, digital photographs, and social media, the boxes in the attic will be filled with obsolete, broken, and useless technical devices, such as computers, cell phones, personal digital assistants (PDAs), and removable storage media. Even more difficult to access is the "digital attic" of cloud-based storage services, such as Google drive and Dropbox, web and mobile applications, such as Outlook, Google Calendar, and thousands of others that hold our personal histories. These technologies are incredibly convenient and useful and completely opaque and intangible.

Over the past 20 years, libraries and archives have developed a research agenda, a set of best practices, and implemented systems and procedures to archive and preserve their own digital materials; they have done a good job preserving their own born-digital and digitally converted data. However, only a small fraction of the personal digital material has been archived (DPC, 2015). The Library of Congress believes that the work that libraries and archives have done can scale down to the individual level and wants libraries and archives to help everyone in America to learn about digital preservation and to have tools and best practices to preserve their own data (Ashenfleder, 2012).

THEORETICAL

Personal digital archives, the modern equivalent of a collection of personal papers, can be defined as the "informal, diverse, and expanding memory collections created or acquired and accumulated and maintained by individuals in the course of their personal lives" (Williams, John, & Rowland, 2009, p. 341). Personal digital materials came into existence when computing technologies were made available to the general public. While the first personal computer was built in 1971 and a variety of computerized game systems were available, it was not until Apple in 1977 and IBM in 1981 released consumer-friendly computers that individuals were able to create digital content (IBM, 2011; Rawlinson, 2017; Wilson, 2015). Libraries and archives began receiving personal digital archives soon thereafter. Many were not sure what to do with these materials; as many of the documents had also been printed, archivists decided to leave the computers and removable storage media in boxes on the shelf. However, as the number of collections with personal digital material continues to grow, librarians and archivists realized that this was not a sustainable model. As an example, the British library decided in early 2000 that they needed to develop new processes for dealing with personal digital archives as they got a very large collection, the W. D. Hamilton Archive, which had a variety of computers and media devices (Williams et al., 2009). The concept of digital curation was expanded to include personal digital archives.

Personal Information Management

Personal information management is the process by which personal digital archives are built. Personal information management is the work of managing and organizing one's digital files; this includes where the files are stored, what the files contain, when the files were created, and why the files were created and saved. It is rare for an individual to create truly intentional personal digital archive; saving digital material may seem arbitrary and chaotic. People keep digital materials for any number of reasons "that may be simultaneously sentimental, practical, and even accidental ... Personal digital archives contain files that capture both the mundane and the extraordinary, and represent moments that people may want to remember forever, as well as some that a person may wish had never happened" (Redwine, 2015, p. 2). Personal information management includes physical, digitally converted, and born-digital materials. This discussion will focus on the digital materials. Types of digital materials include photographs, personal correspondence in email and word processing documents, financial information in documents, spreadsheets, tax software, and online applications.

Managing personal digital archives is very challenging due to the very nature of personal data; it is generated by and stored in a wide variety of computing devices. The files can be rapidly and almost invisibly copied between different devices and application resulting in multiple copies in many different digital places. Digital photographs can be created with a digital camera or a cell phone. The images on the digital camera could be stored on a secure digital (SD) card. The images taken with the cell phone are stored within the phone, but depending on the type of phone, the images may also be automatically synced with the Google or Apple cloud. The photographer may transfer the images on the SD card to his or her personal computer and/or to a cloud data storage provider. The photographer may upload some of the photos to a professional website, Facebook page, Twitter feed, and Instagram account, as well as a personal version of all of those applications (for more on personal data in social media applications, see Chapter 11).

An inventory of the applications, services, processes, and hardware used to create, store, and maintain digital materials may be the best way for individuals to document their personal information environment. Such an inventory would be an invaluable help to digital curators (Redwine et al., 2013).

Personal Information Environment

Format is a key factor in long-term preservation, but for personal information management, the device, service, and/or application may have a bigger impact on the ability to access and extract data. Individuals may not have any idea where their data actually resides. For both cell phones and tablets, the operating system and the service provider have a great influence on where and how the data is stored. Android devices store important information in the Google cloud, while iOS devices use the Apple cloud. Depending on which messaging applications are used, the data may be stored on the device, in the Internet service providers' storage cloud, or another third-party storage technology. To add to the complexity, mobile applications will use internal storage, their own organization's storage, or a commercial third-party cloud storage provider.

Personal Devices: Computer, Tablets, and Phones

Over the past 10 years, the difference between a personal computer, a laptop, a tablet, and a phone has narrowed significantly. The connectivity, functionality, and the computational power and speed have begun to converge. With shared application infrastructures, people are able to access and distribute their data on any of their devices, whichever was available at the moment. A recent study shows that from "a system-wide view, these [information management] practices were not distinct but interwoven in their narratives as they described their data, devices, and choices holistically" (Vertesi, Kaye, Jarosewski, Khovanskaya, & Song, 2016, p. 478). However, the ability to extract and manage data between these devices can be very different.

Data on a personal or laptop computer is controlled by the individual owner. Decisions on data management (see Chapter 7) are made by the individual. However, data in mobile personal devices, such as cell phones and tablets, is opaque and controlled by various service providers: the operating system provider, the Internet service provider, or the application provider. With mobile devices, the data files are hidden. It is very difficult for the average user to find, much less organized, the data files.

Cell phones are handheld telecommunications computers. Of course, cell phones place calls, but most also have textual base communications capabilities, such as text messaging using Short Message Service (SMS) and Multimedia Messaging Service (MMS), instant messaging, email, and web browsing (Ayers, Jansen, Cilleros, & Daniellou, 2005). To manage these communications, cell phones have personal information management applications, such as phone books or contacts lists. Besides call information, data that can be extracted from a cell phone includes photos, videos, the content of texts, contact information, all GPS location history, and emails, as well as information about apps with access to bank accounts and other financial data. Many software packages, both open source and commercial, exist that can copy the data.

The modern tablet computer is a portable computer with a touchscreen interface that is larger than a cell phone and smaller than a laptop computer. The first tablet computers were prototyped in the late 1960s by Alan Kay of Xerox, the first who sketched out the idea in 1971; the first widely sold tablet computer was Apple Computer's Newton (Strickland, 2017). Tablets have the same type of application data as a cell phone. As with cell phones, software is available to extract data.

Personal Information Management Systems

The term *personal information systems* has two very different definitions. One is application based and refers to tools to manage tasks, calendars, appointments, and contacts (Technopedia, 2017). The second definition focuses on the complex personal information environment:

> Personal Information Management Systems (or PIMS) are systems that help give individuals more control over their personal data. PIMS allow individuals to manage their personal data in secure, local or online storage systems and share them when and with whom they choose. Providers of online services and advertisers will need to interact with the PIMS if they plan to process individuals' data. This can enable a human centric approach to personal information and new business models. (EDPS, 2017)

This second definition, managing our information across the web, is the focus of this section.

The social media services that people use, Facebook, Google, Twitter, and so on, provide functionality, computational platforms, and storage; both the software and the hardware are controlled by the service provider. There is a growing movement to reclaim control from these organizations. Tim Berners-Lee has said:

> I would like us to build a world in which I have control of my data ... if you put together all the data from my wearable, my house, from companies like the credit card company and the banks, from all the social networks, I can give my computer a good view of my life. And I can use that. That information is more valuable to me than it is to the cloud. (Hern, 2014)

Personal information management is an active area of research in computer and information science. One proposal is to separate the hardware service from the software service. The consumer could choose an app based on function and a separate hardware platform on which to run that app. "This would therefore bring together, on a personal server, all this user's favorite applications and all the user's data that is currently distributed, fragmented, and isolated" (Abiteboul, André, & Kaplan, 2015, p. 33). In this model, the consumers buy or lease a server, install software and must manage the operating system and the software (Abiteboul et al., 2015). Another research project is Databox, an open source personal networked device that manages personal data by collecting and organizing access points to data in the cloud. It allows individuals to determine which external applications get access to the data. It adds a layer of control over cloud data (Mortier et al., 2016). There are other efforts to developing methodologies for indexing and tracking the personal data held by third parties (Chaudhry et al., 2015).

TECHNICAL

The technical challenges for preserving personal archives are primarily at the data acquisition level, that is, how digital curators actually get to the data from old computers, old storage media, and third-party applications and storage providers.

Data Salvage

Archivists and librarians care deeply about preserving our current history to make it available in the future. It will not be possible to preserve material that is not accessible. Therefore, it is the job of librarians and archivists to help individuals learn to preserve their personal history. They deal with these issues regularly. When a library is presented with a box of computing and storage devices, a process to recover that data, to salvage that data must be planned. As discussed in Chapter 8, data recovery is the process of retrieving and restoring data. Generally, data recovery is a planned process for restoring data from backup media. Data salvage, on the other hand, is the process of retrieving data from old and/or damaged devices and media. The following is an example of a problem that a digital curator would face. This is an email to a curation listserv:

I wonder whether I could draw on the collective wisdom of the list, please: We are trying to recover ... data from a couple of old computers and are looking for an organisation [sic] that would be able to attempt the data recovery for us. Please see below for details:

10MB Hard Drive, 720k 5.25" floppy and DOS 3.3 and an Apple Macintosh Proforma 6200 (vintage 1995/6). The machines are complete but we cannot say when they were last powered on. Both are believed to contain ... data which we would like to recover and possibly preserve.

I'm afraid we don't have any details as to the data types and formats we are to expect on these computers. I'd be very grateful for any pointers that would help us find an organisation [sic] that could assist in the save recovery of the data on these machines.

The organization in this email is looking to find an outsourcing option to recover its data. For a rarely occurring scenario, this is a reasonable course of action. But many libraries and archives find themselves dealing with boxes of old computers and storage media. Data can be salvaged from such storage devices as cell phones, tablets, PDAs, internal or external hard disk drives (HDDs), solid-state drives (SSDs), USB flash drives, magnetic tapes, CDs, DVDs, RAID subsystems, and other electronic devices (DS, 2017). But preservation needs more than merely salvaging the data. Preservation requires organization, descriptions, authenticity, and integrity. These physical storage devices need to be accessioned just as any other object would be. Each physical storage device needs to be assigned an inventory number and described; media metadata would include information on the label type of media: manufacturer, size, and so on. During the object accession process, the curator should ensure that the physical media has been write protected; that is, the curator must ensure that no one can write new data on the media.

Digital Forensics

During the same time that information science researchers, librarians, and archivists were developing theories and best practices for digital curation, the legal professionals, including judges, lawyers, and law enforcement professionals, had similar, yet different, concerns about acquiring, preserving, and using digital content as evidence. Preserving digital content in perpetuity, what libraries and archives aim to do, has a much longer timeframe than preserving evidence. However, authenticity, integrity, organization, and description are equally important to both.

While librarians and archivists were concerned with repository systems, workflows, and data integrity, the legal profession was interested in acquiring data from computers and storage media. This acquisition process includes tracing the evolution of files, extracting information from email systems, databases, and other proprietary systems all without making any changes to the files, the file system data, or the system logs. The legal profession calls this process digital forensics. Digital forensics can be defined as:

The application of computer science and investigative procedures for a legal purpose involving the analysis of digital evidence after proper search authority, chain of custody, validation with mathematics, use of validated tools, repeatability, reporting, and possible expert presentation. (Zatyko, 2008, para. 3)

Digital forensics is the process by which evidence of criminal activity on computers is collected. It is the process of discovering, authenticating, and analyzing data—very much an aspect of curation. It started as a process to catch white-collar criminals. The methods developed in forensics can help curators when they get personal digital archives delivered to their archive, when a box of hard drives, floppy disks, CDs, e-readers, cell phones, tablets, and other data-rich devices are dumped in a box for a curator to figure out.

Digital forensics can be very useful for digital libraries and archives. While much of the terminology has been developed by law enforcement, the tools can support digital curation. Many tools, some open source, can be modified and used in a digital repository environment.

Technical Issues in Digital Forensics

Edmond Locard, a pioneer of forensic science and criminology in the early to mid-20th century, is credited with discovering cross-transfer of evidence. He noted that criminals leave evidence, traces of themselves, whenever they interact with a victim or an object at the crime scene (Nickell & Fischer, 1999; Redwine et al., 2013). in front of Redwine here. Detecting and gathering trace evidence is now a staple of physical forensics. The same principle is also true in digital forensics. Any time someone opens a file, opens an application, or clicks on a link, a log is written, a database is updated, and a trace is left. This poses a problem for both digital curators and digital forensics investigators; their actions also leave traces. These traces can change data, thus corrupting the evidence and impacting the authenticity of the object.

In several areas, trace evidence is important to both digital forensics investigators and digital curators: logs, memory/cache, and files. Log files track activity on a computer; many applications write every action to a log. This log may be an external file or internal to the document or data. These logs allow the application to *undo* actions, restore data after an interruption, and help customize the application for the user. For example, Microsoft applications log all of the keystrokes and actions taken. When a user makes a mistake, the application allows the user to back out of or undo keystrokes. Web browsers use cookies to maintain small bits of information about the user's interactions as well as logs to track specific activities. Trace evidence is also accumulated in the computer's main and cache memory.

The most significant curatorial issues about trace evidence concern the file system. Every action taken to a file is recorded in the file system; when a file is opened, the file system records the date and time and (possibly) the user ID. When a file is changed, the file system records the date and time of the change, the user ID, and the size of the file. When digital curators need to salvage data, they want to ensure that the files have not been altered in the file transfer from the old equipment to the new equipment. The transfer process should not change the file system information: who last opened the file, when the file was created, and when the file was last changed.

Tools for Safe Data Extraction

Many tools, both software and hardware, have been developed for digital forensics to ensure that trace evidence is not modified by the act of accessing and copying the data. Some of the data extraction software applications can be used in stand-alone environment or are built into tools for reading the various storage media. Most organizations do not maintain a stock of old floppy disk and CD/DVD readers or have computers with SCSI adapters for old removable hard drives. A number of hybrid hardware devices have been developed that can read multiple types of storage media. Sometimes called *Rosetta* systems, these devices had the appropriate device drivers and other components to extract data from many different storage media. These devices include software to extract data without changing any of the underlying files. An increasing number of large academic libraries have been acquiring these types of systems to be able to extract data from old media devices. Stanford and Yale are two such libraries.

The output of the data extraction process is generally what is called a forensic image, an exact bit-level copy of the entire storage device. The forensic image file should be named with the inventory number of the physical device. The data extraction process should immediately generate a fixity hash to ensure integrity. Different tools use different file formats for the forensic image. The three most common formats are the following:

- Raw/DD format is used in a number of forensic, virtualization, and other tools. The format does not support metadata and fixity hash data.
- Encase evidence format is a proprietary format.
- Advanced Forensic Format (AFF) supports metadata and fixity hash data but is not widely supported.

Determine Scope of Capture

Creating the forensics image of the storage media is the first step for digital curators. A forensic image is not a user-friendly review of the data. Many decisions need to be made about the scope of what information will be accessible and usable. Often, the data on the storage device is fragmented; some of the data is generally not suitable for humans to view. Determining what data needs to be reconstructed and usable requires policy and process.

The data on a forensic image could be of three types: user data, software, and log data. User data is the primary content collected and created by the user and includes documents, images, audio, video, email, and so on. Software includes the operating system, applications, and other code. Log data, information about the users' application and online activities, includes browser cache, cookies, registry entries, and so on. The curator needs to determine which of these files can and should be made public. Issues of copyright and licensing for software need to be addressed.

Questions about the appropriateness of log data being available need to be answered. Will the log data support the understanding for the academic user, or will it just be an invasion of the users' privacy?

Ethical Concerns in Data Salvage

Curators are aware of the ethical issues when processing collections of personal papers. Ethical guidelines have been developed by professional societies and individual institutions. Deeds of gift, the contract transferring ownership from the individual to the archive, can outline access restrictions, if any, which the data owner wishes to impose. The donor, the person contributing the personal data to the archive, may not understand how much data is available or the various technology devices in the collection. The curator is ethically obliged to help the donor understand the issues with technology:

> Be aware that any digital materials that you donate, including computers, computer disks, and other digital storage media, may contain passwords, web browsing history, other users' files, and copies of seemingly deleted files. Whether or not these files are apparent to researchers will depend on the initial method of transfer and on the repository's access policies and procedures for handling digital material, which may change over time as technology evolves. Discuss any concerns about deleted content with the archivist or curator. (SAA, 2013, para. 12)

The deed of gift needs to discuss issues of reconstructing or reviving deleted files. Computer files are not really deleted. When files are *deleted* through an application or directly through the file system, the file names and the pointers in the file system table are deleted, but the data still exists on the file until it is overwritten by other data. Deleted files that are located in unallocated space that have yet to be overwritten can be retrieved using various applications. Some applications use an overwrite protocol, using zeros and ones to overwrite data onto all sectors of the device, to effectively delete the data. However, even when the data is overwritten, it is possible to rebuild the data.

Looking at deleted information could be very useful to researchers. Researchers use sophisticated technologies, such as electron microscopes and mass spectrometers, to analyze erasures and cross-outs on physical manuscripts. Forensics tools are the digital equivalent and can be used to further scholarly study, which is the equivalent of looking at the paper manuscripts seeing the edits, comments, marginalia, and so on. Is it unethical for researchers to circumvent the original intent of the owner by retrieving and re-creating deleted digital content? As mentioned previously, files are not necessarily collected rationally; were the deleted files intentionally deleted for posterity or just to clean up the file folder? Who decides the original intent of the owner?

Provenance

Provenance refers to the history of an object. In the art world, provenance involves keeping a record of ownership; the means of ownership transfer, such as inheritance, sale through dealer, and auction, among others; locations through its history; conservation activities such as X-rays, infrared photography; and other processes (Flescher, Duffy-Zeballos, Goldman, & Boddewyn, n.d.). In digital curation, provenance also refers to the history of an object. While the data documenting ownership is similar, the method of ownership transfer and the conservation methods are very different. For personal collections, provenance can be particularly important for assuring the authenticity and originality of the data. With appropriate provenance information, the archive can document the circumstances in which the files were acquired, whether they were acquired by the data creator, a family member, or a subsequent owner. By documenting the data recovery process, the librarian and archivist establishes that the files are authentic and the data is unchanged data. The provenance documentation can describe the computing environment in which the digital records were created and stored, including the specific storage devices.

For evidentiary materials, providence, the chain of custody, became a legal term used to describe who has had custody of and/or touched the materials.

> This involves keeping a log of every person who had physical custody of the evidence, documenting the actions that they performed on the evidence and at what time, storing the evidence in a secure location when it is not being used, making a copy of the evidence and performing examination and analysis using only the copied evidence, and verifying the integrity of the original and copied evidence. If it is unclear whether or not evidence needs to be preserved, by default it generally should be preserved. (Kent, Chevalier, Grance, & Dang, 2006, pp. 3–4)

PRACTICE

For most people, personal information management, building personal digital archives, and preservation planning are not high-priority activities. Digital materials are saved by happenstance rather than by design. Building and preserving personal digital archives need to become a regularized and rational process (Becker et al., 2009).

> An important part of personal digital archiving involves determining, either individually or with the help of a curatorial institution, which parts of an individual's "digital stuff" are worth trying to save permanently. The more actively one selects, manages and cares for personal digital archives, the more likely those are to survive the ravages of time on technology. Similarly, the more control an individual has over their personal archives, the greater their ability to save only what they intend. (Redwine, 2015, p. 2)

Librarians and archivists are creating outreach programs to teach the public about preserving their own personal data. These outreach programs are designed to raise awareness of the issues of perseveration without overwhelming people with technical details. The goal is to simplify the process and help people make better choices about their data.

Library of Congress Personal Archiving Initiatives

The Library of Congress began offering advice on personal archiving in 2007. Over time, the single web page has become a full-fledged program to help the general public and provide materials for local libraries and other cultural organizations to help their patrons with personal archiving. The Library of Congress focused on providing basic guidance that gives the nonspecialist some ideas for getting started (Ashenfleder, 2016; LeFurgy, 2013).

Getting Started

The best practice for personal archiving developed by the Library of Congress is based on the institutional best practice. This best practice is framed as four steps to get started, a process for initiating personal information management:

- Identify thing to be saved.
- Decide what to keep.
- Organize files.
- Store in multiple locations (Lazorchak, 2013).

The Library of Congress gives very specific advice on data storage. They recommend following what is commonly known as the "professional photographers' 3-2-1 rule." Each file should have three copies saved on at least two different types of storage with one copy saved in a different (remote) location (Johnston, 2013). For example, each digital photograph file would have three copies—one copy on the hard drive of the personal computer, one on an SD card, and one copy on a flash drive stored at the owner's business.

While using multiple media types does increase the probability that the data will be usable in the future, it also increases the complexity of managing the media. Using removable media like SD cards, flash drives, CDs/DVDs is the piece management. Having an inventory on a spreadsheet that lists the devices and their locations and contents is very helpful for estate planning as well as digital preservation. Using cloud storage for one copy makes sense. Cloud services should be included in the inventory.

Personal Digital Archiving Day Kit

Helping local libraries and other cultural organizations conduct workshops is another aspect of the personal archiving initiative of the Library of Congress. A complete kit is available to help libraries plan, organize, publicize, and execute a Personal Digital Archiving Day workshop. Posters, fliers, evaluation form, handouts, videos, and activities are all downloadable from the site. Examples of some of the materials are the following:

- Keeping personal photographs guidance
- Keeping personal audio guidance

- Keeping personal video guidance
- Keeping personal electronic mail
- Personal digital records
- Keeping personal websites, blogs, and social media

ALA Preservation Week

Since 2005, the American Library Association's (ALA) division, Association for Library Collections and Technical Services (ALCTS), has sponsored Preservation Week. The goal of Preservation Week is to "inspire actions to preserve personal, family, and community collections, in addition to library, museum and archive collections . . . [and] . . . raise awareness of the role libraries and other cultural institutions can play in providing ongoing preservation information" (ALCTS, n.d.). Like the Library of Congress, ALCTS has developed a full set of handouts, program support materials, planning aids, and so on. Preservation Week focuses on preservation of all types of materials but includes digital preservation. Both ALA and Library of Congress encourage libraries to include Personal Archiving in Preservation Week.

SUMMARY

- Personal archiving is the process of preserving an individual's family life, personal life, and professional life as a legacy for future generations. This includes both physical objects and digital materials, both born digital and reformatted to digital, such as photographs, old records, financial records, and personal correspondence.
- Managing personal digital archives is very challenging due to the very nature of personal data. It is generated by and stored in a wide variety of computing devices and Internet services. The files can be rapidly and almost invisibly copied between different devices and applications, resulting in multiple copies in many different digital places.
- Libraries and archives can use digital forensics tools and processes to discover, authenticate, and analyze data from old or broken computing and storage devices. Many tools, both software and hardware, have been developed for digital forensics to ensure that trace evidence is not modified by the act of accessing and copying the data. Some of the data extraction software applications can be used in stand-alone environment or are built into tools for reading the various storage media.
- To help teach the public about these issues of curating their own digital materials, librarians and archivists are creating outreach programs. These outreach programs are designed to raise awareness of the issues of perseveration without overwhelming people with technical details. The goal is to simplify the process and help people make better choice about their data. The Library of Congress and ALA's ALCTS have developed tools to help libraries and archives plan, organize, and run workshops.

> ## Questions for Discussion
>
> 1. What do you see as the primary issues in curating your own personal digital archive?
> 2. What do you see as the primary issues that libraries and archives face in preserving personal digital archives?
> 3. Under what circumstances would you allow researchers to get access to the underlying data to try to recover deleted files?

NOTES

1. https://www.brainyquote.com/quotes/quotes/h/honorharge560011.html
2. This, indeed, happened in my own family. Upon my uncle's death, we found a large box filled with many hundreds of photographs of my grandparents and my great-grandparents. Included in this treasure trove were a dozen Daguerreotypes and tin types of my great-great-grandparents from as early as 1850.

REFERENCES

Abiteboul, S., André, B., & Kaplan, D. (2015). Managing your digital life. *Communications of the ACM, 58*(5), 32–35. Found at http://dl.acm.org/citation.cfm?id=2670528

Ashenfleder, M. (2012). Communicating personal digital archiving to the general public. *Keynote Address at Personal Digital Archiving 2012*. Found at https://www.youtube.com/watch?v=5ySHVTivrQw

Ashenfleder, M. (2016). Your personal archiving project: Where do you start? In *The Signal*. Found at https://blogs.loc.gov/thesignal/2016/05/how-to-begin-a-personal-archiving-project/

Association for Library Collections and Technical Services (ALCTS). (n.d.). *Event ideas for beginners*. ALA. Found at http://www.ala.org/alcts/preservationweek/plan/ideas1

Ayers, R. P., Jansen, W., Cilleros, N., & Daniellou, R. (2005). Cell phone forensics tools: An overview and analysis. *NIST Interagency/Internal Report (NISTIR)-7250*. Found at http://csrc.nist.gov/publications/nistir/nistir-7250.pdf

Becker, C., Kulovits, H., Guttenbrunner, M., Strodl, S., Rauber, A., & Hofman, H. (2009). Systematic planning for digital preservation: Evaluating potential strategies and building preservation plans. *International Journal on Digital Libraries, 10*(4), 133–157. Found at https://publik.tuwien.ac.at/files/PubDat_180752.pdf

Chaudhry, A., Crowcroft, J., Howard, H., Madhavapeddy, A., Mortier, R., Haddadi, H., & McAuley, D. (2015). Personal data: Thinking inside the box. In *Proceedings of the Fifth Decennial Aarhus Conference on Critical Alternatives* (pp. 29–32). Aarhus University Press. Found at http://dl.acm.org/citation.cfm?id=2882858

DigiSapi (DS). (2017). *Data recovery*. Found at https://digisapi.com/in/datarecovery.html

Digital Preservation Coalition (DPC). (2015). *It's personal: Collecting, preserving and using personal digital archives*. Found at http://www.dpconline.org/events/past-events/personal-digital-archives

European Data Protection Supervisor (EDPS). (2017). *Personal information management system*. Found at https://edps.europa.eu/data-protection/our-work/subjects/personal-information-management-system_en

Flescher, S., Duffy-Zeballos, L., Goldman, V. S., & Boddewyn, J. (n.d.). Provenance guide. In *International Foundation for Art Research*. Found at https://www.ifar.org/Provenance _Guide.pdf

Hern, A. (2014). Sir Tim Berners-Lee speaks out on data ownership. *The Guardian*. Found at https://www.theguardian.com/technology/2014/oct/08/sir-tim-berners-lee-speaks -out-on-data-ownership

IBM. (2011). *The birth of the IBM PC*. Found at https://www-03.ibm.com/ibm/history/ exhibits/pc25/pc25_birth.html

Johnston, L. (2013). *Personal digital archiving initiatives at the Library of Congress*. Found at https://www.slideshare.net/lljohnston/johnston-personal-digitalarchivinglecture

Kent, K., Chevalier, S., Grance, T., & Dang, H. (2006). Guide to integrating forensic tech-niques into incident response. *NIST Special Publication*, *10*, 800–886. Found at http:// nvlpubs.nist.gov/nistpubs/Legacy/SP/nistspecialpublication800-86.pdf

Lazorchak, B. (2013). Four easy tips for preserving your digital photographs. In *Perspectives on Personal Digital Archiving*. National Digital Information Infrastructure and Preservation Program of the Library of Congress. Found at http://www.digital preservation.gov/documents/ebookpdf_march18.pdf

LeFurgy, B. (2013). Introduction. In *Perspectives on personal digital archiving*. National Digital Information Infrastructure and Preservation Program of the Library of Congress. Found at http://www.digitalpreservation.gov/documents/ebookpdf _march18.pdf

Library of Congress (LOC). (n.d.). *Personal digital archiving day kit: Planning and organiz-ing your event*. Found at http://digitalpreservation.gov/personalarchiving/padKit/ planning.html

Mortier, R., Zhao, J., Crowcroft, J., Li, Q., Wang, L., Haddadi, H., . . . Brown, T. (2016). *Personal data management with the databox: What's inside the box?* Found at http://www .eecs.qmul.ac.uk/~hamed/papers/CAN2016Databox.pdf

Nickell, J., & Fischer, J. F. (1999). *Crime Science: Methods of Forensic Detection*. Lexington, KY: University of Kentucky Press. Paradigm Project. 2008.

Rawlinson, N. (2017, April 25). History of Apple: The story of Steve Jobs and the company he founded. *Macworld*. Found at http://www.macworld.co.uk/feature/apple/history-of -apple-steve-jobs-mac-3606104/#toc-3606104-6

Redwine, G. (2015). Personal digital archiving. *DPC Technology Watch Report 15-01*. Found at http://www.dpconline.org/docs/technology-watch-reports/1460-twr15-01/file

Redwine, G., Barnard, M., Donovan, K. M., Farr, E., Forstrom, M., Hansen, W. M., . . . Thomas, S. E. (2013). *Born digital: Guidance for donors, dealers, and archival repositories*. Washington, DC: Council on Library and Information Resources. Found at https://www.clir.org/pubs/reports/pub159/pub159.pdf

Society of American Archivists (SAA). (2013). *A guide to deeds of gift*. Found at https:// www2.archivists.org/publications/brochures/deeds-of-gift

Strickland, J. (2017). *How tablets work*. Found at http://computer.howstuffworks.com/ tablets/tablet3.htm

Technopedia. (2017). *Personal Information Management (PIM)*. Found at https://www .techopedia.com/definition/24752/personal-information-manager-pim

Vertesi, J., Kaye, J., Jarosewski, S. N., Khovanskaya, V. D., & Song, J. (2016). Data Narratives: Uncovering tensions in personal data management. In *Proceedings of the 19th ACM conference on computer-supported cooperative work and social computing* (pp. 478–490). ACM. Found at http://dl.acm.org/citation.cfm?id=2820017

Williams, P., John, J. L., & Rowland, I. (2009). The personal curation of digital objects: A lifecycle approach. In *Aslib Proceedings*, *61*(4) (pp. 340–363). Found at https://www .researchgate.net/profile/Peter_Williams9/publication/235272899_The_personal_curation _of_digital_objects_A_lifecycle_approach/links/54e0cfcf0cf2953c22b7b6d0.pdf

Wilson, B. (2015, November 6). The man who made "the world's first personal computer." *BBC News*. Found at http://www.bbc.com/news/business-34639183

Zatyko, K. (2008, December 1). Defining digital forensics. *Forensic Magazine*. Found at https://www.forensicmag.com/article/2008/12/defining-digital-forensics

Chapter 11

CONSIDERATIONS IN ARCHIVING SOCIAL MEDIA

With our blogs and tweets, digital cameras, and unlimited-gigabyte e-mail archives, participation in the online culture now means creating a trail of always present, ever searchable, unforgetting external memories that only grows as one ages.

—Joshua Foer[1]

Social and cultural history is often comprised of whatever diaries and letters remain and that is down to chance and wide open to interpretation.

—Sara Sheridan[2]

INTRODUCTION

Social media is ubiquitous; it is everywhere, on our phones, on our computers, on the news and in our conversations. Never before in history have people been able to communicate to so many so quickly at such a low cost. Celebrities, politicians, thought leaders, and organizations of every type use social media to sell themselves, their ideas, and their products. Social media is not just for the famous or the wealthy; it is available to virtually anyone with a smartphone and Internet connection. Everyone can use social media to express opinions and record activities and feelings.

As platforms that promote sharing of events and emotions to create virtual communities and develop social networks, social media sites are replacing other forms of communication, such as correspondence, diaries, and journals. As such, social media has become an important primary source of cultural and historical information. Archiving social media, preserving the data for the future, has become an important aspect of digital curation.

As society turns to social media as a primary method of communication and creative expression, social media is supplementing and in some cases supplanting letters, journals, serial publications and other sources routinely collected by research libraries. Archiving and preserving outlets such as Twitter will enable future researchers access to a fuller picture of today's cultural norms, dialogue, trends and events to inform scholarship, the legislative process, new works of authorship, education and other purposes. (Osterberg, 2013)

This chapter will approach social media as a curatorial issue; that is, how archives, libraries, museums, and other cultural heritage organizations assess, acquire, and manage social media data that impacts and supports their mission and collection policies. Then the issues of extracting social media data will be explored. Finally, representation of social media data will be discussed within the context of a digital repository.

THEORETICAL OVERVIEW

Social Media in Organizations

When organizations use social media to communicate with the public, whether to create a brand, market, or sell its services, the postings become part of the official and legal records of the organization. Social media has become an essential component of most organizations' communication plan (Madhava, 2011). Because social media postings and pages are organizational records, organizations need to preserve them, not only for their internal records management but also as a legal requirement. Under both federal and most states' law, organizations are required to produce "all potentially responsive information for e-discovery purposes" (Madhava, 2011, para. 3). Depending on the nature of the organization, additional regulatory mandates and rules for preserving social media and website content may exist. For example, Sarbanes Oxley ACT (SOX), a law enacted in 2002 to ensure honest and transparent financial reporting, requires U.S. companies to annually assess "the effectiveness of the internal control structure and procedures of the issuer for financial reporting" (Sarbanes Oxley, 2002). In addition to the financial reporting, the SOX Act requires U.S. companies to develop and enforce records management policies that comply with the act; any business record that discloses business information must be retained for seven years. This requirement extends to social media data, both of the organization and of any of its officers. If the CEO of a U.S. company makes a comment via her personal Twitter account about how well the company is doing, that tweet is considered to be a company record that must be preserved for seven years. Fines up to $15 million may result if these records are tampered with or destroyed.

The National Archives and Records Administration (NARA, 2013) recommends developing a social media records retention policy that covers various topics, such as what tools are being used, who is allowed to create content, what can be said on social media platforms, and the requirements and processes necessary to capture and preserve the data. Social media archiving policies should account for all legal and regulatory requirements (Madhava, 2011). NARA developed a set of best practices for the federal agencies to capture social media data. These best practices can easily be modified for any organization. The first recommendation is to build a foundation at the beginning by developing a cross-discipline working group with records managers, social media and web managers, IT staff, privacy and security staff, and other stakeholders who can then work to create policy and define requirements. Next, find tools that will help to develop methods for evaluating current technologies and best practices against requirements and policy. The final stage is to implement policies, technologies, and methods; ongoing training; and evaluation of the process (NARA, 2013).

Social Media as Collections

In addition to being entertainment, social media has become an incredibly important source of primary material about current events and society's reactions to them. Social media is a primary source about individuals, movements, events, and organizations. Libraries and archives are collecting social media materials as curated collections and research data collection.

Social Media as Curated Collections

Libraries and archives are creating curated collections of social media materials to meet the specific collection needs of their organizations. Librarians and archivists often collect information about people of interest, such as politicians, artists, actors, musicians, thought leaders, inventors, scientists, and so on. These people often use various social media platforms. Information about them is found in fan sites, special interest group sites, and political party sites. "Official" or "real" social media sites for these celebrities and people of interest are reported to be created and maintained by these individuals; however, in many circumstances, these supposedly "real" sites are often managed by designated surrogates. Nevertheless, these sites provide information about these individuals. For example, almost all members of Congress have official Facebook pages, Twitter accounts, Instagram accounts, and so on. The members of Congress use the social media outlets to directly communicate to their constituents. Not only are these social media outlets official records of the federal government, but they also become part of the personal papers of each of these members of Congress. Some members of Congress manage their own social media communications, while others are managed by staffers.

As with individuals, organizations use social media platforms. Again, libraries and archives may include the social media postings of organizations such as political parties, businesses, and other organizations. An archive may collect materials on the history of the automobile. Collecting material from Ford, GM, and other automobile manufacturers would be logical. Archivists and librarians who collect information about political movements would certainly be interested in collecting the social media output of political parties, and archives of journalism would collect the social media output of news organizations.

Many librarians and archivists are interested in collecting material on specific events such as sporting events—the Olympics, World Series, and Super Bowls— or they might archive tragic events such as mass shootings or terrorist events. The Library of Congress was an early and proactive collector of web and social media materials; immediately after September 11, 2001, they began to collect social media and web content surrounding the reaction to the terror attacks on the World Trade Center and Pentagon. As they developed a program for web and social media collection,

> some staff initially expressed skepticism about the research potential of many Web sites, closer examination revealed a wide range of official documents, research studies, audio and video recordings, press releases, agendas and conference proceedings, blogs, electronic newsletters and other sources documenting people, events and activities likely to be of lasting research interest. (LOC, n.d.)

Some of these single events lead to political and/or social movements. For example, the Arab Spring, the name given to the social uprising in Egypt in 2011, was both documented and facilitated by social media. As individuals gathered to protest political and social issues, they filmed and photographed the events, including speeches, marches, and abuse by police and military, providing social commentary all the while. In addition to documenting the events, social media was used to communicate in real time warning protesters of police action, arranging for meetings, and planning for new events. Social media provided access to the events in ways that traditional journalism could not (Eltantawy & Wiest, 2011).

In the United States, the events in Ferguson, Missouri, have become an example of social media facilitating social change. Hashtags have become social movements. The death of Michael Brown and the subsequent protests were the precipitating events to the social movement, Black Lives Matter. The Washington University of St. Louis library has developed a curated collection called Documenting Ferguson. This project is attempting to collect all of the individual social media postings about the events that occurred in Ferguson, Missouri. "The project will document and create a permanent record of experiences related to this tragic event, including citizen protests and rallies; community reactions, meetings, and memorials; and capturing cultural events via social media" (Buck et al., 2014).

Social Media as Data Collections

Social media is an important source of research data (Thomson & Kilbride, 2015). Social scientists have access to a record of behaviors, feelings, and opinions of billions of people. "The Twitter digital archive has extraordinary potential for research into our contemporary way of life," said then librarian of Congress James H. Billington. "Anyone who wants to understand how an ever-broadening public is using social media to engage in an ongoing debate regarding social and cultural issues will have need of this material" (LOC, 2010). Twitter is just one of these great data sources. While these data collections are publicly viewable, getting access to specific sets of data can be difficult for researchers. Some librarians and archivists in research institutions are interested in archiving entire social media data stores.

In 2010, Twitter donated all of its data to the Library of Congress. As noted earlier, James Billington, the Librarian of Congress, was enthusiastic. However, the reality of providing easy and organized access to the data for researchers has been more difficult than originally anticipated. The collection is not yet public, and currently no production date has been set. The volume of data and the volatility of the data, as well as the need for constant update and growth, are the primary challenges of dealing with social media data.

Although archiving all of social media has been a goal, little real progress has been achieved. However, research is ongoing. The Canadian government funded a five-year project to investigate issues of Social Media Data Stewardship, "a set of data- and user-driven principles to guide all aspects of managing social media data including 'its collection, storage, analysis, publication, reuse, sharing and preservation'" (SMDS, 2017, para. 3). They have developed a model of data stewardship that echoes the Open Archives Information System model with data consumers, such as researchers and policy makers; data producers, the social users who enter and upload data; and data intermediaries, the social media platform providers. The research focuses on these three areas (SMDS, 2017).

Social Media Preservation for Individuals

Digital Presence

Digital presence, the term used for a person's accumulated online activity, includes websites, blogs, and social media, such as Facebook, Twitter, Instagram, LinkedIn, and so on. A person's digital presence can be active long after death. Digital presence outlives the physical. The issues of preserving someone's digital presence are more complex than preserving just the digital artifacts. While recent research indicates that most people have low interest in preserving or curating their personal information (Abiteboul, André, & Kaplan, 2015), awareness of a digital presence and the artifacts of a recently deceased loved one may increase the level of interest. Social media is changing not only the manner in which we interact with each other but also the nature of memory. As people share more of their lives online, a great part of self-actualization comes from a "continual production of digital content" (Krtalić, Marčetić, & Mičunović, 2015, para. 4). Social media creates surprisingly accurate representations of who we are (Carroll & Romano, 2010; Steinhart, 2007). Social media becomes the memory of individuals, families, and society.

In addition to memory, the nature of existence is changing with social media. Digital life does not conform to spatial or temporal restrictions; digital beings do not adhere to the normal laws of space and time (Swartwood, Veach, Kuhne, Lee, & Ji, 2011). Digital life can exist in multiple places at once: a Facebook status, a Twitter feed, an Instagram stream. More significantly, digital presence can exist beyond the physical existence; our digital existence outlives us. Digital life exists in a technical infrastructure. Kietzmann, Hermkens, McCarthy, and Silvestre (2011) identified a series of building blocks that support the digital life: relationships, reputation, groups or communities or collections of users, conversations, sharing, and presence, which means online availability. Each of these building blocks requires data to support its specific function. Some data is explicit; that is, it is intentionally entered by keyboard, camera, or other input device by individuals while other data is implicit, which means extrapolated by software, implied by defaults, and collected via GPS and other embedded functions in phones and other ubiquitous devices (Ellis Gray & Coulton, 2013).

Assessment is always an important part of preservation. Assessing social media content for preservation can be complex due to the complexity of the data: photos, videos, posts, comments on others' posts, friends and contacts, and "likes" and other emotion indicators. A recent study indicates that social media users prioritize primary, original content for preservation: photos, videos, text, and original posts. However, people who were very frequent social media users rated friends and contacts as important data to preserve (Kowalczyk, in press).

Digital Estates

The impact of our digital presence is beginning to become evident; people have begun to realize that their digital presence will outlive their physical selves and that their digital assets can be valuable. Digital assets are part of one's legacy. Traditionally, legacies have been tangible and object-based: investments, currency or jewelry, homes, photographs, and family heirlooms. However, memory-holding objects are now digital; many photographs are digitally stored on removable media, such as CDs and hard drives, cell phones, and cloud services. Diaries and journals are on social media; correspondence is in email; and investments and currency are accessible via online accounts with user names and passwords (Carroll & Romano, 2010). Appointing heirs to digital materials may or may not be obvious to estate planners (Carroll & Romano, 2010). Three significant issues arise when planning for a digital estate: identifying sensitive content, anticipating needs for future reuse of the content, and determining selective access to content (Micklitz, Ortlieb, & Staddon, 2013). Just as important as documenting in a digital will which digital assets should be passed on is deciding which assets should be deleted or forgotten (Thouvenin, Burkert, Hettich, & Harasgama, 2016).

In a recent study, people were asked what should happen to their digital online presence and data after their death. Nearly half of the respondents, 47 percent, did not want to make a decision but wanted someone else to decide, either their family or their executor. They indicated that the decision should be made by the people who would be either comforted or hurt by the continuing online presence. A number, 12 percent, of respondents want their data to be archived or frozen so that no changes could be made. Another 27 percent want to have their pages maintained with information about their death and open to others for posting and tagging. However, not all people want their online presence to continue; 29 percent want their online presence deleted (Kowalczyk, in press).

TECHNICAL IMPLICATIONS

Harvesting and Preserving Web Content

Collecting web content, whether for indexing or preservation, is a well-known, well-understood technical process generally referred to as harvesting. Text giants such as Google, Microsoft, Yahoo, and other Internet search organizations use harvesting to create their indexes. The Internet Archive, the organization that has as its mission to preserve the web, uses harvesting technologies to collect its data. The web harvesting process is performed by programs known as crawlers, spiders, or bots. These are generally set up to run automatically so that people do not need to intervene. The harvesting programs can be seeded with an initial set of links. The harvesting program follows links and collects the files. While harvesting websites is relatively straightforward, there are potential problems that can negatively impact archiving. The website may have missing pieces, broken links, or protected subcomponents. The web server may block harvesting of all or parts of the site. When harvesting at high volume, it is not always possible to know exactly what has been harvested. While there are many harvesting programs available, both the Library of Congress and the Internet Archives use an open source software package called Heritrix (Banos & Manolopoulos, 2016; LOC, n.d.).

In order to improve the ability to preserve their websites, the Library of Congress has developed a set of guidelines that document best practice based on their many years of experience. These guidelines are to help web developers create better archives websites:

- Follow web standards and accessibility guidelines.
- Be careful with robots.txt exclusions.
- Use a site map, transparent links, and contiguous navigation.
- Maintain stable URIs and redirect when necessary.
- Consider using a Creative Commons license.
- Use sustainable data formats.
- Embed metadata, especially the character encoding.
- Use archiving-friendly platform providers and content management systems (LOC, n.d.).

Some of these guidelines would not be difficult for web developers to follow. Many of these guidelines are just best practices for good information architecture and web development; following standards, creating accessible sites, and using site maps are all components of good web design. However, some of the guidelines might be new to web developers. It could be possible to convince web developers to think about using more stable URIs/URLs. Using stable URIs/URLs helps not only with preservability but also with the maintainability of the website; stable URIs/URLs could also be thought of as persistent identifiers, which, as discussed in Chapter 5, is a great aid to curation. Sustainable data formats and embedded metadata should be familiar concepts. Convincing sites to use them, however, may be difficult. Sustainable formats do not always provide the functionality that site designers want; a JPEG file while more sustainable is not as dynamic as Flash. And embedding metadata takes time and effort and does not produce immediate results for the website. Some organizations are concerned about making their web content available to web harvesting processes and block them via the robots.txt file. Well-behaved harvesting programs read that file and ignore the paths and links documented in the file. It is important to let these sites know that the robots.txt exclusions will block archiving as well.

Tools are available to help web developers, librarians, and archivists proactively create archive ready websites whether or not a website will archive well. Application such as Google Webmaster Tools has many functions that can improve the ability to archive the website, including site map management, broken link testing, metadata testing, crawler testing to emulate a crawl or robots.txt testing, and others. The Clear+ web archiving methodology has been implemented as a web service called ArchiveReady (Banos & Manolopoulos, 2016). An excellent suggestion for improving the credibility of websites comes from Stanford University Libraries; they suggest checking with the Internet Archives' Wayback machine: "Since many web archives use the same technologies, plugging a web address into the Internet Archives' Wayback Machine and clicking around can give you a quick sense of whether there are major barriers to the archiving or re-presentation of your content" (SUL, 2017, para. 7).

Social Media Data Extraction

Getting data from social media sites is much more complicated than web harvesting. Since its inception, the web has been standards-based, which has made developing and deploying harvesting tools relatively simple. However, social media is not a monolithic technology; each social media site has its platform. Each platform has a completely different set of underlying technologies. There are virtually no standards in social media technology. Unlike the web, there is no single off-the-shelf harvesting program that will collect data from Facebook, Twitter, Instagram, and other social media platforms.

Each individual social media platform has its own unique way of providing access to the underlying data. The most prevalent method of access is an application programming interface (API). Each API is unique. For example, the "amount and types of data displayed varies greatly from session to session and from user to user. Mapping preservation applications to the Facebook API allows full access to the entire population of data for any targeted user's Facebook profile" (Madhava, 2011). Social media platforms change their APIs as their functionality and policies change. Programs that use these APIs for data acquisition need to change as the APIs change.

Many tools and web services help organizations archive social media data. NARA (2013) lists 59 social media preservation tools that range from simple extraction to full preservation services. The social media text data extraction and preservation market is volatile; services come and go frequently, and the functionality changes rapidly. NARA has developed a set of guidelines for federal agencies for choosing tools to extract social media data:

1. Evaluate and test the available tools for social media capture to determine if the tools meet your needs, budget, and skill level. Agencies may be able to find free or low-cost tools to capture content that can then be managed in a recordkeeping system.

2. Consider using tools that provide transparency related to processes and capture. For example, open source tools can be modified by the agency as necessary.

3. Use the export capabilities that certain platforms have built into their native systems. For example, the social networking platform Yammer converts content into CSV files and makes the files available for downloading.

4. Utilize open APIs to create customized tools that will allow appropriate export and download.

5. Ask the platform provider directly for social media content, such as Twitter (NARA, 2013, p. 22).

A report on the state of social media archiving from the Digital Preservation Coalition (DPC) states that many institutions implement the same tools for social media data acquisition that they use for web harvesting. Many of the social media harvesting tools are very new and have not been sufficiently tested. "Because of the novelty of archiving social media data, standards and best practice do not yet exist to benchmark the qualifications of a long-term strategy for preserving this content" (Thomson, 2016, p. 25). While some standards exist that can be used, they are insufficient for effective preservation of social media data (Thomson, 2016).

PRACTICAL APPLICATION

Social media and web content qualify as "big data." Big data is defined as data that is high in volume, velocity, variety, and volatility. Big data is big; it is high in volume consisting of many terabytes of data. Big data has high velocity; that is, the data is produced at an amazing rate of speed. Big data has variety; in the case of social media and web data, that means many file formats, many vendors, and many sources of data. Big data has high volatility; social media and web data change rapidly. Big data operates on a completely different scale than traditional data processing. When libraries and archives collect big data, the traditional modes of collection and collection processing will not work with data at scale.

Collecting social media and web materials challenges the manner in which librarians and archivists acquire materials. Traditionally, librarians and archivists evaluate the source of material looking for authenticity and originality. Collections of material are processed; items are assessed, documented, and organized. When collecting digital content at scale from social media and the web in huge quantities, the sheer volume of items makes traditional processing impossible; individual items cannot be reviewed or documented with carefully crafted and thorough metadata.

The volume precludes item-level selection. Collection at scale requires changes in that quality control. If a library or archive is collecting all of the material on the specific topic, the option for rejecting materials based on file formats, image quality, or bit rate cannot be sustained. If we are collecting all of the materials, then we must accept all of the files. This may change the nature of preservation service offerings. Rather than committing to preserve everything perfectly within context, the repository services may need to be expanded to preserve the bulk of the data as well as can be reasonably expected. This will undoubtedly complicate our preservation services; however, collecting social media and web data will certainly enhance the collections.

Ethical Issues in Social Media Collections

Collecting social media and web content has ethical implications. When collecting materials on sensitive topics, such as protests and political issues, identifying individuals involved in these activities may be problematic. This is particularly true when there is photographic evidence of incriminating activities. When archives develop collections that cross social media platforms, connections can be made between users' handles that would not be otherwise obvious. When a social media collection crosses social media channels and can be associated with other data, new insights and a broader view of events can be developed; however, this may also make individuals more vulnerable as their identity is revealed. Developing standards of practice for attribution in sensitive situations is necessary.

When capturing social media data, many platform providers deliver all of the content, including *deleted* materials. In many systems, data is never truly deleted; it is marked as deleted and generally not shown to public, but it is still in the system. For example, when a person creates a tweet and then deletes it, the tweet remains in the Twitter database with the status of *deleted*. If that tweet has a hashtag that is being collected, it is included in the download. This raises an interesting question of how to process and deal with that tweet. Would the library or archive keep the deleted tweet in the full archive? Would the deleted tweet be retrievable and viewable? Would the tweet be marked as deleted, removed from public view, but still be viewable by researchers? Would the tweet be actually deleted from the archive? Would it matter who the tweeter was—whether a private individual, a celebrity, or an elected or government official?

"The ethical considerations around social media archives are riddled with technical, theoretical, and practical complications, and the best way to tackle them is not to ignore the issues and take a 'collect it all' approach, as some are advocating, but to address them head on and develop concrete solutions where possible or guidelines, best practices, and even a set of values where you can't find solutions" (Jules, 2016).

SUMMARY

- Social media has become an incredibly important source of primary material about current events and our reactions to them. Social media is a primary source about individuals, movements, events, and organizations. Libraries and archives are collecting social media materials into ways as curated collections and research data collection.

- *Digital presence* is the term used for a person's accumulated online activity, including websites, blogs, and social media, such as Facebook, Twitter, Instagram, LinkedIn, and so on. A person's digital presence can be active long after death. The impact of our digital presence is beginning to become evident; people have begun to realize that their digital presence will outlive their physical selves and that their digital assets can be valuable. Digital assets are part of one's legacy. Digital estate planning is increasingly important.

- Standards of professional ethics have not yet been developed for social media collections. Community efforts to discern and define ethical behavior need to occur.

Questions for Discussion

1. Have you ever considered your social media presence as an entity different from yourself? What do you think about that concept?

2. What types of archived social media or web collection have you encountered?

3. When you are a digital archivist, what types of social media and web materials would you like to collect?

4. What types of policies will need to be in place in a library or archive to handle a digital bequeath in someone's will?

5. Have you ever tried to collect materials using any of the social media extraction tools? What was your experience like?

6. How would you deal with some of the ethical issues of curating social media collections?

NOTES

1. Found at https://www.brainyquote.com/quotes/quotes/j/joshuafoer503099.html?src=t_archives

2. Found at https://www.facebook.com/permalink.php?id=525094707519212&story_fbid=1476038065758200

REFERENCES

Abiteboul, S., André, B., & Kaplan, D. (2015). Managing your digital life. *Communications of the ACM*, *58*(5), 32–35. doi:10.1145/2670528

Banos, V., & Manolopoulos, Y. (2016). A quantitative approach to evaluate website archivability using the CLEAR+ method. *International Journal on Digital Libraries*, *17*(2), 119–141.

Buck, L., Clay, R., Davis, S., Foster, M. J., Freeland, C., Ghasedi, N., … Zeller, M. (2014). *Documenting Ferguson: Project explanation and purpose*. Washington University, St. Louis Library. Found at http://digital.wustl.edu/ferguson/DFP-Plan.pdf

Carroll, E., & Romano, J. (2010). *Your digital afterlife: When Facebook, Flickr and Twitter are your estate, what's your legacy?* Berkeley, CA: New Riders.

Eltantawy, N., & Wiest, J. B. (2011). The Arab spring | Social media in the Egyptian revolution: Reconsidering resource mobilization theory. *International Journal of Communication, 5,* 18.

Ellis Gray, S. & S. E., & Coulton, P. (2013). Living with the dead: Emergent post-mortem digital curation and creation practices. In *Digital Legacy and Interaction* (pp. 31–47). New York, NY: Springer International Publishing. Found at http://eprints.lancs.ac.uk/66096/

Jules, B. (2016). *Some thoughts on ethics and DocNow.* Found at https://news.docnow.io/some-thoughts-on-ethics-and-docnow-d19cfec427f2

Kietzmann, J. H., Hermkens, K., McCarthy, I. P., & Silvestre, B. S. (2011). Social media? Get serious! Understanding the functional building blocks of social media. *Business Horizons, 54*(3), 241–251.

Kowalczyk, S. T. (in press). Life and after-life: Perceptions of preserving digital presence.

Krtalić, M., Marčetić, H., & Mičunović, M. (2016). Personal digital information archiving among students of social sciences and humanities. *Information Research, 21*(2), paper 716. Found at http://InformationR.net/ir/21-2/paper716.html

Library of Congress (LOC). (n.d.). *Library of Congress guide to creating preservable websites.* Found at http://www.loc.gov/webarchiving/preservable.html

Library of Congress (LOC). (2010, April). *Twitter donates entire tweet archive to Library of Congress.* News Release. Found at http://www.loc.gov/today/pr/2010/10-081.html

Madhava, R. (2011). 10 things to know about preserving social media. In *Information Management.* Found at http://content.arma.org/IMM/September-October2011/10thingstoknowaboutpreservingsocialmedia.aspx

Micklitz, S., Ortlieb, M., & Staddon, J. (2013, May). "I hereby leave my email to . . . ": Data usage control and the digital estate. In *Security and Privacy Workshops (SPW), 2013 IEEE* (pp. 42–44). IEEE. Found at http://citeseerx.ist.psu.edu/viewdoc/download?doi=10.1.1.678.8371&rep=rep1&type=pdf

National Archives and Records Administration (NARA). (2013). White paper on best practices for the capture of social media records. Found at https://www.archives.gov/files/records-mgmt/resources/socialmediacapture.pdf

Osterberg, G. (2013, January). Update on the Twitter archive at the Library of Congress. In *Library of Congress* (Vol. 1).

Sarbanes Oxley. (2002). U.S. Code › Title 15 › Chapter 98 › Subchapter IV › § 7262. In *Management Assessment of Internal Controls.* Found at https://www.law.cornell.edu/uscode/text/15/7262

Social Media Data Stewardship (SMDS). (2017). *About.* Found at http://socialmediadata.org/about/

Stanford University Library (SUL). (2017). *Web archiving resources.* Found at http://library.stanford.edu/projects/web-archiving/archivability/resources

Steinhart, E. (2007). Survival as a digital ghost. *Minds and Machines, 17*(3), 261–271.

Swartwood, R. M., Veach, P. M., Kuhne, J., Lee, H. K., & Ji, K. (2011). Surviving grief: An analysis of the exchange of hope in online grief communities. *OMEGA—Journal of Death and Dying, 63*(2), 161–181. Found at http://ome.sagepub.com/content/63/2/161

Thomson, S. D. (2016). Preserving social media. *DPC Technology Watch Report 16-01.* Found at http://www.dpconline.org/docs/technology-watch-reports/1486-twr16-01/file

Thomson, S. D., & Kilbride, W. (2015). Preserving social media: The problem of access. *New Review of Information Networking, 20*(1–2), 261–275. Found at http://eprints.gla .ac.uk/111476/1/111476.pdf

Thouvenin, F., Burkert, H., Hettich, P., & Harasgama, R. (2016). Remembering and forgetting in the digital age—A position paper. *Information Research, 21*(1), paper memo2. Found at http://InformationR.net/ir/21-1/memo/memo2.html

Chapter 12

CONSIDERATIONS IN CURATING
RESEARCH DATA

You can have data without information, but you cannot have information without data.
—Daniel Keys Moran[1]

INTRODUCTION

The digital revolution has fundamentally changed both the practice and the output of research. Due to increasingly sophisticated technologies, research has become more interdisciplinary and interdependent as researchers tackle bigger and more complex problems. Research output, in the form of digital data, is being created at an increasingly fast pace. The dramatic growth of scientific digital data generation is referred to as the "data deluge" (Borgman, Wallis, & Enyedy, 2007; Hey & Trefethen, 2003; Reed, 2010).

Preserving research data and ensuring its continued access have emerged as major priorities for funding agencies and academic institutions. Multiple reasons justify this growing interest in digital data preservation. The data itself has significant research value as it can be reused to fuel new ideas and insights. The data is also part of the scholarly record as evidence of the rhetorical structure of scholarly communication (Rusbridge, 2007), and, as such, preserving it becomes part of the mission of archives and libraries. Preserving data is also important to the research communities as it is necessary for replication and validation of research results (Swan & Brown, 2008).

Providing long-term access to digital research data has a number of challenges. Digital data requires constant and perpetual maintenance (Hedstrom & Montgomery, 1998). Technologies change, equipment ages, and software is superseded. Many organizations look to their libraries and archives to provide guidance and support when developing preservation environments for their research data because of their missions, the experience in preserving digital materials, and their commitment to the long-term stewardship of information.

THEORETICAL OVERVIEW

Libraries and archives want to preserve research data in order to facilitate data sharing. Data sharing requires an environment that supports open data; the open data movement is similar to the open access movement for scholarly publication. In order to have research data to preserve for the long term, that data needs to be available, which means that research organizations, including libraries and archives, need to understand and support the research process.

Data Sharing

One of the primary goals of preserving digital research data is to facilitate its reuse over time. In fact, most of the definitions of the term *digital preservation* include data reuse. For example, digital preservation can be thought of as "the managed activities necessary for ensuring both the long-term maintenance of a bytestream and continued accessibility of its contents" (Beagrie et al., 2002, p. 11). Lesk (2008) contends that preservation is tightly coupled with access; funding for preservation and curation activities will be based on the perceived usefulness and accessibility to the data. Reusing research data is an important component of digital curation.

While researchers are the main constituency for data reuse, others need access to research data, including educators, policymakers, and the general public. Making data broadly available can promote public understanding of research, evidence-based advocacy, educational uses, and citizen-science/research initiatives. Data sharing is not as simple as just making data available. Preparing data for reuse is more difficult than just preserving the bits for posterity. "It is the variety and complexity of data, and its context, that make it much more difficult to preserve so that others might make use of it" (Johnston, 2017, p. 4). There are a number of barriers to sharing data. Describing data so that others can find it, understand it, and make good and appropriate use of it is an arduous and expensive process. Finding repositories to house the data is another significant issue.

Perhaps the biggest barrier is the attitudes of researchers. Many researchers do not want to share their data. They feel that they will lose their competitive edge if others can use their data. Others do not see the value of their data; while the data is useful for their studies, they cannot see why or how anyone else could use it. Still, others worry about others misusing their data or others trying to discredit their work. These attitudinal issues were identified many years ago and are still problematic (Duca, 2017). Publishers, funders, universities, governments, and professional associates are making data sharing a mandate; in order for researchers to get funded, publish, and have a good professional reputation, they are required to share their data. These mandates can help promote data sharing, but they also are exposing the lack of technical and monetary support for data sharing (Kowalczyk &

Shankar, 2011). Data sharing is too large a task for a single organization. Data sharing and preservation are shared responsibilities for publishers, scholars, and professional organizations (Antonijević & Cahoy, 2014). Governmental data is a special case of data sharing.

Open Data

For the past 15 years, a number of open data initiatives included efforts to provide public access to government collected and controlled data and have worked to gain access to this data. Researchers and archivists developed a set of open data principles (Sunlight Foundation. 2010). These 10 open data principles are the following:

1. Completeness—all of the underlying data should be available while still following legal requirements for privacy.
2. Primacy—the data should be the primary course data, including its contextual metadata.
3. Timeliness—the data should be released as quickly as possible.
4. Ease of physical and electronic access—the data should have as few technical and use barriers as possible. Downloading should be simple. Data should be in easy to use formats.
5. Machine readability—all data should be easy to process. For example, all PDF files should have embedded text for searching and processing. Statistical data should be in formats that can be used by statistical software.
6. Nondiscrimination—access to the data should not require registration or other identification.
7. Use of commonly owned standards—open standards should be used for storing and accessing data.
8. Licensing—licensing restrictions should be minimal.
9. Permanence—government data should be available and accessible in perpetuity.
10. Usage costs—no fees should be imposed for accessing government data.

Few open data initiatives have the impetus of law. Most are executive directives that encourage governments to share data. In the European Union (EU), sharing data is not mandatory; however, all EU institutions are "invited to make their data publicly available whenever possible" (EU-ODP, 2017, para. 4). The EU Open Data Portal provides access to data published by EU institutions.[2] In the United States, "open and machine-readable data [as] the new default for government information" was mandated by executive order in 2013 (White House, 2013, para. 2). However, as an executive order, this can be easily overturned by subsequent administrations. U.S. government data is available via the data.gov portal.

The Research Process

Preserving research data is a complex process; as the technology that creates data improves, the process can become even more complex. Understanding the workflow of research and the lifecycle of data can help digital curators become more proactive and work with researchers to create data that is more *preservable*. In digital research, data is created and stored in file formats; context is created in every step of the research process. All of this data needs to be managed so that it can be accessible and usable for the long term.

Data Creation

Research is based on data. Data can be generated or gathered from existing data sources. Data can be *generated* by observations, instruments, or experiments, or data can be *gathered* via databases, vendors, web crawlers, and other processes. Data comes from research methodologies, such as surveys; field studies; case studies; direct observation in experimental situations; analysis of instrument generated data; analysis of existing data sets, modeling, and simulation; and text or language analysis. Many researchers use both unique data that they generate and data that they gather from existing sources.

Data creation is an ongoing process throughout the research lifecycle. As data is analyzed, additional data is created. For survey data, the analysis data such as the output from statistical programs could be considered ancillary or supporting data as it is used to support conclusions that are reported in published papers and can be recreated and verified with relative ease. For data that is longitudinal or merged from many sources, the original data can be less important than the final integrated dataset.

Research Data Formats

Research methodology is an important component of preservation because each methodology has a set of requirements, which often dictates a set of data formats. Vendors may prescribe the format for both data created by instruments and data gathered from databases, websites, or applications. Data could be created in a community standard, or data could be created in a format created specifically for a particular study or a specific research domain. The format of the original data affects efforts to integrate data from different sources and for data quality processing, such as normalization and data cleaning. The proliferation of complex formats greatly increases the complexity of preservation (Barateiro, Antunes, Cabral, Borbinha, & Rodrigues, 2008; Ross, 2007).

File formats can be proprietary, community-based syntactic and semantic standards, or syntactic standards. Proprietary formats are formats owned by one or more organizations or individuals with legal restrictions of use and limited transparency and/or software for rendering and processing. Standard formats are formats in the public domain or owned by an organization that makes these formats available with no legal restrictions and has publicly available documentation and software for processing and/or rendering. Proprietary formats used for instrumentation data, internal systems data, or vendor data are often migrated to standard formats. Standard formats used were image standards, such as TIFF, JPEG, or research domain or community XML standards like FITS,[3] BSML,[4] and FGDC.[5] Studies of research practices have shown that researchers often confused domain data standards with generalized computing data standards. These are generally generic syntactic data computing or storage format without any semantics, such as CSV, ASCII files, and relational or XML-based databases.

A major U.K. data repository ran a test to identify all of the file formats that had been deposited. Using Droid, a well-known format identification tool, they found that the tool recognized less than 40 percent of the formats. Their sample contained 107 file extensions that were unidentifiable (JISC, 2017). Research data in these generic, proprietary, and unknown formats creates a major barrier to preservation, as they require additional context to describe the meaning of the data as well as specialized and often expensive software that needs a specific computing environment to render properly.

Context for Research Data

If the goal of preservation is continuing access, funding for preservation and curation activities could be based on the perceived usefulness and accessibility to the data. Access requires metadata. And metadata is expensive. There is a direct relationship between the cost of metadata creation and the benefit to the user (NISO, 2008). Not only is metadata a key factor for preserving research data, but it is also vital for replicating results in the peer review process, data reuse, and creating knowledge from data.

Creating metadata is a demanding task that is both complex and time-consuming. Within the lifecycle, metadata can be created at virtually any point: prior to data creation, when files are saved, or when submitting to a repository. Data sources, instrumentation used, instrumentation settings, experimental conditions, software used, software configurations, and samples used are some examples of contextual information that can result from the process of creating research data and that needs to be encoded as metadata. Much of this data is implicit, captured in configuration files, lab notebooks, text documents, human subjects testing application forms, and file names. In a small number of domains using specific methodologies, contextual data is captured as data is generated and stored in a standard format.

The contextual data falls into four categories: (1) data about the experiments/research output, (2) the relationship among files, (3) data quality control algorithms or software, and (4) social data, such as usage statistics or discussion forum data where feedback about the data is gathered. Experimental/research output contextual data is generally explicitly stored in lab notebooks, spreadsheets, documents, and automated workflows. This data is crucial to the quality of the research; this is the data that is the most important. Structural context such as the relationships among files is more problematic. Much of the structural context is implicit in file names and directory structures. In some domains, most of the explicit data is stored in opaque application files; that is, the data about the relationships between files is stored inside of complex software applications. Structural context can be an important component of the research because it can document the relationships of files in time sequence over the course of the research. Software is very important for some data. In many types of research areas, the data can only be used within the software that created it, the software that did the analysis, and the software that rendered or visualized the data. Increasing in importance to the researchers is social data that exists in web usage logs, blog entries, or listserv environments. While this data is primarily explicit, much of the data is free text—so unstructured as to be difficult to use.

In most cases, the researcher is responsible to manage data for the life of the project, meet standards of good practice, and "work up data" for use by others (Lyon, 2007, p. 9). The process of working up the data involves metadata. It can be very difficult for researchers to find either the data or any contextual metadata as projects are completed. As funding ends, graduate students and staff who may have created and managed the data leave. With them goes all of the knowledge of the data.

Metadata is for both human use, as in search and discovery, and automatic processing. The metadata needed for automated preservation activities is difficult to create manually. Many of the tools being developed to help scientists document their data focus on data production and publishing more than preservation. Within some domains, automated tools for creating provenance or lineage and file-level technical data have been developed as well as some tools for creating scientific metadata, including description of experiments, treatments, participant responses, data cleaning efforts, and information about the data creators.

Rusbridge (2007) describes both the positive and negative navigation of these barriers. For projects with stable staffing and good communication, good sense can be sufficient to manage the data well enough to produce sound scientific results. But many projects produce data that is both unknowable and unusable—that is, without context, without the associated experimental conditions, in undocumented files, and in incomprehensible spreadsheets. It is this second scenario—unidentifiable or unusable data—that is the primary barrier to preservation. Data that cannot survive the short term certainly cannot be preserved.

Storing Research Data

Researchers have two primary options at the end of a project: (1) to maintain their own data, hopefully in an orderly manner or (2) to transfer responsibly to another entity. While some researchers do nothing to their data once a project is complete and the data remains as it was, most researchers must take an action to free workspace within their computing and storage infrastructure, such as copying or moving files. Very few researchers decide to delete data; those who do are generally pruning the data, removing intermediate results files that they considered to be unimportant.

Most researchers maintain their own data on removable media, such as CDs, DVDs, or external hard drives. Some research data can be supported in a lab or work group environment. Individual researchers are able to transfer the control of their data to a lab-supported data archive. The research lab takes responsibility for managing the data storage environment but generally does not commit to long-term preservation. Institutional data archives can also support research collection.

These archives take responsibility for data management, long-term preservation, and ongoing access. A small number of researchers have begun to use commercially available storage services, such as Amazon and Google, for their research collections. These services provide a stable technology base that provides online access for a relatively low cost. For researchers in some research domains, data can be stored in a well-supported digital repository; researchers in the biomedical field can, depending on the nature of the data, use the Protein Data Bank,[6] GenBank[7] (the gene sequencing database), and many others.

Digital Science Infrastructure

The term "Big Science" has been used since the early 1960s to describe the well-funded research laboratory that requires massive capital investment to yield results (Weinberg, 1961). Much of the work on preserving scientific data comes from *Big Science*. With funding from agencies such as the National Science Foundation in the National Institutes of Health, *Big Science* built big infrastructure, often referred to as cyberinfrastructure, to support its digital science. The cyberinfrastructure systems included such features as massive data storage, workflow components to manage the allocation of resources and the movement of data, complex algorithms for processing input data, automatic metadata capture for structure and provenance, and a portal for managing access to services and data. Long-term curation was an underlying principle of most cyberinfrastructure projects; the software and hardware were developed for sustainability. Some of these server infrastructure systems lasted only as long as the federal funding; however, others have evolved into domain- or community-supported systems that continue to provide support to researchers.

While *Big Science* is the most visible and receives most of the grant funding, the bulk of the scientific data created is from *little science* or any laboratory that does not require significant capital investment. This data is often called the "long tail" of scientific data (Heidorn, 2008). This name comes from the chart visualization of research data (see Figure 12.1). The left of the chart, the head, represents the huge data sets of homogenous data stored in common standards that is curated in well-funded and well-managed repositories. The right of the chart, the tail, represents a massive number of small, heterogeneous data sets stored in idiosyncratic standards curated by individual researchers stored on small servers or removable media (Kowalczyk, 2014). So while progress has been made in preserving data in *Big Science,* much work remains to preserve the data created by *little science*.

Digital Humanities Infrastructure

Digital humanities encompass many types of research domains, methodologies, and data types. Digital humanities projects often entailed digital scholarly editions, specialized applications for specific research projects, and specialized applications for a specific research domain. These projects were expensive, idiosyncratic, and hard to maintain by the researchers and/or their departments. Institutional support

Figure 12.1.
The Long Tail of Research Data

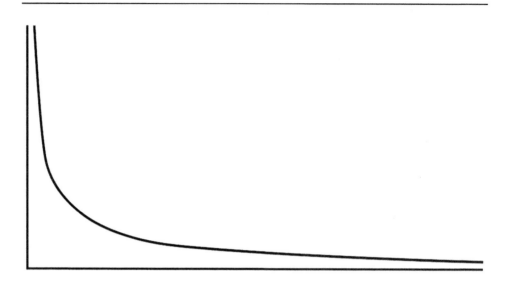

for digital humanities includes the trend toward digital humanities centers in colleges and universities; many of these centers have not been as successful as initially expected due to the resource-intensive nature of digital humanities projects, such as text digitization and encoding or specialty applications development. Cross-institutional activities, including funding agency initiatives to develop shared technical infrastructures, have had mixed results. All of these efforts have not provided the desired results; infrastructure for digital humanities is unavailable to many researchers (Borgman, 2009). Little institutional or federal grant funding is available for digital humanities infrastructure.

Much of the work in digital humanities deals with textual data. One of the biggest barriers to digital humanities was getting textual data in digital form; digitizing materials or negotiating for access to digital materials was the first step of most digital humanities projects (Cunningham, 2011). With the advent of massive digitizing efforts by many libraries and Google, digital data for researchers in the humanities is now becoming available (Williford & Henry, 2012). For many humanists, using these massive data sets is difficult. They have little or no technical support, no storage, no software, and no computers with sufficient power to process so much data. Some large academic institutions and their libraries are providing infrastructure for digital humanities researchers.

One initiative to develop infrastructure for digital humanities comes from the HathiTrust Digital Library, a shared and secured digital repository. The HathiTrust Digital Library is one of the largest collections of digital books and documents available to researchers and offers long-term preservation and access services, including bibliographic and full-text search and reading capabilities for public domain volumes and some copyrighted volumes. The HathiTrust Digital Library has funded a Research

Center (the HTRC) to provide computational research access to the HathiTrust Digital Library collection. This is a technology infrastructure that allows researchers to access the data in a secured environment, process the data, get research results, and store and preserve the output. The HTRC provides services for data discovery, service discovery, results management, and data management.

Data discovery provides an interface for searching the HTRC collection for specific subsets of data to be processed as well as to create and save individualized subsets as subcollections of the data for ongoing use. Service discovery allows researchers to find available algorithms for analyzing, visualizing, and processing the data with individualization of these algorithms via parameters. One of the most important aspects of the HTRC is its results management function. This allows researchers to persistently store the output of the research process. This data is then managed within the HTRC (Kowalczyk et al., 2016).

Efforts such as the HTRC can provide models for curating research data—infrastructures that securely and persistently manage and preserve data with support from research organizations and libraries. Preserving the data from its inception is a better model than waiting until the end of the project. It is much less expensive and much easier to capture the essential information about the data as it is being processed than trying to extract metadata from file names, notebooks, and documents. This model can and should be replicated.

TECHNICAL IMPLICATIONS

In addition to the other important technical aspects of preservation of metadata, format, authenticity, and integrity, curating research data has two additional major technical challenges. The first is the sheer size of the data, and the second is the complexity of the relationships between the various files.

Accessing Research Data

Dealing with huge research data sets, some of which are hundreds of terabytes, is difficult. In addition to purchasing and deploying huge data storage technologies, organizations that archive research data need to have sufficient network bandwidth to move this data. Moving data is not just for ingesting data. It is required whenever someone wants to access the data for downloading or processing. Providing access to research data can be as difficult and complex as storing the data.

Two primary ways provide access to research data: (1) moving the data to the tools and (2) moving the tools to the data. Moving the data to the tools is the most common model. Long before digital repositories and formal requirements for sharing data were enacted, researchers would share data by moving data from one computer to another using tools, such as email and the file transport protocol (FTP). This model is still used as individual researchers connect through their social and professional networks. This moving data to the tools model works for small data within a small research community; however, it does not scale well for large data, and it is not accessible or findable for researchers who are outside of that small research community. Data that could be valuable for researchers in another domain will be very difficult to identify (Kowalczyk & Shankar, 2011).

The second model of data access is just the opposite; rather than moving data to the researcher, the software tools for access and analysis are moved to the data. In other words, the specific tools needed to access and use the data are integrated into an accessible interface, such as a web portal, and made available to researchers. The tools could be specific to a data format, such as geospatial data and map applications, or specific to a research domain, such as climate data or protein structures. While this solves the problem of moving massive amounts of data, it presents new access issues. In this model, researchers need to discover not only what is just data but also the appropriate toolsets. Some of the research portals provide search and discovery mechanisms for the tools as well as the data (Kowalczyk & Shankar, 2011).

Managing Context and Data

As mentioned earlier, research data is more complex than most other types of digital materials that libraries and digital archives manage. The research process is a cycle that could produce multiple versions of the same data file. In addition, many intermediary files are created. Identifying which are the *final* files can be difficult (see Chapter 7 for more on data management). Some research processes use workflow applications that manage the data inputs and outputs, sequence a series of processing steps to be performed, manage errors and other problems, and record the flow and provenance as metadata. Data is just one output of the entire research process. For researchers, a published, peer-reviewed paper is the actual real research product. In fact, any given data sets may be related to multiple research papers. In addition to formal published papers, many researchers also give presentations on the same findings at conferences; these presentations are often delivered using PowerPoint or Google slides or other applications.

For example, a group of researchers has developed a large survey. The resulting data set had thousands of rows and 120 columns. When using a statistical package to analyze the data, the researchers created 60 spreadsheets with results and 60 log files from the statistical package. From this data, the researchers wrote three different papers that were peer reviewed and published in three separate journals as well as to conference presentations. The researchers are planning a follow-up study that will build on what was learned. It is likely that several additional papers will be written that will use both the existing data and the new data.

Managing all of the elements of a research project is challenging. Rather than thinking about each element as a separate logical entity, it can be helpful to think of all of the output as a single logical object, a research object. The research object is composed of multiple files that support a research initiative. A research object would aggregate researchers' papers, presentations, and data; provide a structured set of relationships between the components; and include bibliographic and file-level metadata for each component.

Any given research project could have multiple research objects. The example of the researchers with the large survey with multiple data files, three papers, and two presentations could be organized in any number of ways. One way would be to have a single research object for all of the files from the entire project—all of the papers, presentations, and data files. A more granular and perhaps the most sustainable way to organize this data is to have multiple individual research objects that are interconnected: one research object for the data files themselves, one for each paper as an individual research object, and one for each presentation as an individual research object. Each of the publications and presentations would link to the research object that aggregates the data. If the two presentations were of two of the published papers, it would be logical to include the presentations within the research object of the papers; that is, if the presentations are derivatives of the papers, then the presentations should be part of the papers research object. The goal of the research object is to increase transparency of research outcomes, increase the ability for results verification, and increase the ability for data reuse (Bechhofer, De Roure, Gamble, Goble, & Buchan, 2010).

Research objects could be implemented in several ways. Using the Metadata Encoding and Transmission Standard (METS), the structural metadata format discussed in Chapter 4, a repository could link all of the component elements of a research object. Another option would be to use the Open Archives Initiative Object Reuse and Exchange (OAI-ORE), a standard for describing aggregations of web resources. Or a repository could use its own relational or linking model. The logical representation of the research object could be implemented in any of the various repository systems. A repository would not necessarily need to physically have and manage all of the components of the research object as long as the links are stable and maintained.

PRACTICAL APPLICATION

Digital curators build collections of data from both locally held data stored and managed by the repository and data hosted remotely and stored and managed in remote systems to support the researchers in their communities. However, building a sustainable infrastructure for preserving and accessing research data needs broad support. "A multi-institutional approach is the only one that now makes sense. But the purpose of collections remains the same: to support the creation and dissemination of new knowledge" (Avery, Baughman, & Ruttenberg, 2012, p. 1). The collaboration can be with publishers to support scholarly publishing in both the sciences and the humanities (Choudhury, Ray, & Furlough, 2009). Europe and the United Kingdom are leaders in collaborative data curation. Their open data infrastructure project is an innovative approach to developing large-scale repositories for long-term curation of data.

While libraries and archives are trying to open their repositories to data, the number of local, institutional data repositories is still low (Duca, 2017). For most researchers, the preservation infrastructure of a repository lies beyond their reach. They do not have access to a repository (Kowalczyk, 2014; Lyon, 2007). Libraries and archives are working with their communities to understand the data lifecycle and develop tools and methods to help researchers find repositories for their data.

"Rather than focusing on acquiring the products of scholarship, the library is now an engaged agent supporting and embedded within the processes of scholarship" (Avery, Baughman, & Ruttenberg, 2012, p. 2).

SUMMARY

- Many libraries and archives are actively involved with researchers and research organization in the process of preserving research data because of their missions, the experience in preserving digital materials, and their commitment to the long-term stewardship of information.
- Understanding the workflow of research and the lifecycle of data can help digital curators become more proactive and work with researchers to create data that is more *preservable*. Data creation processes can influence file formats choices, which in turn, impact the preservability of the data.
- Creating metadata is a demanding task that is both complex and time-consuming. Within the lifecycle, metadata can be created at virtually any point: prior to data creation, when files are saved, or when submitting to a repository. Metadata for research data involves technical information about the equipment, conditions of the research, and descriptions of the results.
- Researchers generally do not use repositories for archiving their data. Most use removable media, such as CDs/DVDs or hard drives.
- Accessing large data can be difficult. The primary models for access data is move the data to the tools or move the tools to the data.
- Research data has many component parts. Using structural metadata to link the elements is essential for preservation and reuse.

Questions for Discussion

1. Where in the research lifecycle could digital curators intervene to help researchers?
2. Why is data sharing important? Why should libraries and archives care and/or support data sharing in their organizations?
3. Do you see other options for accessing research data other than the two models described?
4. How can libraries and archives collaborate to promote data preservation and data sharing?

NOTES

1. https://www.brainyquote.com/quotes/quotes/d/danielkeys230911.html
2. https://www.europeandataportal.eu/en/
3. https://fits.gsfc.nasa.gov/rfc4047.txt
4. http://xml.coverpages.org/bsml.html
5. https://www.fgdc.gov/
6. https://www.rcsb.org/pdb/home/home.do
7. https://www.ncbi.nlm.nih.gov/genbank/

REFERENCES

Antonijević, S., & Cahoy, E. S. (2014). Personal library curation: An ethnographic study of scholars' information practices. *Portal: Libraries and the Academy, 14*(2), 287–306.

Avery, C., Baughman, S., & Ruttenberg, J. (2012, March 10). 21st-century collections: Calibration of investment and collaborative action. *ARL Issue Brief, 1.* Found at http://www.arl.org/storage/documents/publications/issue-brief-21st-century-collections-2012.pdf

Barateiro, J., Antunes, G., Cabral, M., Borbinha, J., & Rodrigues, R. (2008). Using a grid for digital preservation. In G. Buchanan, M. Masoodian, & S. J. Cunningham (Eds.), *Digital libraries: Universal and ubiquitous access to information* (Vol. 5362, pp. 225–235). Berlin, Germany: Springer. Found at http://www.springerlink.com/content/k71v8x6081738x18

Beagrie, N., Bellinger, M., Dale, R., Doerr, M., Hedstrom, M., Jones, M., . . . Woodyard, D. (2002). Trusted digital repositories: Attributes and responsibilities, *RLG-OCLC Report.* Mountain View, CA: Research Libraries Group and OCLC. Found at http://www.oclc.org/research/activities/past/rlg/trustedrep/repositories.pdf

Bechhofer, S., De Roure, D., Gamble, M., Goble, C., & Buchan, I. (2010). Research objects: Towards exchange and reuse of digital knowledge. In *The Future of the Web for Collaborative Science (FWCS 2010).* Nature Precedings. Found at https://eprints.soton.ac.uk/268555/1/fwcs-ros-submitted-2010-02-15.pdf

Borgman, C. L. (2009). The digital future is now: A call to action for the humanities. *Digital Humanities Quarterly, 4*(1). Found at http://digitalhumanities.org/dhq/vol/3/4/000077/000077.html

Borgman, C. L., Wallis, J., & Enyedy, N. (2007). Little science confronts the data deluge: Habitat ecology, embedded sensor networks, and digital libraries. *International Journal on Digital Libraries, 7*(1–2), 17–30. doi:10.1007/s00799-007-0022-9

Choudhury, S., Ray, J., & Furlough, M. (2009). Digital curation and e-publishing: Libraries make the connection. *Charleston Conference.* Found at https://jscholarship.library.jhu.edu/handle/1774.2/35005

Cunningham, L. (2011). The librarian as digital humanist: The collaborative role of the research library in digital humanities projects. *Faculty of Information Quarterly, 2*(1). Found at http://fiq.ischool.utoronto.ca/index.php/fiq/article/view/15409/12438

Duca, D. (2017). Where are we with open research data infrastructures in the UK? In *Research Data and Related Topics.* Found at https://researchdata.jiscinvolve.org/wp/2017/07/13/open-research-data-infrastructures-uk/

European Union Open Data Portal (EU-ODP). (2017). *The EU Open Data Portal.* Found at http://data.europa.eu/euodp/en/about

Hedstrom, M., & Montgomery, S. (1998). *Digital preservation needs and requirements in RLG member institutions: A study commissioned by the Research Libraries Group.* Mountain View, CA: Research Libraries Group. Found at http://www.oclc.org/research/activities/past/rlg/digpresneeds/digpres.pdf

Heidorn, P. B. (2008). Shedding light on the dark data in the long tail of science. *Library Trends, 57*(2), 280–299.

Hey, T., & Trefethen, A. (2003). The data deluge: An e-science perspective. In F. Berman, G. C. Fox, & A. J. G. Hey (Eds.), *Grid computing: Making the global infrastructure a reality* (pp. 809–824). Chitchester, England: John Wiley & Sons, Ltd. Found at http://eprints.ecs.soton.ac.uk/7648/1/The_Data_Deluge.pdf

JISC. (2017). *Putting preservation into practice using shared preservation infrastructure.* Found at http://www.dpconline.org/docs/miscellaneous/events/2017-events/1692-2017-june -jisc-rdss-research-data-shared-service/file

Johnston, L. R. (2017). Introduction to data curation. In *Curating research data volume one: Practical strategies for your digital repository.* Association of College & Research Libraries. Found at http://hdl.handle.net/11299/185334

Kowalczyk, S. T. (2014). Where does all the data go: Quantifying the final disposition of research data. *Proceedings of the Association for Information Science and Technology, 51*(1), 1–10.

Kowalczyk, S. T., & Shankar, K. (2011). Data sharing in the sciences. *Annual Review of Information Science and Technology, 45*(1), 247–294.

Kowalczyk, S. T., Sun, Y., Peng, Z., Plale, B., Willis, C., Zeng, J., . . . Auvil, L. (2016). Big data at scale for digital humanities: An architecture for the HathiTrust research center. In *Big Data: Concepts, Methodologies, Tools, and Applications, 345.*

Lesk, M. (2008). Recycling information: Science through data mining. *The International Journal of Digital Curation, 3*(1), 154–157. Found at http://www.ijdc.net/index.php/ ijdc/article/view/71/50

Lyon, L. (2007). *Dealing with data: Roles, rights, responsibilities and relationships. Consultancy report.* Bath, UK: UKOLN and Joint Information Systems Committee (JISC) Committee for the Support of Research. Found at http://ie-repository.jisc.ac .uk/171/1/13ealing_with_data_report-final.pdf

Reed, M. (2010). *Data deluge.* Found at http://www.datadeluge.com/

Ross, S. (2007, September 17). Digital preservation, archival science and methodological foundations for digital libraries. *Proceedings of the 11th European Conference on Digital Libraries (ECDL).* Budapest, Hungary: Springer. Found at http://www.ecdl2007.org/ Keynote_ECDL2007_SROSS.pdf

Rusbridge, C. (2007). Create, curate, re-use: The expanding life course of digital research data. *EDUCAUSE Australasia 2007.* Melbourne, Victoria, Australia: EDUCAUSE. Found at http://hdl.handle.net/1842/1731

Sunlight Foundation. (2010). *Ten principles for opening up government information.* Found at https://sunlightfoundation.com/policy/documents/ten-open-data-principles

Swan, A., & Brown, S. (2008). *To share or not to share: Publication and quality assurance of research data outputs: Main report.* London, UK: Research Information Network, Joint Information Systems Committee (JISC) Committee for the Support of Research, and the National Environment Research Council UK. Found at http://www.rin.ac.uk/ system/files/attachments/To-share-data-outputs-report.pdf

Weinberg, A. M. (1961). Impact of large-scale science on the United States. *Science, 134*(3473), 161–164. Found at http://www.jstor.org/stable/1708292

White House. (2013). Open government. In *Open Government Initiative.* Found at https:// obamawhitehouse.archives.gov/open

Williford, C., & Henry, C. (2012). One culture. In *Computationally intensive research in the humanities and social sciences: A report on the experiences of first respondents to the digging into data challenge.* Council on Library and Information Resources. Found at http:// www.clir.org/pubs/reports/pub151

GLOSSARY

Administrative metadata: a description of the elements necessary for managing resources, such as rights information, file creation information (when, what equipment), and technical information (file size, file format, format specific parameters, and fixity information). Also known as technical metadata.

Archival file: the highest quality file stored in the most sustainable format to be considered the master file for an object.

Archival Information Package (AIP): the information required for a digital repository to archive and manage digital content. This is one of three major information packages in the Open Archival Information System conceptual model.

Checksum: a method for detecting bit-level errors in digital files or transmission. A unique number is calculated based on the bits of the file. By recalculating the checksum and comparing it to the original number, a repository can verify that the bits of the file have not changed.

Codec: encodes and decodes a digital signal or stream. The codec has a function that encodes the data for transmission and storage and a function to decoder that reverses the process.

Commercial software: a computer code that is either purchased or licensed by a company. It may or may not be modifiable by the customer. Product support is often available for purchase from the company.

Cost model: a framework for defining, allocating, and estimating the multiple components of the total cost of a product or service.

Data archiving: the process of migrating data to remote storage for long-term retention. In some circumstances, data that is infrequently used is archived. In other cases, high-quality archival versions of files are archived.

Data backup: the process of copying files in order to be able to restore the data in case of a service disruption, data corruption, or data loss.

Data governance: the set of processes to manage shared decision making about access to, quality of, and security for data.

Data management: the process of developing and implementing practices and processes to manage files throughout the lifecycle—including acquiring, storing, and managing data/files.

Data management plan: a formal document required by federal research-funding agencies that describes the data that will be created and how it will be managed and stored so that it can be preserved and shared over time.

Data migration: the primary strategy for preserving data. It is a process of converting data from one file format to another. Data migration can also be mean moving data between different storage devices.

Data profiling: the process of determining the criteria for evaluating data quality.

Data quality: a measurement of fitness or adequacy of the data for its intended purpose.

Data salvage: the process of retrieving data in accessible media and/or formats.

Derivative file: a lower quality copy of the archival file that can be used for as a web delivery version.

Descriptive metadata: the contextual metadata about the intellectual content of the information object. Common descriptive metadata formats include MARC (and its many variants), Dublin Core, MODs, and VRACore.

Digital archive: an organization that manages one or more digital collections. A digital archive can also refer to a repository system.

Digital curation: the process of managing data throughout its lifecycle, which includes creation, selection, maintenance, archiving, and preserving data for continuing access to the intellectual content.

Digital forensics: the science of recovering, extracting, and investigating digital information while maintaining the chain of evidence and without leaving any traces.

Digital object: the set of computer files that comprise a logical information asset. For example, a photograph that has been digitized might have an archival image file, a full screen deliverable file, a thumbnail version, a descriptive metadata file, and a structural metadata file. The digital object consists of all of those files.

Digital presence: an individual's online activities, such as social media.

Digital preservation: the process of ensuring that information is accessible and usable over time.

Digital will: a legal document that allows individuals to leave instruction about the final disposition of their digital documents, files, photos, and social media presence.

Disaster recovery planning: a process to determine the steps and allocate the resources needed to resume business processing after a disruptive problem. This process is also known as business resumption planning.

Dissemination Information Package (DIP): the information required for a digital repository to provide external access to archived digital content. This is one of three major information packages in the Open Archival Information System conceptual model.

Dublin Core: a descriptive metadata schema designed for web resources. Dublin Core (DC) has 15 elements all of which are optional and repeatable.

File: a container for holding information. It is stored in a file system.

File format: defining the layout of a file.

File Transport Protocol: a standard method to move files between computers over a network. FTP is one of many protocols that can be used, including SFTP (SSH File Transport Protocol) and MFTP (Multicast File Transfer Protocol).

Fixity: an attribute of permanence and immutability. In digital curation, ensuring fixity is a key component of integrity that is implemented via a checksum.

Harvesting: the process of gathering data from various sources.

Ingest: the process of adding new data to a repository system.

JHOVE: a software tool for format identification, validation, and characterization of digital files. JHOVE stands for JSTOR/Harvard Object Validation Environment and is pronounced "jove."

Lifecycle: a description of the stages of an activity from its inception to its conclusion. For digital curation, a number of lifecycles describes the various stages of data from its creation through its final disposition.

Maturity models: management tools to measure an organization's ability in a specific area. Maturity models usually have a five-level scale from zero (no ability) to five (fully actualized ability).

Metadata: information about a data object. Metadata provides context for the information object. There are three types of metadata—descriptive, administrative, and structural.

Metadata Encoding and Transmission Standard (METS): a structural metadata standard widely used in digital libraries and archives. METS organizes the component files of a digital object. The METS standard is managed by the Library of Congress.

Metadata Object Description Schema (MODS): descriptive metadata schema that is a subset of the MARC bibliographic standard.

MIX: the Metadata for Images in XML standard designed to capture and store technical information about digital still image files. MIX is a NISO standard (ANSI/NISO Z39.87-2006).

Normalization in digital curation: a subset of data migration. It is the process of converting data to a common—that is, normal—file format to make the ongoing preservation process simple. For example, a digital library or archive could normalize all of their digital document to PDF/A during the ingest process. In database management, normalization is the process of reducing/removing data redundancy.

Open Archival Information System (OAIS): a conceptual model that describes the functions of a digital repository system for preserving digital content.

Open source software: computer code that is freely available for others to use and/or modify. Product support may be available by the community of users.

Persistent identifier (PID): a reference to digital resource. Because a URL is fragile and breaks when the resource moves, a PID separates the name of the resource from the location of the resource.

Personal information management: the process individuals use to organize, maintain, find, and use their own data, such as documents, digital photos, email, and so on.

Preservation planning: the process of developing an action plan to care for and maintain the collection over the long term.

Provenance: metadata that records all of the processes that have been used to create, modify, and manage a digital file.

Quality assurance: a set of processes and procedures to prevent errors and defects.

Recovery point objective (RPO): an element of a disaster recovery plan that indicates the maximum time during which data may be lost from a service disruption.

Recovery time objective (RTO): an element of a disaster recovery plan that indicates the amount in which an organization needs to restore a business process after a disruption of service.

Repository: a system that stores and manages logical digital objects, the composite files, and the relationships between those files in order to provide ongoing access to the information within the digital objects.

Risk avoidance: the process of avoiding problems that could negatively impact the organization.

Risk mitigation: the process of developing plans to minimize or reduce negative impacts of potential problems.

Structural metadata: the contextual information that documents the relationships between the discrete computer files that are part of a digital object. For example, a book can have hundreds of individual image files. Structural metadata provides information about the proper order and sequence of the files. A common structural metadata format is the Metadata Encoding and Transmission Standard (METS).

Submission Information Package (SIP): the information required for a digital repository to ingest digital content. This is one of three major information packages in the Open Archival Information System conceptual model.

Technology emulation: software and hardware systems that mimic the technical environment needed to execute an old, obsolete program or system. The emulation environment can communicate to the program or system in its own language and then translates that communication to be able to interface with newer operating systems and hardware. This is one of the strategies for preserving data.

Turnkey vertical application: a software and/or hardware system that is designed for a specific purpose that needs little or no modification to run properly.

Virtualization: the process of creating a virtual (not real) version of a thing. For example, virtualization software can create multiple virtual servers out within a single machine.

Workflow: a sequence of steps to complete a process from its beginning to its end.

A HANDBOOK FOR TEACHERS

Digital Curation for Libraries and Archives supports a master's level course on digital curation. It introduces students to the concepts of curating digital materials, sets digital curation within the broader context of library and information organizations, and provides an overview of the research in curating and preserving digital data. This handbook provides activities that will develop some of the skills necessary to create collections and curation plans for digital materials.

COURSE DELIVERABLES

The two course activities that students have found to be challenging and engaging are to build a born-digital collection and to develop a curation plan for born-digital collections. These two activities mirror two important activities of digital curators. The course schedule given later in the text is designed to help students have sufficient information to be able to complete the tasks.

Digital Archival Collection

Students will create an archival collection of digital materials on a topic of their own choosing. This topic should be of archival interest and have readily available digital artifacts. The digital artifacts can be Twitter posts, YouTube videos, news postings, blog postings, digital images, and so on. Students will collect the artifacts, create metadata, and create a collection in our Omeka system. The collection should have an introductory page with a clear description of the collection, its importance, and the nature of the artifacts collected. The collection should have a minimum of 30 artifacts. Use the exhibit function of Omeka to add contextual material and build subcollections by format, theme, or chronology. Item metadata should be clear and help researchers find appropriate materials.

Digital Archival Collection Presentation

Students will present their digital archival collections. Each should prepare a talk using PowerPoint or other presentation software describing the archival collection, its importance, and the process by which the collection was created (data acquisition, metadata decisions, and interface issues). In addition, each student should give a demonstration of the collection created. Students should be prepared to answer questions about their collection.

Digital Curation Plan

Students will develop a curation plan for several sets of data: scientific data, humanities data, and a set of social media data. For this assignment, students will identify which files will be preserved and will provide a rationale for decision and a plan to curate the digital data. The curation plan will include an inventory of data, files, formats, metadata, and an assessment of the resources required to curate the collection, including staffing requirements and technologies necessary to sustain the data.

COURSE SCHEDULE

This course schedule basically follows the outline of the book. It can certainly be modified to meet any schedule. This schedule is based on a three-hour class meeting weekly for a 15-week semester. Guest speakers can enhance students' learning experience. Having a guest speaker form a local university library's digital repository team adds a practical aspect to the *repository* session. The speaker can often show performance reports, real workflow processes, and underlying data structures that are not available from the public or staff interface. I also like to ask researchers to come to the *humanities* and *scientific data* sessions.

As noted earlier, the final project is a digital curation plan for three real, authentic datasets. For a large, creative, and challenging project, I usually give students a week to work on the project and meet with me if they have questions. This meeting is optional. I find that students do not really ask questions until they have to apply concepts in a real-life situation. Usually, I hold the consulting session in the classroom during the normal class time. I ask them to have completed about half of the project. Before I meet one-on-one, I ask what their big concerns are. If several bring up the same issue, I address the issue to all of the students. I then meet with each student in the order they entered the room. The students self-report; I have never had a problem with the queue. Students ask questions to clarify issues and review concepts that confuse them. I find this to be a really rewarding exercise. I learn the issues that students struggle and revise the class, reading materials, and activities accordingly.

Week 1	Introduction
Week 2	Curation models
Week 3	File formats
Week 4	Metadata
Week 5	Data assurance
Week 6	Repositories
Week 7	Data management
Week 8	Class presentations
Week 9	Disaster planning
Week 10	Curating humanities data
Week 11	Curating social media
Week 12	Curating scientific data
Week 13	Consulting session
Week 14	Personal archiving
Week 15	Final project

CLASS ACTIVITIES/ASSIGNMENTS

Every semester, I create a Google Drive folder for my class. I set the sharing options as "anyone with the URL can update." I make a subfolder for each activity. This way, I can collect in class exercise documents and watch student participation in real time. I teach this as a blended class—some of the sessions are online, and some are face-to-face. All of the activities can be used in either mode. The activities are designed to give students a variety of learning experiences. Some activities help students work in small groups; others are individual tasks. Activities help students learn how to find and analyze technical information, how to design new services for patrons, and how to evaluate collections.[1]

INTRODUCTION ACTIVITIES

Activity 1—The goal of this activity is designed to help students uncover their preconceived notions of preservation, see the broad range of concepts possible, and begin to know their classmates.

Introducing Digital Curation Concepts with a Concept Map

1. Break up into groups of two or three.
2. Have a discussion with your partner about digital curation.
   - What words and concepts do you use to describe digital curation and preservation?
   - What words and concepts do you use to describe how people use digital curation and preservation?
   - Make a list of these words.
3. Using these words, create a concept map with the Popplet tool.
4. Save your work as a PDF (see the export option—please use all of your names in the file name).
5. Upload the file to Google Drive folder.
6. We will review and discuss the concept maps.

Activity 2—The goal of this activity is designed to help provide students with a basic understanding of some of the most common technical terms that they will come across and be sure that we all agree on definitions. It also shows me the students' technical knowledge.

Technical Glossary

A number of terms* will come up in our readings and discussions over this semester. Please research and write definitions for those terms in this Google Doc.

Group 1—Terms 1–3
Group 2—Terms 4–6
Group 3—Terms 7–9
Group 4—Terms 10–12
Group 5—Terms 13–15

In 15 minutes, we will review and discuss the definitions maps.
*These are the terms that I usually use. I add or subtract based on the readings and number of students in the class—bit, byte, file, directory, file system, operating system, file format, mime type, character set or character encoding, Unicode/UTF8, Database, RDBMS, XML, program, and API.

MODELS EXERCISES

Curation Models

The goal of this activity is to help students see the scope of preservation efforts, as well as to locate preservation resources.

National Curation Models Investigation

In this assignment, you will investigate national curation models.
Pick one or two from the list given next. Investigate the national curation efforts for the country (or political organization) that you have chosen. Prepare a short (no more than 90 seconds) presentation to discuss the attributes, features, and model of the curation programs. Use Flipgrid* to record and share your findings.

- Australia
- United Kingdom
- The Netherlands
- European Union
- United States

*Flipgrid (flipgrid.com) is a web and mobile tool for recording and sharing short videos.

METADATA

Activity 1—The goal of this activity is to help students understand what type of metadata could be automatically gathered when preserving websites.

Extracting Metadata

Break into groups of two. Find three websites of different types with different types of content.

1. Look at each site.

   What type of data could/should be curated and preserved?
2. Think about how you could gather metadata about this material.

   Look at the source code.

   What could you "harvest"?

   Are there barriers to retrieve this data?
3. Prepare a three- to five-minute report on your findings for the class—use the Metadata Lab Google Presentation.

Activity 2—The goal of this activity is to understand the nature of the types of digital materials, what is important about each type of material, and what metadata could be collected.

Significant Properties for Preservation

Work in groups to develop a list of significant properties for a data format. What are the most important aspects that need to be documented and preserved? Document your ideas on this Google Doc.

Group 1—Microsoft Word
Group 2—Adobe Acrobat
Group 3—Visual images
Group 4—Digital audio
Group 5—Digital video

FILE FORMATS

This activity is designed to show students how to research file formats, how to use the Library of Congress's (LOC) resources, and how to decide on the "preservability" of formats.

Exploring File Formats

Go to the LOC's Sustainability of Digital Formats.

Go to the Content Categories. In your group, prepare a five-minute report on the file formats that are recommended for your type of materials using this Google Presentation. Use these questions to prepare your report.

1. Describe the file formats.
2. Look for the file format standard documentation.
3. What file formats are recommended for preservation?
4. Are there file formats that are not recommended for preservation?

Group 1—Still images

Group 2—Sound

Group 3—Textual

Group 4—Moving images

Group 5—Web archiving

DATA ASSURANCE ACTIVITY

The goal of this activity is to help students envision and develop a plan for assuring the quality of the data for their digital archival collection assignment. This activity can be used for an at-home assignment or an in-class activity. When using this as an in-class activity, I have the students work independently to create a Google presentation and then share it with a partner and then with the whole class. This helps me see what confusions students have.

Build a Data Assurance Workflow

Think about the type of materials you will include in your digital archival collection assignment. Develop a workflow for the various types of materials you plan to have in your archival collection. Develop a few diagrams using the components used in the lecture/videos. Use either Google Presentations or Google Docs to document your workflows. If you need new components, you can feel free to define and use them.

REPOSITORY ACTIVITIES

Activity 1—The goal of this activity is to look at policy and licensing issues for institutional repositories.

Data Licensing Activity

For this exercise, you are going to develop a content license for an organization's digital repository. Work in groups of two or three. Use the materials covered in class, the list of materials in the Data License Resources section, and any other resources that you can find to develop the license. Use this Google Doc to describe your digital repository and your data license.

Data License Resources

- DCC Guidelines for Licensing Data
- Institution specific licensing options
  - Penn State license
  - IU license and data guidelines
  - ICPSR
- Generic licenses
  - Creative Commons
  - Open Data Commons

Activity 2—The goals of this activity are to interact with the staff side of a real repository system and see the functionality in action.

If possible, install a copy of DSpace (an open source, turnkey system) or get a license to a test version of CONTENTdm. Accounts need to be created prior to class. I walk the students through a set of tasks. After one initial walkthrough, students would then do several more individual documents and image uploads.

Using Repository Systems

- Add a collection.
- Add a document.
- Add an image.

DATA MANAGEMENT ACTIVITIES

The goal of this activity is to formulate a workshop or program for a specific audience on the topic of data management. This task helps students articulate why data management is important and to reflect on the different needs of different types of people. Students also engage in thinking about outreach to various constituents.

Data Management Plans Activity

Outreach is a key component for a successful data management program in a library. For this week's assignment, develop materials for a data management workshop for researchers in your organization.

- Pick an organization (real or imaginary).
- Develop an agenda (topics to be covered).
- Create some publicity materials:
  - A poster (using PowerPoint or Google Slides),
  - A short video, using FlipGrid or another video app, or
  - A flier (using Word, PowerPoint, or Google apps)

- Your outreach materials should explain the workshop and let people know why they could come, what you will teach them, and how this will benefit them.

If you create a video, please upload a document or a URL with the agenda.

DISASTER PLANNING ACTIVITIES

The goal of this activity is to familiarize students with the issues of disaster planning. The students need to make choices and trade-offs. They need to think through options.

Develop a Disaster Recovery Plan

Develop a disaster recovery plan for your digital archive. Decide on the type of archive that you will be supporting. For your starting point, think about the type of archive that you will use in your final project. Use the materials covered in class, the readings, the Open Archival Information System framework, and any other resources that you can find to develop this disaster recovery plan. This table would be a good place to start.

Recovery point objective (RPO)—the acceptable latency of data that will not be recovered

Recovery time objective (RTO)—the acceptable amount of time to restore the function

Create a Google Doc and share it with me using the "anyone with the URL can edit." Please describe your digital archive, the collections, and the disaster recovery plan.

CURATING ARTS AND HUMANITIES DATA ACTIVITIES

The goal of this activity is to see various models to support humanities computing and preservation.

Table 8.5.

Sample Disaster Plan

Critical System	RTO/ RPO	Threat	Prevention Strategy	Response Strategy	Recovery Strategy
Digital Repository	4 hours/ 2 hours	Server failure	Secure equipment room, backup server, UPS	Switch over to backup server, validate UPS functions	Fix/replace primary server; move back to primary server
Digital Repository	4 hours/ 2 hours	Storage failure	Secure equipment room, backup server, UPS; maintain store of spare disks	Swap out damaged hard drive with spares. Restore data	Obtain more spare disk drives
Building Security	2 hours/ 2 hours	Security system deployed	Locate system in secure area; UPS; install protective enclosure around sensor units	Deploy guards at strategic points	Obtain/install replacement unit/ sensors

Digital Humanities Centers Lab Activity

In groups of two, review the digital humanities center assigned to your group. Explore the site. Look for services, projects, organizational structure, organizational affiliations, and any other pertinent information.

- What types of projects are supported?
- What academic disciplines are supported?
- What services are offered?
- Is there any affiliation with the libraries?

Group 1
  UCLA Center for Digital Humanities
  IDAH—Indiana University
Group 2
  Maryland Institute for Technology in the Humanities
  Initiative for Digital Humanities, Media, and Culture at Texas A&M University
Group 3
  University of Virginia Library Scholars' Lab
  Northwestern University Digital Humanities Laboratory
Group 4
  Center for Public History and Digital Humanities at Cleveland State University
  Princeton University's Center for Digital Humanities
Group 5
  Loyola Chicago's Center for Textual Studies and Digital Humanities
  University of South Carolina's Center for Digital Humanities

CURATING SOCIAL MEDIA ACTIVITIES

Activity 1—The goal of this activity is to learn about the similarities and differences of social media service agreements and think about how this impacts libraries and archives as they want to collect and preserve social media data.

Social Media Policy Review

Break into groups of two or three. Find and review the policies for each site concerning data use/sharing and death/inactivity of account holders. Summarize the findings in this Google Doc. Then talk about the ramification for archives when trying to gather and preserve this data and add these to the Google Doc. We will discuss as a group.

Group 1
  Facebook
  SlideShare
Group 2
  Twitter
  LinkedIn

Group 3
  Instagram
  Snapchat
Group 4
  YouTube
  WordPress

Activity 2—The goal of this activity is to look at one of the web archiving services and see how libraries are creating web collections.

Social Media Archives Lab Activity

Go to Archive-It. Explore the collection. Find some websites that have been archived. Go look for the same website(s) in the Internet Archive. Analyze and compare the experience of looking for an archived website by answering the following questions:

- Are the interfaces effective?
- Could you find what you were looking for?
- What are the benefits of each archive?
- What are the limitations of each archive?
- Could you see using either of these services in your professional life?
- Could either of these resources be useful for your digital collection project?

Activity 3—The goal of this activity is to help students understand the issues in curating social media data, including selection, acquisition, and inventorying.

Social Media Footprint

Digital footprint refers to the compilation of content on the Internet that can be associated with a person and, thus, potentially available to anyone performing a search on that person. The list of possible content visible online is seemingly endless and can include YouTube, comments on a news article or blog, photos on Flickr or Instagram, and posts on Facebook and Twitter. For this assignment, you are asked to pick a public figure and inventory this person's public digital footprint. This document will be the basis for the social media collection that you will use in the final assignment to develop a digital curation plan.

Search various Internet search engines and digital social media for this person. Inventory the social media sites, the number of entries per site, the types of data shared, and any other information that is pertinent. Please create this inventory as table in a document or spreadsheet using either Microsoft Office products or Google products. As part of your inventory, please include a paragraph or two explaining whom you are profiling, why you chose this person, and why this material is important.

Please upload the document or the URL (be sure to share your document).

CURATING SCIENTIFIC DATA ACTIVITIES

The goals of this activity are to explore the wide variety of available data collections and give student experience evaluating the functionality and the scope of a scientific data resource.

Data Collection Lab Activity

Scientific data collections are becoming more visible and usable. Please break into groups and review the data collections assigned to you.

- What type of collection is this—research, community, or reference?
- How is this collection maintained?
- What type of data is available in this collection?
- Can you tell what file formats are available?
- Are there tools for viewing and/or processing the data?
- What metadata is available for this collection?

Group 1
  NOAA Digital Coast
  Academic Commons—Columbia University
Group 2
  NOAA hurricane data
  IUScholarWorks
Group 3
  Goddard Space Flight Center's Global Change Master Directory
  Dryad
Group 4
  Protein Data Bank
  Harvard Dataverse Network
Group 5
  National Snow and Ice Data Center
  American Mineralogist Crystal Structure Database
Group 6
  National Nuclear Data Center
  Biological Magnetic Resonance Data Bank

PERSONAL ARCHIVING ACTIVITIES

The goal of this activity is to give students a creative way to think about the issues in personal archiving.

Personal Archiving Lab

Create a poster or handout to promote personal archiving. You could create an information poster—what it is and why it is important. You could create an advertising poster for your library's new program on personal archiving. You could create an infographic. Or you could dream up another type of poster. Be creative. Have fun with this!

Make it graphic and colorful. Use PowerPoint, Google Slides, or other graphical software package. Please submit a PDF or a link to a Google Doc.

NOTE

1. Some of the activities use web resources from universities and digital curation institutes. These resources can change without warning and need to be reviewed prior to the class activity.

AUTHOR INDEX

SUBJECT INDEX

About the Author

STACY T. KOWALCZYK is an associate professor at Dominican University in the School of Information Studies. In addition, she serves as the director of Dominican University's Master of Science in Information Management (MSIM) program. She was an associate director of the Indiana University Libraries Digital Library Program, where she managed new projects and services, and the former associate director of software development for the Harvard University Libraries, where she worked on the Harvard Library Digital Initiative. Kowalczyk teaches courses in digital libraries, digital curation, systems analysis and design, information architecture, human computer interaction, and library and data management systems. She has published research in leading journals and presented papers at refereed international conferences. Kowalczyk holds a PhD in information science from Indiana University and a master's degree in library science from Dominican University.